Language Development
of
Exceptional Children

Language
Development of
Exceptional
Children

By

HAROLD D. LOVE, Ed.D.

Chairman, Special Education Department
University of Central Arkansas
Conway, Arkansas

JAMES C. MAINORD, Ph.D.

Associate Professor, Special Education Department
University of Central Arkansas
Conway, Arkansas

DAVID NAYLOR, Ed.D

Associate Professor, Special Education Department
University of Central Arkansas
Conway, Arkansas

CHARLES C THOMAS • **PUBLISHER**
Springfield · Illinois · U.S.A.

Published and Distributed Throughout the World by

CHARLES C THOMAS ● PUBLISHER

Bannerstone House

301-327 East Lawrence Avenue, Springfield, Illinois, U.S.A.

© *1976, by* CHARLES C THOMAS ● PUBLISHER

ISBN 0-398-03573-3

Library of Congress Catalog Card Number: 76-16084

Printed in the United States of America
C-11

Library of Congress Cataloging in Publication Data

Love, Harold D
    Language development of exceptional children.

    Bibliography: p.
    Includes index.
    1. Handicapped children--Education--Language arts.
I. Mainord, James C., joint author. II. Naylor,
David, 1939-   joint author. III. Title.
LC4028.L68   371.9   76-16084
ISBN 0-398-03573-3

This book is dedicated to the memory of A. J. Meadors who as an educator and a humanitarian influenced the lives of many people.

PREFACE

THE overall intent of this book is to serve as a guide for reviewing the literature on a new and emerging area in the study of exceptional children. The authors, through this text, contend that language development is another major facet of humanistic development through which exceptional children can be more clearly understood. Furthermore, the authors wish to express their contention that language growth and development represent an important developmental area which separates these children from children who fall within the range of normal or unremarkable development. It is through such areas as listening, thinking, gesturing, speaking, reading and writing that exceptional children demonstrate their developmental imbalances.

To that end, the authors have presented a review of theoretical explanations, empirical investigations and practical information which reflects the status of knowledge relevant to exceptional children. As a referential guide to the language development of exceptional children, it is hoped that this manuscript will serve as an introductory text for this emerging field of study. The information contained herein may also serve as a supplementary text for specific courses in special education and developmental psychology.

The completion of a manuscript cannot be accomplished without the support and contribution of several professional associates. Through their efforts, encouragement, and professional insight we were able to compile the information included in this text. As with most projects of this scope it is difficult to recall and mention all of the contributors. However, we appreciate their work and feel gratified at the notarization of their efforts. Initially we wish to acknowledge the devotion and encouragement given by our wives, Sue Love, Mary Dean Mainord, and Janie Naylor, through the many hours required for the completion of the text.

We wish to thank Mrs. Jean Thompson for the typing, re-typing, and editing of this manuscript. We thank Rhonda Atkinson for her assistance in preparing and editing several chapters of this book.

Further acknowledgments should be given to Jane Baldridge, Ed Mashburn, Mike Willbanks, and Peggy Pack Young for their reviews of literature contained in some of the chapters.

We further wish to acknowledge the efforts of Hazel Carrell, Shirley Gosbey, Gloria Hill, Elaine Houston, Ada Lewis, Carol Rasco, and Barbara St. Claire who aided in the development of the information concerning the role of the parents in fostering the language development of exceptional children.

To these many professionals we are deeply indebted.

H.D.L.
J.C.M.
D.N.

CONTENTS

Language Development
of
Exceptional Children

Chapter 1

OVERVIEW OF THE THEORETICAL POSITIONS CONCERNING LANGUAGE DEVELOPMENT

OTHER than mechanical noises made by most animals, no form of life lower than the amphibian is capable of making laryngeal sounds. Karlin, Karlin, and Gurren (1965) state that speech is characteristically and distinctly a human function. Even with birds there is a great advance in the various sounds which foreshadow the production of vowels. The parrot is capable of making certain sounds, but there is no symbolization involved; this bird merely repeats a few sounds over and over again.

Insects appear to have elaborate systems of gestural communication; for example, bees have a complicated but concise system of navigational signals which dominate their social organization (Frisch, 1954).

Bartel (1975) informs us that the nature of language has been strenuously debated by psychologists, linguists and, more recently, psycholinguists. A large part of the argument has arisen because some persons have failed to distinguish between *language* and *speech*. Speech has a verb form to speak; language does not. When we speak we utter words in a systematic way and we convey meaning. A speaker and a listener understand each other if they know the language being spoken. Therefore, without language, meaningful speech is impossible. Bartel (1975) further states that the distinction between language and speech is related to two psychological terms, *competence* and *performance*. This distinction was first made by linguist Noam Chomsky (1957). Competence refers to the underlying knowledge of any given language possessed by an individual. Performance refers to the actual expression of that competency when a human being understands or produces well-formed sentences.

3

Several theories concerning the origin of speech have been offered by various authors, and some explanations were accompanied by a certain amount of scientific data. Karlin, Karlin, and Gurren (1970) offer seven theories concerning the origin of speech and language in man. From their work, it appears that the earliest theory of speech was that of *divine origin*. The basis for the divine origin theory is the Bible, which is replete with statements about language and the languages throughout the world. In the beginning, according to the Bible, the whole earth was of one language and one speech. The sons of Noah journeyed east and decided to build a city with a tower reaching toward heaven. The Lord, finding them guilty of presumption, decided to confound their language so they could not understand each other's speech, thus permanently interrupting construction. The tower was called Babel, and the Lord scattered the people over the face of the earth.

The literature lists the legends of several races and tribes which touched upon the divine origin theory. The belief in divine origin of speech, therefore, is not limited to Judeo-Christian theology. For example, the Norsemen believed that their speech was a gift given to them by the God of Thunder, Thor.

Lefevre (1894) was one of the first people to write about the origin of speech and language in man, and he came forth with the onomatopoetic theory which assumed that primitive words arose while man was imitating the various sounds in nature such as the babbling of a brook, the whistling of the wind in pine trees, the barking of dogs, the crackling of fire, and so on. This theory could possibly account for a small part of the origin of sounds.

Judd (1926) wrote about the interjectional theory. His theory is based upon the belief that the earliest speech sounds came about through involuntary exclamations — sounds emitted during periods of excitement, fear, sorrow, and astonishment.

Karlin, Karlin, and Gurren (1970) indicate that the interjectional theory and the onomatopoetic theory failed to consider speech as a form of social intercourse and as a means of communication between man and his neighbors. These three authors indicated that the psychological gesture theory of Wundt (1916), the oral gesture theory of Paget (1930), the philological vocal play theory of Jespersen (1922), and social control theory of de Laguna

(1927) should be considered and studied.

Paget's oral gesture theory theorizes that when man invented tools his hands became so occupied that he could no longer use them for the communication of ideas. Therefore, man had to use the movements of the mouth, tongue, and lips as oral gestures to displace hand gestures. The vocal play theory postulates that language grew out of the sounds made by happy primitive youths, and according to Darwin (1871) people must consider that primitive men made musical sounds before they actually learned to talk. Social change had a lot to do with the development of speech and language according to de Laguna (1927). As the environment became more complicated and man associated with his neighbors more often, speech came about through human cooperation. It became a necessity for living together, protecting one's home and things, and cooperating with one's neighbors in agriculture, building, religion, and so on.

One of the unusual and controversial explanations of language development in children comes from the theoretical views of Noam Chomsky. His theoretical postulates of language development emphasize an innate quality which predisposes the developing child to acquire the speech and language systems which are unique to his environment. The major postulate of Chomsky's theory is generative-transformationalism that enables the child to learn, to internalize, and to express the language which is unique to his culture. This theoretical postulate proposes that the child has the basic ability to acquire language and during development will acquire major or essential components of the language system. The transition of language from simple prespeech forms of developmental language to the use of complex expressive language occurs rapidly, and most children of near-average or above-average intelligence will accomplish this transition by the age of six. There is, however, little empirical evidence to verify the major positions of his theory. There is little empirical evidence which substantiates a range of age in which this transformation should occur. According to Chomsky, language acquisition is innate within the brain, and some aspects of language are so complex they cannot be learned. It is perhaps this conceptualization that generated much of the criticism from stage and learning theorists (Lerner, 1971).

Language and Thinking

Many scholars have examined the role of language in thinking, but the relationship is still not fully understood. Language is a tool which permits us to speak, helps us to learn, recall, remember, transmit, and control our environment.

Lerner (1971) used an example which illustrated the dependency of language on thought when she wrote about the experience of Helen Keller as she became aware that things have symbolic names to represent them. This discovery at age seven changed her behavior from that of an undisciplined animal to that of a language-oriented human being. Anne Sullivan, her teacher, described the events (Keller, 1961).

> I made Helen hold her mug under the spout while I pumped. As the cold water gushed forth, filling the mug, I spelled "w-a-t-e-r" in Helen's free hand. The word coming so close upon the sensation of cold water rushing over her hand seemed to startle her. She dropped the mug and stood as one transfixed. A new light came into her face. She spelled "water" several times. Then she dropped on the ground and asked for its name and pointed to the pump and the trellis and suddenly turning around she asked for my name . . . . All the way back to the house she was highly excited, and learned the name of every object she touched, so that in a few hours she had added thirty new words to her vocabulary.

Lerner (1971) also wrote about Helen Keller's first awareness of language. Helen described how she felt when she first felt cool water gushing over one hand and spelled the word *water* into the other hand (Keller, 1961).

> As the cool water gushed over one hand she spelled into the other the word *water*, first slowly, then rapidly. I stood still, my whole attention fixed upon the motion of her fingers.
>
> Suddenly I felt a misty consciousness as of something forgotten — a thrill of returning thought; and somehow the mystery of language was revealed to me. I knew then that "w-a-t-e-r" meant the wonderful, cool something that was flowing over my hand. That living word awakened my soul, gave it light, hope,

joy, set if free . . . . I left the well-house eager to learn. Everything
had a name, and each name gave birth to a new thought.

Linguists agree that the structure of language is very complicated and diversified. This has attracted the attention of scholars
from many disciplines, and much has gone into developing the
theories and concepts concerning the nature of language. Wallace
and McLoughlin (1975) mention three major theorists who have
made contributions to the knowledge of language acquisition.
The three mentioned are Skinner (1957), Chomsky (1965), and
Lenneberg (1967). Noam Chomsky has already been discussed in
this chapter, therefore we shall mention the behaviorist model
proposed by Skinner and the language model proposed by
Lenneberg.

Skinner (1957), instead of using just the word *language*, uses
the words *verbal behavior* to explain the phenomenon of acquiring language. As a behaviorist Skinner believes that language is learned by the child when observing a model. Naturally
the environment would play a vital role in Skinner's theory. The
people in the child's environment offer reinforcement by listening, paying attention, commenting and observing, and
Skinner believes these are all important in acquiring language.
The verbal community shapes the child's verbal behavior, and the
arrangement of the reinforcement variables is extremely important.

Lenneberg (1964) is not an environmentalist, and his language
model is based upon biological beliefs. He thinks the environment offers only raw material that the child may use in learning to
communicate. According to Lenneberg, the brain matures both
neurologically and chemically, and language is learned by a ma-
turational process.

Inner Language

Inner language or inner speech is the language one uses to
communicate with oneself. It is the result of the integration of
experience and can be developed only if all the sensory systems
and the brain function together effectively and at the same time.
Gearheart (1973) believes that it is this integration of experience,

together with the capacity to transfer freely between and among all systems, which gives language meaning and significance.

According to Myklebust's (1954, 1965) semiautonomous systems concepts of brain function, there is the distinct possibility that as information moves through a sensory channel it might conflict with the normal transmission or reception of another channel; he calls this "overloading." Gearheart (1973) cites several examples of overloading, which include the child who learns better while listening to a lecture if he closes his eyes. Everyone probably does this at times, but if a person learns better that way, then his visual information input could easily be interfering with the auditory. The opposite could also be true, and the child must adapt to what is best for him. Another example is the child who can read silently and understand what is read, but when asked to read aloud he cannot or has great difficulty doing so.

Disturbances of inner language are not as well understood as receptive and expressive language skills. Inner language disturbances are believed to involve the process of establishing verbal imagery for words and concepts.

Auditory Receptive Language

The ability to understand spoken language is called auditory receptive understanding. Children who have a problem in this area can usually hear what is said, but they have problems deciphering it. It is, in other words, a problem of comprehension. Receptive language problems have been called word blindness, word deafness, aphasia and auditory verbal agnosia. Many children who have been described as *learning disabled* suffer receptive language difficulties. These children often have trouble remembering the names of people and things, and they have trouble placing a symbolic name with an object. Some children do not understand various speech sounds, and they often have difficulty with words, sentences, and reading in general. During training and education these children must be made aware of different sounds and must receive a great deal of individual attention and emphasis upon sound discrimination.

Language Development Systems

Dr. Heimer Myklebust has been writing, conducting research, teaching, directing clinical and laboratory experiences, etc., for the past thirty-five years. He has amassed a huge amount of research concerning deaf and aphasic children and adults. Much of his early work was in the area of language development problems associated with auditory disorders. In *Learning Disabilities: Educational Principles and Practices,* a book he co-authored with Doris Johnson in 1967, they write about children who have learning disabilities of neurogenic origin. Myklebust believes these children have behavioral problems but the cause is neurological.

Infant babbling is a very important prerequisite to spoken language, and Myklebust (1967) points out that the congenitally deaf child does not babble, nor does the autistic child. He believes that the child must identify with the mother to develop a language pattern completely, and the deaf and autistic child does not. In other children the auditory system gets on the wrong channel, so to speak, and they do not identify properly either.

Theory of Learning

If one is to understand Myklebust's approach to language development, one must also understand his theory of learning. He proposes (Johnson and Myklebust, 1967) that learning depends on the proper opportunity as well as upon the presence of three types of integrities: psychodynamic factors, peripheral nervous system (PNS) functions, and central nervous system (CNS) functions. Myklebust proposes that learning has a hierarchy of experiences, and if any of these experiences are altered to any great degree, then learning is affected. These levels of experience overlap developmental periods that operate at the same time in normal children. The developmental levels offered by Myklebust are

1. *Sensation.* This is the lowest level of behavior and refers only to activation of sensorineural structures. Detriments at this level

include deafness and blindness. The two are peripheral nervous system involvements which cause a sensory deprivation.

2. *Perception*. This is the interpretation of sensation and the engagement of anticipatory behavior.

3. *Imagery*. A way in which to describe some of the processes which are covered by the term *memory*.

4. *Verbal Symbolic Behavior*. This type of behavior is highly inclusive and encompasses not only verbal but nonverbal types of learning and recall. It refers to the ability to represent experience.

5. *Conceptualization*. This is the highest level of experience attained by man. Conceptualization must have common elements involved and around those classification and categorization take place.

Myklebust believes strongly in proper assessment, teaching to be directed at the appropriate level and type of disability. For example, teaching sound discrimination may be helpful to one child but detrimental to another. After excellent, specific methods of mediation Myklebust believes in a sound evaluation of the entire program.

McDonald's Theory

One of the most representative theoretical positions of language development of children is the tenents and postulates of McDonald (1967). McDonald's theory is frequently presented with a diagrammatical representation of the major components necessary for the normal developmental acquisition of language. This diagrammatical representation was originally presented as "McDonald's House of Language" (1967). The original representation, however, has been altered and adapted to the present "McDonald's Tree of Language" (1967). The theory suggests that there are six important components of language development.

1. The structural and functional integrity of the subject
2. An accepting and stimulating environment
3. Time for maturation and learning
4. A broad range and background of experiences
5. Sequential steps for concept formation

6. Perceptive and expressive language development

The first component of McDonald's theory implies that the subject should have the constitutional adequacy necessary for language development to occur. This component implies that the child's anatomical makeup should be within the range of normal for normal growth and development of language to occur. Structurally, it is imperative that the child make it through embryonic and fetal development with those structures necessary for language learning to be intact. Physically, the child must have an intact central nervous system, an intact auditory mechanism for sound discrimination necessary to comprehend the verbal cues from his environment, and intact oral and nasal cavities necessary for the production of sounds and speech.

The structures, which may be structurally intact, must be functioning for the acquisition of language to occur. Special educators are becoming increasingly aware of the problems encountered by children who, though structurally adequate, produce atypical behaviors resulting from functional disorders. A child who has normal auditory acuity, suggesting that his auditory mechanism is structurally intact, but who exhibits perceptual inabilities resulting from a dysfunction in his auditory modality is one example. Even though the child is within the range of normal hearing, he may not be able to detect subtle differences in sounds, recall sequences of sounds, or associate meaning with the verbal cues in his environment. The functional disorders may also be observed in his other perceptual avenues, such as visual, tactile, or kinesthetic. McDonald implies that both a structural and functional problem within the physical anatomy of the child might impede the development of language in children.

The second major component of McDonald's theory stresses the importance of environmental influences on the acquisition of language in children. This component further suggests that the environment has a significant impact on the nurturing of speech and language development of children. The children must be exposed to an atmosphere that is conducive for them to express their ideas, to ask questions about their environment, and to use verbal communication to satisfy their wants and needs. This component is most easily seen in children who pair initial attempts at speech with an environment that offers security, acceptance, and the freedom to try out their newly-developed repertoire of behavior. The environment which encourages and accepts the child's verbal abilities will aid in the development of positive emotional responses from the child toward further speech and language development.

The deleterious effects of an unaccepting environment can be observed in the chronically regressed schizophrenic child and children with the bizarre behaviors and mannerisms that are so characteristic of autism. It is these children who present the most bizarre, unusual, and abnormal speech and communication characteristics. The fundamental feature of both conditions is that of psychological causation, possibly originating from an environment that was not conducive to normal growth and development of the personality and, subsequently, language. The environmental impact of language development is further noted in the amount or the degree of stimulation. Stimulation originating from a very early age has been suggested as a necessary ingredient to facilitate language development of children. It is because of stimulation that children acquire early perceptions that are so fundamental to the development of language concepts. Stimulation of the child comes from a variety of environmental sources including family; stimuli within the home; the speech models within the home; the amount of family conversation; the quantity and quality of parental interactions with a child; and the availability of books, magazines, toys, play activities, and play materials that will aid the child in the development of many early language concepts. It is through the availability of environmental stimuli that the child develops early perceptions and, later, concept formations which will increase and enrich his developing vocabulary. The effects of environments considered nonstimulating or lacking in stimulation have been underscored frequently in the literature. Nonstimulating environment has been indicated as the common denominator of two exceptionalities. The children who are commonly referred to as socially disadvantaged or cultural familial mentally retarded are often considered products of environments which are ill-suited to provide proper stimulation.

Like most authorities in the area of language development, McDonald highlights and emphasizes that language development is a developmental phenomenon dependent upon maturation of the child. Further emphasis is given to the premise that language is a learned behavior and is guided by and follows the laws of learning. He does emphasize, however, that learning and maturation are controlled by a time factor. In other words, language development occurs with the aid of maturation and learning over a period of months and years.

McDonald implies that experiences come to the child in the form of sensations. The sensations represent the initial step of the sequential hierarchy leading to the various forms of language development. The sequential hierarchy from sensation to language development is explained by McDonald in the following statement:

> Experiences come to the organism in the form of sensations. At first, the senses respond only to the presence or absence of an adequate stimulus .... As time passes and maturation and learning take place, the child becomes able to discriminate among stimuli. He can now detect that one sound is in some way different from another sound .... Later he learns to attach meaning to certain of the stimuli to which his senses respond; that is to say, perception occurs. Percepts become organized into concepts which are the building blocks of one's language structure (McDonald, 1967).

The language structure eventually develops into the various modes for the reception and expression of symbolic language. Receptively, the child incorporates the symbolic comprehension of language through the listening and reading modes. Expressively, the child develops sequential competencies of gesturing, speaking, and writing the production of symbolic language.

Gerald N. Getman

Dr. Gerald Getman is developmentally oriented and probably is more visually oriented than most of the perceptual-motor theorists. Dr. Getman's theory is based on the sequential learning which we associate with very young children. He believes that visual perception can be developed through training which assists the child in the following. Kephart (1971) points out that these stages overlap, but they do follow a sequential pattern.

General motor patterns. The child learns by moving. The body explores with the eyes, providing the primary guidance system.

Special movement patterns. This includes the all-important eye-hand coordination and other integrated body-sensory skills.

Eye movement patterns. Vision begins to replace the hands in exploration of the environment. Acquisition of information requires less and less manipulation.

Visual language patterns. The child learns to master auditorization. Control of the various muscles (throat, lip, tongue, etc.) is acquired, so that gesturing may be replaced by a more efficient procedure, oral language. Getman emphasizes the role played by the eyes in learning oral language.

Visualization patterns. Other authors would likely call this development of visual memory. It includes the recall of earlier learning, integration of new learning with old, and interpretation of new learning.

The Delacato System

There has been a great deal of controversy surrounding the work and writings of Carl Delacato. Delacato (1963) relates language performance to the following functions:

1. Birth and early development
2. Sleep patterns
3. Creeping abilities
4. Walking patterns
5. Bi-ocular and binocular abilities
6. Singing ability and tonal ability
7. The predominant eye
8. Handedness and footedness
9. Perceptual patterns

One of the most controversial theoretical positions offered to explain receptive and expressive language problems, reading disabilities, and mild locomotor disturbances is the patterning theory of neurological organization developed by Doman and Delacato. Their theoretical views of neurological development of children were designed while they were associated with the Institute for the Achievement of Human Potential. This theoretical framework has as its ultimate objective to duplicate in brain injured, retarded, reading disabled, and language disordered children the same quality of neurological organization that is observed among normal children. The theory proposes that language and reading disabilities result from the breakdown of sequential development in the five stages of neurological organization. According to their theory, neurological organization is achieved through proper and orderly development of the following five sequential stages: (1) spinal cord-medulla, (2) pons, (3) midbrain, (4) cortex, and (5) cortical or hemispheric dominance. From conception until full development, the orderly development of the child's nervous system necessitates full organization throughout each of the sequential steps. It is in this respect that Doman and Delacato propose "ontogeny recapitulates phylogeny." This phrase is translated to imply that the ontogenic development of the child recapitulates or parallels the phylogenic evolutionary development of the nervous system among the human species.

Spinal cord-medulla, as the first stage of neurological organization of the child, was based on, or corresponds to, the neurological development of the earliest vertebrate animals. These animals were most clearly represented by sharks and rays. Propulsion or locomotion for these early animals was made possible by the spinal cord of the nervous system. With these animals, who had simple brains, the medulla structure was the dominant portion of the brain.

The pons and midbrain stages of neurological evolution were most clearly developed among amphibians. These animals spend part of their life in an aquatic environment and remainder of their existence on a terrestrial environment. While in the water, the amphibian's movement was characterized by homolateral locomotion — that is, they moved through the water by a simultaneous movement of the limbs on one side of the body, which was followed by a simultaneous movement of the limbs on the other side of the body. Homolateral movement was controlled or regulated by the pons on the amphibian's brain. Changing to the land environment created the requirement for the amphibian to move in a style characterized as cross-pattern — when the right front leg moves forward, there is a simultaneous forward movement of the left rear leg. The cross-pattern movement was possible because of the evolvement of the midbrain, a new step up in the evolution of the nervous system.

Following the amphibians were the reptiles, who also moved in a cross-pattern gait. However, they developed larger brains than their predecessors. The reptiles were followed by the mammals, who developed larger brains and evolved larger and more complex structuring of the cortex. It is within the class of mammals that one finds the largest, most intricate and complex brain — the human brain.

According to Delacato, the difference between man and the lower forms of animals is the evolvement of two halves of the human cerebral cortex. The division of labor of the two cerebral hemispheres allows man to see three-dimensionally and to develop speech and other modes of communication. The establishment of cortical hemispheric dominance represents the fifth and final stage of neurological organization.

Doman and Delacato proposed that some exceptional children, particularly those with reading and communication disorders, may have the component skills necessary to perform such functions, but their lack of neurological organization impedes or prevents the acquisition of the skills. It became necessary for the therapist to pinpoint at which of the five stages the child is lacking neurological organization.

Perhaps the following example would serve to explain the failure of complete neurological organization in producing a reading problem. A child who sleeps in a patterned tonic neck reflex attitude is simulating the movements noted in the earlier animals where the pons was the dominant area of the brain. The tonic neck sleeping position assumes that the child, while lying on his stomach with his head turned to the left, the knee of the left leg is bent and raised toward the waist, and the left arm is bent at the elbow with the hand toward the face. The child's right arm will also be stretched along the body as will the right leg. Should the child's head be turned in the opposite direction, there should be a complete body reorganization or the child will awaken. Delacato suggests that such a reorganization will occur among normal reading children. This alteration or reversing of the body organization implies that the child is organized at the pons level. Delacato assumes that this child is organized at the pons level because the movements are similar to the homolateral pattern observed among the amphibians while living in the aquatic environment. Therefore, Delacato recommends the parents should posture children who do not sleep naturally in the tonic neck reflex attitude. The theory also suggests that if children cannot crawl in a cross-pattern style, it may be indicative of insufficient neural organization at the midbrain level. The reader is requested to recall that the cross-pattern fashion of locomotion occurred because of the evolvement of the midbrain observed among the earliest amphibians and reptiles.

The therapeutic treatment of the patterning theory has been publicly criticized by a number of health and educational representatives in a joint conference, meeting specifically to discuss the controversial patterning theory. A statement was issued depicting their concern with the use of such treatment procedures with children having learning problems. The conference expressed concerns ranging from a lack of theoretical verification of the Doman-Delacato treatment procedures to a suspicion of the claims of success with exceptional children without any supportive research. They also expressed a joint concern toward the *developmental profile*, which to date has no validity nor reliability data supporting the efficacy of the diagnostic instrument.

Because of the restrictions that the Doman-Delacato treatment place on certain developmental activities (walking, listening to music, etc.), the conference indicated concern for this aspect of treatment because they found no published research to document their position.

The authors wish to express that the above discussion was not intended to support or discount the patterning theory, but due to its controversial nature they believe the reader should be exposed to the major elements of the theory.

Raymond H. Barsch

Dr. Raymond Barsch developed many of his ideas and materials while serving as Director of the Teacher Preparation Program for Teachers for the Physically Handicapped and Neurologically Impaired at the University of Wisconsin. Dr. Barsch has a theory called *movigenics* (two Latin words, *movere*, meaning to move, and *genesis*, meaning origin and development). Movigenics to Barsch is a theory for education, and he speaks of it with enthusiasm and writes about it in a highly readable manner. The movigenics theory is based on the ten concepts which follow:

1. The fundamental principle underlying the design of the human organism is movement efficiency.

2. The primary objective of movement efficiency is to economically promote the survival of the organism.

3. Movement efficiency is derived from the information the organism is able to process from an energy surround.

4. The human mechanism for transducing energy forms into information is the perceptocognitive system.

5. The terrain of movement is space.

6. Developmental momentum provides a constant forward thrust toward maturity and demands an equilibrium to maintain direction.

7. Movement efficiency is developed in a climate of stress.

8. The adequacy of the feedback system is critical in the development of movement efficiency.

9. Development of movement efficiency occurs in segments of sequential expansion.

10. Movement efficiency is symbolically communicated through the visual-spatial phenomenon called language.

These ten constructs are the basis of Barsch's movigenics. Gearheart (1973) states that "On this base, a movement efficiency matrix, composed of fifteen parts and made up of three major organizational units, is presumed to exist within each individual. Each individual is then in a constant search for more movement efficiency, more grace and ease in both physical and cognitive movement."

Barsch uses five component parts of the first unit of his movement efficiency matrix which permits the development of maximum postural-transport orientation — muscular strength, dynamic balance, body awareness, spatial awareness, and temporal awareness.

Dr. Barsch offers six percepto-cognitive models — these are gustatory, olfactory, tactual, kinesthetic, auditory, and visual. These six in various combinations provide the vehicle whereby the learner can acquire information. These six modes make up the second unit of the matrix.

Implications of Movigenics

Barsch (1965, 1967, 1968) arrived at a movigenic theory and constructs through his motor curriculum. He planned specific activities in a developmental motor program and described these activities in several publications. He separated the two fields of learning disabilities and motor training, and stated that it was by chance that their development coincided. Dr. Barsch contends that although children with learning disabilities need motor training, there are many children who do not have learning disabilities who also need motor training.

One of the most important implications of the movigenic framework is that the roles played by language development and auditory skills in learning are relatively neglected. We need guidelines to help the teachers bridge the gap from motor skill development to academic skills, and in the movigenic curriculum this task is not clearly specified.

Bryant J. Cratty

Dr. Bryant Cratty is a prolific writer, and in his writings he expresses his views concerning perceptual/motor theorists, and in his writings he says that he apparently believes some of the theorists make claims which are difficult to substantiate. Dr. Cratty believes in the value of perceptual/motor training for children with learning disabilities, and in his book written in 1971 he states, "Movement games may help the child with learning problems, may aid the active normal child to learn better, and may improve the academic progress of the culturally deprived and retarded child."

Cratty states that the inability of children to play games well or to participate successfully in athletics may lead to a lowered social acceptance by peers, lower their self-concepts and therefore reduce their academic performances. Naturally, this is more the case with boys than with girls, but it must be pointed out that a large proportion of children having learning disabilities are boys. Dr. Cratty is quick to point out that hand/eye coordination is extremely important in writing, and that general coordination is important in a large number of academic tasks.

Newell C. Kephart

The late Dr. Newell Kephart was director of the Glen Haven Achievement Center at Fort Collins, Colorado, and is one of the best known of the perceptual/motor systems advocates. Dr. Kephart developed a well-ordered theoretical construct, and from it has evolved a system of training activities which he designed to remedy diagnosed learning deficiencies. In 1971 Kephart stated, "It is logical to assume that all behavior is basically motor, that the prerequisites of any kind of behavior are muscular and motor responses."

It is Kephart's theory that the child develops a series of strategies for handling increasing quantities of outside information per unit of time. Concurrent with these two lines of development is an intricate matching procedure between outside information and established internal responses. The following information comes from one of Kephart's early books entitled *Learning Disability: An Educational Adventure,* published in 1968:

> *Motor Stage.* The child's initial encounters with the universe are motor encounters. The child moves and as a result of this movement an encounter with the environment occurs . . . .
>
> It is during this stage that the child develops the tools for environmental encounters. He learns what the parts of his body are, what responses they can make, how to produce these movement responses, and how to recognize what response has occurred . . . .
>
> . . . The first control, therefore, of the environment organism

interaction is a motor control and involves the control of the organism itself. As these motor experiences increase in number the resulting learnings develop in a sequential fashion ...

It is probably inaccurate to suppose that all of the activity of this stage in development is purely motor. When the organism moves, certain perceptual information is automatically generated. Thus, in the muscles and joints there are sensitive end organs which are stimulated when movement occurs. It is therefore technically impossible to have movement without a resulting effect.

In developing language, reading, and writing skills and other forms of communicative arts, Kephart believes in several processing patterns or stages. It has already been mentioned that he believes all behavior is basically motor and that this behavior must be used in developing all types of communicative language. Kephart states that the eye learns to see what the hand feels, and therefore eye/hand coordination must be developed. At a very early age the eye explores, and, according to Kephart, the hand moves after the eye to confirm what the eye is experiencing. Later the child will use the hand just for assurance in a new situation, but the motor and perceptual data have merged, and Kephart refers to this phenomena as perceptual/motor match.

Another major step in the learning process, according to Kepart, is the establishment of figure/ground relationships. If a child is able to separate figure from ground, he has the ability to concentrate on different items relating to the environment and to the background.

Laterality is also in the sequence of his motor basis of learning. According to Kephart, the directions we recognize and use every day in our activities are all related to the wholeness of learning. Right, left, up, down, before and behind are all relative and must be recognized before the child can learn in a meaningful way. Body image is another motor base of achievement, Kephart states, and each individual's body is the point of reference around which relative impressions of the environment must be organized. The child must learn to use the body in a meaningful way and to be proud of the use of the body. Kephart believes that locomotion, or the ability to move about, is important in learning correctly. Special attention must be paid to the child who has a deficiency in locomotion, or he will not be successful in spatial exploration.

Kephart considers visual/motor capabilities to be extremely important in developing communicative skills which are necessary for learning and abstract thinking. Kephart puts more emphasis on visual and motor input than he does on auditory input.

Summary

This chapter has attempted to synthesize the available literature concerning language development of children. The theories presented in this chapter are representative of diverse positions on the acquisition and use of language. Some of the theories were specifically selected because they relate more to the language development of exceptional children. The behaviorist's position concerning language development of children was given only a brief description as it will be treated with greater detail in the next chapter.

BIBLIOGRAPHY

Barsch, Ray H.: *A Movigenic Curriculum Bulletin.* No. 25. Madison, Wisconsin, Department of Public Instruction, Bureau for the Handicapped, 1965.
———*Achieving Perceptual-Motor Efficiency.* Seattle, Spec Child, 1967, vol. 1.
———*Enriching Perception and Cognition.* Seattle, Spec Child, 1968, vol. 2
Bartel, Nettie: In Hammill, Donald D., and Bartel, Nettie R.: *Teaching Children with Learning and Behavior Problems.* Boston, Allyn, 1975.
Chomsky, N.: *Syntactic Structures.* The Hague, Mouton, 1957.
———*Aspects of a Theory of Syntax.* Cambridge, MIT Pr, 1965.
Cratty, B.: *Active Learning: Games to Enchance Academic Abilities.* Englewood Cliffs, P-H, 1971.
Darwin, C.: *The Descent of Man and Selection in Relation to Sex.* London, J. Murray, 1871.
Delacato, Carl H.: *The Diagnosis and Treatment of Speech and Reading Problems.* Springfield, Thomas, 1963.
de Laguna, G. A.: *Speech: Its Function and Development.* New Haven, Yale U Pr, 1927.
Frisch, K. von: *The Dancing Bees.* London, Methuen and Co., 1954.
Gearheart, B. R.: *Learning Disabilities: Educational Strategies.* St. Louis, Mosby, 1973.
Jesperson, O.: *Language: Its Nature, Development and Origin.* New York,

Henry Holt, 1922.
Johnson, Doris I., and Myklebust, Helmer R.: *Learning Disabilities: Educational Principles and Practices*. New York, Grune, 1967.
Judd, C. H.: *The Psychology of Social Institutions*. New York, Macmillan, 1926.
Karlin, Isaac W., Karlin, David B., and Gurren, Louise: *Development and Disorders of Speech in Childhood*. Springfield, Thomas, 1970.
Keller, Helen: *The Story of My Life*. New York, Dell, 1961.
Kephart, Newell, C.: *Learning Disability: An Educational Adventure*. Lafayette, Kappa Delta Pi Pr, 1968.
―――*The Slow Learner in the Classroom*, 2nd Ed. Columbus, Merrill, 1971.
Lefevre, A.: *Race and Language*. New York, Appleton, 1894.
Lenneberg, E.: A biological perspective of language. In Smith, F. and Miller, G. A. (Eds). *New Directions in the Study of Language*. Cambridge, MIT Pr, 1964.
―――*Biological Foundations of Language*. New York, Wiley, 1967.
Lerner, Janet W.: *Children With Learning Disabilities*. Boston, HM, 1971.
McDonald, Eugene T.: *Articulation Testing and Treatment: A Sensory-motor Approach*. Pittsburgh, Stanwix, 1967.
McDonald's tree of language. From a lecture presented by Dr. Eugene T. McDonald, Research Professor of Speech Pathology, Penn State University, 1967.
Myklebust, H.: *Auditory Disorders in Children*. New York, Grune, 1954.
―――*Picture Story Language Test: The Development and Disorders of Written Language*. New York, Grune, 1965, vol. 1.
Paget, R.: *Human Speech*. New York, HarBrace, 1930.
Skinner, B. F.: *Visual Behavior*. New York, Appleton, 1957.
Wallace, Gerald, and McLoughlin, James A.: *Learning Disabilities: Concepts and Characteristics*. Columbus, Merril, 1975.
Wundt, W.: *Elements of Folk Psychology*. Translated by Schaub, E. L. London, G. Allen and Unwin, Ltd., 1916.

Chapter 2

OVERVIEW OF LEARNING: THEORETICAL POSITIONS AND THEIR RELATION TO LANGUAGE DEVELOPMENT

A COMMON contention among learning theorists is that learning is a process not isolated from language, but an integral process of language development. They posit that all modes of language function are learned — that is, they are guided by factors associated with the learning process. Since this position is so commonly held among learning theorists, the authors felt that one chapter of this book should be devoted to the theoretical positions of learning that are related to language development.

First, it must be understood that there is no single theory of learning completely adequate to explain how children learn. Furthermore, no theory can satisfactorily explain how language is learned. What is attempted here is a compilation of the major conceptualizations to date used to explain the learning process. The authors have elected to present the major theoretical positions of contiguity and reinforcement to serve as explanatory vehicles and to demonstrate their relationship with language learning. Since no single theory can be expected to fully account for and explain how children learn language, readers are advised either to be eclectic or to adopt the learning position that best suits their understanding.

The contiguity theory of learning emphasizes that learning has occurred when a habit has been formed between stimulus and a response, or, as contiguity theorists suggest, whenever a specific stimulus and a specific response occur together. In the strictest sense, the learner, while in the presence of certain stimuli, produces certain predictable behaviors or responses. In other words, there is a simultaneous occurrence of stimulus and response to such a degree that the learner will behave exactly the way he behaved the last time he was in the presence of the stimulus. Behaving in exactly the same manner he behaved the last time he was in the presence of that stimulus can be facilitated, according to the contiguity position, by a continuous repetition of that stimulus and response. For example, if a young child in the presence of a ball (stimulus) says ball (response), it is hoped that the next time he is in the presence of a ball the appropriate labeling response could be elicited. Contiguity theorists suggest that we can strengthen the bond (habit formation) if we so arrange the learning situation to incorporate repetition of the response (ball) in the presence of the stimulus. Because of the continuous exposure, repetition, or drill that the child is subjected to, a strong and stable response can be effected whenever he is instructed to verbally identify that object.

The major contiguity theory is that of classical conditioning, first introduced by Pavlov, a strict behaviorist. Ivan P. Pavlov (1849-1936) is widely known as the founder of the stimulus-response theory, or classical conditioning. Pavlov's work is based on the doctrine of association. Aristotle first provided the basic principle of association by contiguity. This old but basic principle states that if a response occurs in the presence of a particular pattern of stimuli, then the pattern of stimuli will elicit the response (Bugelski, 1971). His theory of classical conditioning depicts the stimuli in a situation as prodding the organism into action. Previously neutral stimuli, as the result of being paired with a stimulus already capable of eliciting such a response, acquire the ability to control behavior and thus cause learning (Snelbecker, 1974). By his now-famous experiment, Pavlov demonstrated this theory by conditioning a dog to salivate at the sound of a bell. The bell (conditioned stimulus) was paired with the offering of food (unconditioned stimulus) in order to condition the salivation (unconditioned response) to occur when only the bell was rung (conditioned response). Pavlov contended that the basis of all behavior was learning and suggested that many of the learned behaviors developed because of conditioning. Pavlov proposed that there are classes of stimuli which elicit certain behaviors or responses that do not have to be learned — that is, the learner has responses to specific kinds of stimuli that are innate or, as one might say, unlearned. For example, an infant will produce a rooting and sucking response whenever his cheek is stroked in the area of his mouth. We cannot say that this is a learned response, but we believe it is a response which innately or naturally occurs. Pavlov initiated this idea with his most famous laboratory experiments of classical conditioning. He labeled certain classes of stimuli as unconditioned and certain classes of responses as unconditioned. He proposed that an organism will naturally respond (unconditional response) to a stimuli that he referred to as an unconditional stimulus.

Another stimulus-response theory is Edwin R. Gutherie's (1886-1959) one-trial learning theory. Gutherie's central proposition was that learning consists of conditioning responses to stimuli. This emphasizes the association, or a conditioning, of a stimulus to a response. Gutherie believed that learning takes place in one trial and no further trials are needed. Expressing the point, he said,

> Whenever a response is made, the response is at once then and there learned or conditioned to the stimulus or stimuli that are present at the time. The stimuli that preceded the response must now be eliminated or somehow disappear. If the stimuli remain, the learner will make new movements and continue to do so until the stimuli do disappear. If a movement is made and the stimuli leading to it are no longer about or active, the movement will have been learned once and for all to those stimuli. There is no time for practice (Bugelski, 1971).

Bugelski (1971) states that Gutherie offered two reasons for the need of practice — the same stimuli are not likely to appear again in exactly the same form, and the movements made in response to a given stimulus do not change the stimulus situation. Another important aspect of this theory is his principle of postremity which posits that we always learn the last thing we do in a response to any specific stimulus situation. This implies that one is always learning as long as he continues to react to whatever stimuli are present. A final aspect of this theory is the belief that rewards and punishments are equally irrelevant for learning. He looked upon rewards and punishments as techniques for eliminating stimuli that preceded the response and which protected the learning that had occurred.

A particularly important and relevant concept of the contiguity theory is the observation that the learner may develop emotional responses. Contiguity theorists indicate that emotional responses cannot always be accounted for, but they suggest that one can arrange the learning situation to maximize the probability that the learner will develop healthy emotional responses.

From the point of view of the contiguity theorists, emotional responses can be either positive or negative. They further suggest that the learning situation be arranged to increase the probability that positive emotional responses will develop within the child. Emotional responses develop because of the precise arrangement of specific stimuli paired in the presence of the child. For example, the young child in his first experience with formalized reading instruction is exposed to two important stimuli being repeatedly paired together. Hypothetically, one could label reading as a stimulus condition while at the same time labeling the teacher as the second stimulus condition. When reading instruction (stimulus 1) occurs, reading behavior always occurs in the presence of the teacher (stimulus 2). If there is a fracture in the teacher-child relationship, or if personality conflicts interfere with a healthy interaction with the child and the teacher, the likelihood is great that his feelings toward the teacher will have significant carryover in his advancement in reading. In other words, because reading always occurs in the presence of the teacher, the child may eventually direct the same feelings he has for the teacher toward reading. He does not like the teacher, therefore he does not like reading. In this case one could charge that a negative emotional response toward reading occurred because of his unfavorable feelings toward the teacher. Laboratory experiments in contiguity studies have repeatedly verified that a response to one stimulus condition may be transferred to a second stimulus condition if those stimulus conditions have been paired on frequent occasions. The reader is directed to the classical conditioning studies of Pavlov for a deeper understanding of the concept of pairing.

As it was previously stated, one should arrange learning

situations, or, specifically, pairing situations, in such manner that positive emotional responses will occur. Consider the favorable results that might have been obtained if the relationship between the child and the teacher had been more positive — if the teacher had been empathetic, understanding and encouraging, the child would have had a more favorable attitude toward the teacher. As a result, the child would have paired reading with a teacher he liked. The child would then give the same response toward reading he gives toward the teacher because they have been paired together on repeated occasions.

Positive and negative emotional responses can also account for deviations in early speech acquisition. If the child's initial attempts to learn to speak are always made in an atmosphere of tension, anxiety, pressure and frustration, he may begin to pair speaking with the feelings he acquires because of that climate. The result of that pairing is most detrimental to his future language growth and development. On the other hand, if a child's early attempts at speech always occur in the presence of acceptance and warmth, his future growth and development in language are greatly facilitated.

Instrumental conditioning (operant), derived from Edward L. Thorndike, primarily asserts that behavior is controlled by its consequences, and we learn to do that which produces pleasant effects and to avoid that which has unpleasant effects (Snelbecker, 1974). The reinforcement approach to learning received its greatest impetus from Skinner in his text, *Science and Human Behavior* (1953). In this approach it is emphasized that the consequences invoked upon either behavior or response determine the strength and frequency of that behavior or response. The response, in this framework, represents directly observable and measurable behavior. Responses occur in the presence of environmental stimuli that are significant or powerful enough to produce or evoke a response. Those who advocate the reinforcement position state the probability of a response occurring in the presence of the stimulus on subsequent occasions is related to the consequence that is given following the response. A consequence that is rewarding or desirable to the learner is used to effect an increase in the behavior or response rate. The learner's environment is the source for stimuli that influence responses from the child. If the responses are rewarded, the reinforcement position proposed that there should be an increase in the probability that the learner will respond to that environmental stimulus on repeated occasions.

The teacher or therapist can control the responses generated by the child by arranging the environment in such a fashion that the favorable possibility of the learner attending to a specific stimulus or a specific class of stimuli is increased. Such an arrangement decreases the probability that the learner will attend to irrelevant stimuli and thereby will avoid inappropriate or incompatible responses. The techniques of reinforcement are used to lead the learner not only to attend more to relevant stimuli but also to respond correctly to those stimuli.

Learning occurs when the learner's responses become conditioned to stimuli. The conditioning of responses is facilitated by the use of reinforcing stimuli presented to the learner after the appropriate response has occurred in the presence of a specific stimulus. Learning, however, is most complex and involves more than specific responses to specific stimuli. The focus of the educator's view of learning lies with the capability of the learner to generalize his responses to similar stimulus conditions and to differentially respond to stimulus situations that require discriminations.

The young child who says cookie when desiring a cracker, potato chip, or other similar munchy snack indicates that his response has generalized to similar stimuli. Originally, the response of "cookie" was conditioned to a cookie. The response, however, became generalized, and similar stimuli (cracker, potato chips, etc.) produced the same response. Other examples of generalization may involve verbalizing "mama" as the name or title of the babysitter, verbalizing "bye-bye" when the mother leaves the child at the babysitter's, and saying "bye-bye" to the babysitter when the mother picks up the child on her return.

However, it is imperative for children to be able to transfer responses to different stimulus conditions when the responses are appropriate. In many instances, responses generalized or transferred to different stimulus situations may be inappropriate and, consequently, the learner's response judged erroneous. As a result, the learning process among children must entail a second important dimension — discrimination.

Discriminations are obtained when one observes that the subject emits a differential response to discriminative stimuli. Reinforcement advocates indicate that one can facilitate the acquisition of discriminative or differential responses by selective reinforcement of responses. This reinforcement plan is most frequently referred to as differential reinforcement. By differentially reinforcing correct responses, the tendency for the child to give correct or discriminative responses is tied to the reinforcement history associated with that response. Positive reinforcement for correct or discriminative responses, while not reinforcing incorrect responses, provides the basis of differential reinforcement and discrimination learning.

Differential reinforcement can be applied to young children for the acquisition of correct labeling responses. It is through differential reinforcement that children no longer label all adult women *mama*. The discrimination was made by the child to use the label *mama* only in signaling or labeling the mother. Labeling of familiar animals serves as another example of how discriminative responses are acquired through differential reinforcement. The child who previously overgeneralized cat to all four-legged and furry animals can learn the appropriate discriminative response of cat only when the cat serves as a discriminative stimulus and the parents reinforce that response. When the label *cat* is used in the presence of a dog and the parents do not reinforce that label, the child learns that reinforcement of the cat response only occurs when that discriminative stimulus is present.

Major emphasis on learning from the reinforcement approach to learning is placed on the stimulus that is delivered or acquired after a specific response has occurred. The stimulus is always dependent upon the subject's emission of a response or chain of responses. Consequences are, in effect, stimuli presented that are contingent upon the emission of certain responses. The selection of appropriate consequences is central to the future emission of certain behaviors. In other words, certain consequences may be used to increase specific responses whereas other consequences serve to decrease the likelihood that the behavior will reappear. Actually, consequences can affect behavior in one of three ways. A given consequence may (1) strengthen, (2) weaken, or (3) have no effect at all on the behavior (Neisworth and Smith, 1973).

The reinforcing stimulus, usually represented by a desirable or pleasurable event (consequence), is given after the occurrence of a desirable response. If that reward significantly strengthens or increases the response, one can infer that the increase in the response resulted from the given consequence. This provides the basis for positive reinforcement. One can only label a reinforcing stimulus as a positive reinforcer if the stimulus promotes an increment in the behavior. In other words, a positive reinforcer is defined by the way in which it effects a specific behavior. If Johnny's rate of written words correctly spelled increases after rewarding each correct word with a baseball card, one can define the card as a positive reinforcer. Furthermore, the therapist can then indicate more correctly that (s)he was using positive reinforcement.

It is important for the reader to keep in mind that giving a child any kind of reward does not constitute a program of positive reinforcement. Attempting to increase a child's response rate or behavior with chocolate candy will not be a reinforcer if the child detests chocolate candy. The child who does not like chocolate candy may actually engage in behavior designed to avoid receiving the chocolate candy. Furthermore, a child who likes chocolate candy may not value chocolate candy as a reward for his work if it is received right after he has polished off two candy bars prior to coming into the therapy session.

One of the important innovations in reinforcement theory was originated by Premack (1965) and has been used with great success in many therapeutic and classroom modification programs. The Premack principle incorporates two classifications of behavior, namely low probability and high probability behavior. The principle states that one might find an increase in low probability behavior if it is followed consecutively by high probability behavior. If one could consider the completion of an arithmetic assignment as a low probability behavior of a child who does not particularly like arithmetic, one could arrange to have play time (high probability behavior) contingent upon the completion of the arithmetic assignment. In this case the low probability behavior is rewarded by the opportunity to engage in play time. If the teacher or therapist notes a significant increase in the completion of math assignments, one could then infer that play time as a high probability behavior served as a positive reinforcer. Remember that the judgment of a reward as a positive reinforcer can only be made by the effect it has on behavior.

Another important concept central to positive reinforcement is that referred to as the *favorable situation*. It is most frequently defined as that situation in which the desired behavior is most likely to occur. Before one can significantly effect a behavior change it is imperative that the learning situation must be arranged to reduce the probability of unacceptable or incompatible behaviors occurring. In most instances there are two important factors related to the favorable situation; they are referred to here as the physical arrangement of the setting and the level of motivation that has been built up within the learner. The physical setting should be arranged to reduce the possibility of the learner's attention being shifted to irrelevant stimuli — use the physical setting to increase the probability he will produce the desired response. For example, the therapist's ability to gain the child's attention for language training will be reduced considerably if the child's attention is directed toward toys and other play materials scattered about the room. The arrangement of the physical environment is extremely important when working with children who are hyperactive or hyperdistractable.

Effecting a favorable situation for learning is also enhanced by preplanning for an optimal level of motivation of the child. A child who has been deprived of food for a number of hours prior to the therapy session is more likely to engage in behaviors that will be reinforced with food. Consider the example of a four-year-old child who is delayed in speech and is in language training to increase his verbal productions. The objective of the language therapist for the four-year-old is to verbally label the breakfast foods of egg, toast, juice, and jam. To effect a favorable situation, the therapist instructs the parents to deprive the child of breakfast before he reaches the therapy room. Upon arrival at the therapy room, the child is hungry, or, in this scheme, highly motivated. The therapist uses pieces of egg, toast, juice, and jam as edible reinforcers which represent components of his breakfast. Since the objective is to shape the child's verbal labeling of breakfast foods, the therapist places only the food stimuli on the table in order to orient the child's attention toward the discriminative stimuli. The therapist has, then, increased the probability that the child will request the food items as opposed to other distracting stimuli that might have been present and, therefore, might have produced incompatible responses. The favorable situation is probably more intensified, however, because of the child's motivation for engaging in behavior that will lead to acquiring food. Because of the favorable situation the therapist is in a better situation to evoke approximations of verbal responses from the child. The therapy session employs a contingency requirement for the child to receive his breakfast. In other words, for the child to receive a bite of breakfast he must give a verbal approximation of the food items he desires.

Because the four-year-old has a previous history of delayed speech, the therapist should not expect the child to be able to identify correctly the food items on the first trial. Therefore, the therapist should break down the final performance into sequences of steps that can be put together later as the language therapy progresses. The language therapy program for the four-year-old is constructed to reinforce approximations of the final performance that have been evoked from the child by the therapist. By reinforcing each successive approximation of the final performance the behavior will, hopefully, become appropriately conditioned. The emission of the *j* sound, in other words, represents an approximation of *jam* and should initially be reinforced by giving the child a bite of the jam breakfast food. Breaking down the final appropriate response requires that the complete or whole response be task analyzed. Task analysis refers to the breaking down of behaviors or responses into smaller units or steps. When shaping a new behavior or response like *jam* one should break the response down into small enough steps to be learned easily. It is quite possible that no amount of reinforcement will teach a child to verbally label the breakfast foods in one step. A process of chaining or working backwards through a series of steps can be implemented successfully (Neisworth and Smith, 1973). This procedure has the advantage of not only strengthening a specific approximation but also increasing the probability that a closer response or approximation will occur (Reese, 1966). In the example of the four-year-old the reinforcement of the *j* sound enhances the probability that the closer approximation of the *-am* sound will occur. Once the two approximations are shaped, the final step in training would involve the reinforcement of the child for saying *jam*. It is important to keep in mind, however, that more primitive approximations of lip movements, grunts, or random sounds may serve as initial approximations or beginnings to be reinforced once the shaping process is begun.

The second type of reinforcement in this approach is referred to as negative reinforcement. Strictly speaking, negative reinforcement implies that the behavior which terminates or avoids an aversive stimulus becomes strengthened. An aversive stimulus in this context refers to those classes of stimuli that are painful, noxious, or undesirable as perceived by the learner. The learner frequently is exposed to situations which necessitate the emission of behavior to prevent aversive stimuli. Negative reinforcement is most frequently used, sometimes unknowingly, by parents in the home and teachers within the classroom. The child who picks up his toys and cleans up his room to avoid punishment is operating under a negative reinforcement scheme. The behavior of picking up the toys and cleaning up the room is reinforced because it is the behavior which avoided the aversive stimulus. The child at school consistently does his homework in order to avoid both the scorn of the teacher and a low grade on his report card. In both examples the behaviors were strengthened. Therefore, the intent of negative reinforcement is always to increase or strengthen behavior.

Consider the example of a young autistic child whose tolerance of adults being present is quite minimal. The adults serve this example as stimuli that the autistic child seeks to avoid. As a consequence, the child engages in behaviors that will, hopefully, remove the adults from his presence.

Previously, however, the behaviors employed by the child were socially unacceptable and incompatible with the repertoire of behaviors which should be exhibited. By taking advantage of the autistic child's dislike of other people, the therapist could use a contingency plan for shaping new and more socially acceptable behaviors within the child. Successfully removing the therapist from the child's immediate environment is contingent upon the emission of a socially acceptable response or behavior predetermined by the therapist. Behaviors such as eye contact for two-second intervals, shaking hands with the therapist, accepting a toy from the therapist, or even the verbal response of saying hello to the therapist may serve as examples of socially acceptable behaviors that will lead to the removal of the therapist who has disarranged the autistic child's isolation. One should, however, be aware of the potential danger of using negative reinforcement in this manner. Continued repetition of such a scheme may enhance the child's reluctance to interact socially with other individuals. However, such techniques may prove to be valuable in altering the psychotic child's unacceptable behavior.

The third major consequence that may follow behavior is punishment. Punishment refers to the application of an aversive stimulus to those behaviors judged to be socially inappropriate and to those responses which interfere with or interrupt learning. Punishment as a tool in the behavior modification scheme is employed to reduce the frequency of behavior that is judged to be undesirable. This consequence can only be defined by the manner in which it affects behavior. The child who previously emitted curse words in the classroom at an average rate of twenty-five times per day may serve as a likely candidate for punishment. The intent, then, behind the administration of this consequence is to reduce the behavior significantly below the level that it is presently being emitted. If punishing the cursing behavior after each occurrence of the behavior brings about a reduction in the rate of emission, one could define the consequence as punishment. It is only through the reduction of behavior that the aversive agent can be judged as punishment.

The teacher or parent who is confronted with cursing behavior may have more success, however, in using a technique that is less dramatic than spanking as a means to reduce the unwanted cursing. He might employ a technique of extinction. Extinction involves the withdrawal of or withholding of a positive reinforcer from a response or behavior that has been previously maintained and strengthened by reinforcement. In the example of the child who frequently used inappropriate cursing behavior one could infer that the cursing was maintained (reinforced) because of the manner in which it operated on the environment. If such behavior brings attention to the child, it could be inferred that attention served as the reinforcer which governed the frequency and the context with which it occurred. By employing an extinction plan the teacher or parents withhold the reinforcer that affects the cursing behavior. In other words, they no longer attend to the behavior, therefore removing the reinforcer which maintains the behavior. It is imperative, however, that the teacher and parents attend to those verbalizations made by the child which do not contain the unpleasant cursing. At this point they are differentially reinforcing the verbal behavior of the child. By reinforcing the desired verbalization of the child and ignoring the undesirable language, the frequency of cursing behavior should decrease significantly. The teacher and parent should be advised, however, to expect a sudden elevation in cursing behavior when the extinction phase is first begun. Unfortunately, all too often, teachers and parents may return to their previous inappropriate method of handling the cursing when the sudden elevation in cursing overpowers them. At this point they again reinforce the behavior, but this time the cursing behavior is at its most intense level. As a consequence, their attempts at reducing the behavior inadvertently strengthen the behavior and increase the intensity of the behavior. Another important part of the reinforcement approach to learning involves the monitoring of behavior in order to determine the frequency, regularity, consistency, and pattern of the behavior prior to the initiation of treatment. It is in this manner that one can measure or chart the behavior as it occurs within specific contexts or in the presence of certain environmental conditions. This is sometimes referred to as the baseline or operant level of behavior. This technique can be employed to chart the frequency of such language behaviors as rate of lip movements, rate of specific vocal behaviors, gesturing to obtain desired objects, words read per minute, child-initiated conversations, and so on. It is through the establishment of the baseline of behavior that one can judge whether or not the reinforcer that is employed will increase the behavior. If the behavior increases above the predetermined baseline, or operant level, one is able to define the reinforcing stimulus as a positive reinforcer. The effectiveness of an aversive stimulus can be evaluated similarly. If the rate of behavior falls below the preestablished operant level, the consequence invoked by behavior can be evaluated as aversive, thus defining the procedure as punishment.

Another important value that the determination of an operant level has in the reinforcement approach is the information gained in setting up a favorable situation. Returning to the example of the four-year-old nonverbal child discussed earlier in this chapter, one can use this example to note the relationship between operant level of behavior and favorable situation. Consider the advantage the therapist might have if (s)he were able to record the most frequently emitted vocal operants of the child prior to the initiation of therapy. Perhaps the therapist might have found that this four-year-old emitted some vocal sounds more frequently than other sounds. By charting the frequency of those vocal sounds the therapist could conceivably rank those sounds in a range from most to least frequently emitted. If, for example, the child, under normal conditions, emitted the m sound, the j sound, and the t sound more frequently than any other vocal operants, the therapist could more easily concentrate the training efforts toward shaping verbal responses which contain those sounds. The therapist has, then, increased the probability that the desired verbal labeling will occur. The therapist now has the advantage of using the j sound to shape jam, the m sound to shape milk, and the t sound to shape the verbal label of toast. This example serves to promote the advantage that charting baselines of behavior, or responses, may possibly have for future treatment using a reinforcement approach.

LANGUAGE THERAPEUTIC APPROACHES
WITH EXCEPTIONAL CHILDREN

The application of learning theoretical models to language

training of exceptional children is clearly established in the literature. Many of the experimental investigations using a learning theory approach have operated under the premise that their laws were as applicable to language development as other varieties of humanistic behavior. The present section is included to provide the reader with a guide by which more specific readings may be pursued. These suggested readings will be listed under relevant content areas. These readings reflect research with exceptional children which has used learning theoretical models to account for and explain language growth and development.

Cerebral Palsy

Benassi, B. J., and Benassi, V. A.: Behavioral strategies for a deaf and cerebral palsied child. *J Commun Disord,* 6:165-174, 1973.

Deaf

Pirreca, M. D., and Fitch, J. L.: Increasing mean length of response by application of reinforcement principles. *J Commun Disord,* 6:175-183, 1973.

Emotionally Disturbed

Hamilton, John, and Stephens, Lynn: Reinstating speech in an emotionally disturbed, mentally retarded young woman, *J Speech Hear Disord,* 32:383-389, 1967.

Kerr, N., Myerson, L., and Michael, J. A.: A procedure for shaping vocalizations in a mute child. In Ullmann, L. P., and Krasner, L. (Eds.): *Case Studies in Behavior Modification.* New York, HR&W, 1965.

Rosen, M., and Wesner, C.: A behavioral approach to Tourette's syndrome. *J Consult Clin Psychol,* 41:308-312, 1973.

Learning Disabilities

Fauke, Joyce, Burnett, Joseph, Powers, Mary Ann, and Sulzer-Azaroff, Beth: Improvement of handwriting and letter recognition skills: A behavior modification approach. *J Learn Disabil,* 6:296-300, May 1973.

Haring, M. G., and Hauch, M. M.: Improved learning conditions in the establishment of reading skills with disabled readers. *Except Child, 35*:341-351, January, 1969.

Nolen, P. A., Kunzelmann, H. P., and Haring, N. G.: Behavioral modification in a junior high learning disabilities classroom. *Except Child, 34*:163-168, 1967.

Mental Retardation

Baer, Donald, *et al.*: The development of imitation by reinforcing behavioral similarity to a model. *J Exp Anal Behav, 10*:405-415, 1967.

Barton, E. S.: Operant conditioning of social speech in the severely subnormal and the use of different reinforcers. *Br J Soc Clin Psychol, 11*:387-396, 1972.

Birnbauer, J. S., Bijou, S. W., Wolf, M. M., Kidder, J. D., and Tague, C.: A programmed instruction classroom for educable retardates. In Krasner, L., and Ullmann, L. P. (Eds.): *Research in Behavior Modification.* New York, HR&W, 1965.

Bricker, W., and Bricker, D.: Development of receptive vocabulary in severely retarded children. *Am J Ment Defic, 74*:599-607, 1970.

———A program of language training for the severely handicapped child. *Except Child, 37*:101-111, 1970.

Brown, Lou, Huppler, B., Pierce, L., York, B., and Sontag, E.: Teaching trainable-level students to read unconjugated action verbs. *J Spec Ed., 8*:51-56, Spring, 1974.

Daly, David A., and Johnson, Hettie Pippin: Instrumental modification of hypernasal voice quality in retarded children: Case reports. *J Speech Hear Disord, 6*:500-507, 1974.

Garcia, E. E., and DeHaven, E. D.: Use of operant techniques in the establishment and generalization of language: A review and analysis. *Am J Ment Defic, 79*:169-178, 1974.

Gray, B. B., and Fygetakis, L.: The development of language as a function of programmed conditioning. *Behav Res Ther, 6*:455-460, 1968.

Hedrich, Vivian: Applying technology to special education. *Am Ed, 3*:23-24, 1972.

Jacobson, Leonard, Bernal, Guillermo, and Lopez, Gerardo: Effects of behavioral training on the functioning of a profoundly retarded microcephalic teenager with cerebral palsy and without language or verbal comprehension. *Behav Res Ther, 11*:143-145, 1973.

Jeffrey, D. B.: Increase and maintenance of verbal behavior of a mentally retarded child. *Ment Retard, 10*:35-40, 1972.

Kent, Louise R.: A language acquisition program for the retarded. In McLean, J. D. (Ed.): *Intervention with the Retarded.* Baltimore, Univ Park, 1972, pp. 151-190.

MacAulay, B., A program for teaching speech and beginning reading to nonverbal retardates. In Sloane, H., and MacAulay, B. (Eds.): *Operant Procedures in Remedial Speech and Language Training*. Boston, Houghton Mifflin, 1968, pp. 102-124.

Socially Disadvantaged

Heitzman, Andrew J.: Effects of a token reinforcement system on the reading behavior of black migrant primary school pupils. *J Ed Res, 67*:299-302, 1974.

Lloyd, Mike: Say it right and they will too. *Am Ed, 8*:5-6, 1961.

Staats, A. W., and Butterfield, W. A.: Treatment of nonreading in a culturally deprived juvenile delinquent: An application of reinforcement principles. *Child Devel, 36*:209-231, 1965.

Speech Problems

Bar, A.: Increasing fluency in young stutterers vs. decreasing stuttering: A clinical approach. *J Commun Disorder, 6*:247-258, 1973.

Brookshire, R. H.: The use of consequences in speech pathology: Incentive and feedback functions. *J Commun Disord, 6*:88-92, 1973.

Curlee, Richard F., and Perkins, William A.: Effectiveness of a DAF conditioning program for adolescent and adult stutterers. *Behav Res Ther, 11*:395-401, 1973.

Egolf, D. B., Shames, G. H., and Seltzer, H. N.: The effects of time-out on the fluency of stutterers in group therapy. *J Commun Disorders, 4*:111-118, 1971.

Fried, Christopher: Behavior therapy and psychoanalysis in the treatment of a severe chronic stutterer. *J Speech Hear Disord, 37*:347-372, 1972.

Goldiamond, I.: Stuttering and fluency as manipulative operant response classes. In Krasner, L., and Ullmann, L. P. (Eds.): *Research in Behavior Modification*. New York, HR&W, 1965, pp. 106-156.

Gray, B. B., and Fygetakis, L.: Mediated language acquisition for dysphasic children. *Behav Res Ther, 6*:263-280, 1968.

Ingram, R. J., and Andrews, G.: Behavior therapy and stuttering: A review. *J Speech Hear Disord, 38*:405-441, 1973.

Moore, W. H. Jr., and Ritterman, S. I.: The Effects of response contingent reinforcement and response contingent punishment upon the frequency of stuttered verbal behavior. *Behav Res Ther, 11*:43-48, 1973.

Rhodes, R., Shames, G., and Egolf, D.: Awareness in verbal conditioning of language themes during therapy with stutterers. *J Communication Disorders, 4*:30-39, 1971.

Shaw, Candyce K., and Shrum, William F.: The Effects of response-contingent reward on the connected speech of children who stutter. *J Speech Hear*

*Disord, 37(1):*75-88, 1972.

BIBLIOGRAPHY

Bugelski, B. R.: *The Psychology of Learning Applied to Teaching.* Indianapolis, Bobbs, 1971.

Neisworth, John, and Smith, Robert M.: *Modifying Retarded Behavior.* Boston, HM, 1973.

Premack, David: Reinforcement Theory. In Levine, David (Ed.): *Nebraska Symposium on Motivation.* Lincoln, U of Nebr Pr, 1965.

Reese, Ellen P.: *The Analysis of Human Operant Behavior.* Dubuque, Wm C Brown, 1966.

Snelbecker, G. E.: *Learning Theory, Instructional Theory, and Psychoeducational Design.* New York, McGraw, 1974.

Chapter 3

STANDARD AND INFORMAL MEASUREMENT OF LANGUAGE PROCESSES: THEIR APPLICATION IN THE ASSESSMENT OF EXCEPTIONAL CHILDREN

SPECIAL educators, psychologists, psychometrists, and educational diagnosticians are becoming increasingly concerned about extant individual differences in the manner in which children learn. Special educators are far more in tune with those areas of individual variation among children that Kirk (1972) describes as "interindividual differences." The concept of interindividual variation reflects a contemporary accounting for differences between children. Interindividual variation uses the concept of a norm, an average or a point of central tendency in order to demonstrate a child's departure from those reference points. For example, a child having one brown eye and one blue eye may be considered to depart from an observed norm since the occurrence of such eye colors is so infrequent within the population of homosapiens.

The development of standardized tests with representative points of central tendency have accented the accountability of interindividual differences. These standardized instruments have enabled professional educators to quantitatively determine observed deviations from the norms expressed by those measurements. Perhaps the most widely used tool in discovering interindividual differences between children is the standardized intelligence test. This instrument allows the examiner to pinpoint the existing discrepancy between the established norm and the child's performance on the instrument. The mentally retarded child, for example, is identified most frequently by his performance on tests of learning aptitude. He is identified and subsequently labeled *mentally subnormal* because he performs a specified number of standard deviations below the mean on tests of intelligence. On the basis of this discrepancy the mentally retarded child is assigned to a special classroom or to an adjusted learning situation to begin or to continue his academic and vocational training. Unfortunately, this constitutes the only index of individual variation for many mentally handicapped children. The interindividual concept of individual differences does not typically lead to the development of specific curricular approaches for individual children. Since most assessment tools provide only a composite score, they tend to disguise the areas of strength and weakness among individuals. A more thorough challenge of composite scores will be found later in the chapter.

Special educators are far less in tune with the individual differences in children that Kirk (1972) describes as "intraindividual variation." The determination of intraindividual variation requires a more penetrating assessment of children. It is for specific reasons that children require study and assessment extending beyond comparisons solely between children (Smith, 1968). For example, there tends to be a difference in the way average or subnormal children learn. As Lerner (1970) suggests, some children learn best by listening, some by looking, and some by touching or performing an action. Wepman (1968) refers to each of these ways of learning as a perceptual modality and further suggests that children have one optimal modality for learning. Such an observation by teachers begs the recognition that children have a much greater learning facility when they can use one perceptual modality rather than another. Likewise, children may have inefficient pathways for learning. These modalities may be so inefficient that little or no advances in learning will be observed (Wepman, 1968) if taught through those pathways.

The intraindividual differences concept challenges teachers to become cognizant of the child's strengths and weakness — his best and his most inefficient perceptual modalities. Before the appropriate approach to learning can be determined for a child, his strengths and weaknesses in learning through auditory, visual and tactile modes need to be evaluated (Lerner, 1970). Such a determination of strengths and weaknesses (intraindividual variation) can facilitate plans for corrective or academic instruction and provide a more meaningful basis for homogeneous grouping (Wepman, 1964).

Inadequacy of Mental Age as a Diagnostic Measurement

The most frequently occurring quantitative assessment of mentally subnormal children is mental age. Mental age is an important vehicle in obtaining an index of a child's ability to master learning tasks. In this regard mental age is frequently used to decide whether a child is ready to begin instruction in a new skill. A common use of the mental age concept is to explain to parents and teachers the status of the child's level of mental maturity. Mental age further offers special advantage for identifying candidates for *adjusted* learning situations or special educational placement. Such learning situations and classes would contain children with the commonality of mental maturity.

However, it is imperative for the teacher and equally important for the researcher to be sensitive to the fact that children grouped together for instruction or data collection on the basis of mental age do not necessarily constitute a homogeneous collection of subjects. Mental age is nothing but a composite score, arrived at by arranging a number of subtest scores which in turn tap a number of intellectual factors (Kessler, 1970). One must realize that although a composite mental age is obtained, it represents a compensation of strengths and weaknesses.

Robinson and Robinson (1965) point out that although the concept of mental age is useful as an index of a child's ability to master cognitive learning tasks, there are significant differences in learning ability among individuals whose mental ages are the same but whose chronological ages are different.

Although mental age is a necessary and important consideration in the development of a suitable program of instruction, it offers little information for the teacher in the way of systematic instruction for each individual child (Smith, 1968). The mental age does not inform the teacher that the child is a *visual learner*, an *auditory learner*, or a *haptic learner*.

Inadequacy of Mental Age and IQ
in Predicting Reading Ability

Since reading is a form of language, the authors wish to point out the possible inadequacy of using mental age in the prediction of specific reading skills. The status of mental age and IQ as important variables purporting to account for reading achievement has been seriously questioned by authorities. Their arguments have generally centered around the following: (1) inconsistency of observed abilities within children on tests of intelligence, (2) limitations of mental age and IQ in predicting reading achievement, and (3) a tendency to find discrepancies between mental maturity and reading ability for bright and below average pupils.

There is a fallacious assumption that mental age represents the level at which the pupil, whether educable mentally retarded or intellectually average, consistently performs. The same IQ score or mental age derivative, however, may result from an even, across-the-board performance or from combinations of high and low points which can be mirror opposites (Kessler, 1970). Harris and Rosewell (1968) point out that "On psychometric tests such as the Stanford-Binet or Wechsler tests, wide scatter is frequent, so that conventional measures of mental level and IQ are often poor indicators of capacity for learning to read."

It is conceivable that the child's areas of weakness are those which tend to have the greatest relationship with reading.

The significance of subscore variation yielding a composite mental age manifests itself most obviously when comparing two children of equal mental age. Although they are equal in composite mental age, it is quite conceivable that their areas of strength and weakness may be totally different. One child's intellectual strength may be found in those areas having a significant correlation to reading achievement. In this case, mental age would be a good predictor of reading capacity. The other child, however, may exhibit weaknesses in those intellectual areas which tend to be related to reading achievement. For this child, a composite mental age would tend not to be a good predictor of reading achievement.

Somewhat related to the argument presented above is the belief that children having equal IQ's or comparable mental ages do not develop equal levels of reading achievement (Spache, 1968). Taking the IQ score or mental age derivative at a face value would lead one to suspect that children develop equally in the acquisition of skills in word attack, word recognition, vocabulary, comprehension, and reading rate. Spache also points out that " ... children who test similarly in intelligence do not necessarily develop similar degrees of reading skills. Nor can an intelligence test predict capacity for all these skills with equal accuracy."

Bond and Tinker (1957), in a study of the relationship between mental age and reading achievement, revealed the inconsistency of such a comparison. Their study, which included 379 subjects, pointed out that agreement between the two measures could only be found for those subjects whose IQ ranged from 90 to 100. For those subjects having IQ scores in excess of 110, their mental ages tended to exceed their measured level of reading capacity. Subjects whose IQ scores fell below 90 exhibited reading ability scores superior to their obtained measures of mental maturity. Such a finding would indicate that the IQ score would tend to be an insensitive indicator of reading for bright students and students who are slow learners or educable mentally retarded.

Inadequacy of Grade Equivalents and Standard Scores in Reporting Reading Skills

It is the concern of the authors that the reporting of composite reading scores such as standard scores, grade levels, and grade equivalents have a tendency to disguise or conceal the actual reading skills of subjects. The composite reading scores, unfortunately, may be interpreted as an even *across the board* performance in reading skills. Actually, the composite score depicts a blending or regression toward a central performance in reading, and in fact might refer to a subject who is accelerated in some reading skill areas, average in others, and deficient in other reading skill areas. For example, a subject who has a composite reading level score of 3.0 (grade 3, 0 months) may have a sight vocabulary of 4.0, a comprehension level of 1.5 and a phonetic analysis level of 3.0. Such results demonstrate the possibility of misguidance on the part of the teacher when planning a reading program for this child. The composite reading score does not reveal the areas of strength or apparent areas of weakness of the reader. Subsequently, the teacher does not know precisely what the pupil can do. More importantly, (s)he does not know which tasks in the reading act (s)he cannot do (Gallant, 1970).

It would be more advantageous, statistically and clinically, to use raw scores from the reading subtests to serve as a breakdown of reading criteria. Statistically, the use of composite scores would alter the variation character of the performance score. Since an even, across-the-board performance cannot be expected in reading skills, a composite reading score would tend to shrink the amount of variance in reading skills that could be predicted. Clinically, the raw score inspection will facilitate planning to adjust the reading program to the individual reader's profile. Without a raw score breakdown, the clinician would only have an interindividual reading assessment of the subject. Such interindividual assessment will not typically lead to the development of a specific prescription for remediating reading difficulties (Smith, 1968).

Awareness of Perceptual Modalities as Predictors of Reading

A more penetrating intraindividual assessment is required to determine " ... the strengths and weaknesses of the child in terms of auditory and visual use of stimuli, and the degree to which other manifestations of disability are present in reading skills. It is for these specific reasons that children often in reading require study extending beyond comparisons solely between children" (Smith, 1968).

Given the premise that extended evaluation beyond interindividual assessment should be made, it would be well to have a means of determining optimal and deficient perceptual modalities that would lend themselves as predictors of relevant reading skills. The authors endeavor to incorporate the above premise to propose that measuring instruments which tap specific modality areas may be useful in forecasting or predicting reading skills among exceptional children.

Such an evaluation plan would seem to be congruent with four of the five major philosophical tenets of Smith (1971) concerning the educational program for retarded children. He indicated that

1. The inevitable differences that exist among mentally retarded children, who are classified on some basis into a single population or group on educationally relevant dimensions, requires that the instructional environment be designed so that each youngster's likelihood for learning is increased.
2. The nature of the instructional environment designed for each elementary age retarded child should be based on pertinent educational information about the child being considered.
3. Special class teachers of mentally retarded children must develop sufficient diagnostic skills to allow them to systematically gather data on appropriate educational dimensions in an informal and unencumbered way within the classroom.
4. Special education teachers who are involved in programming instruction for the mentally retarded should be sufficiently skilled to translate educational and detailed psychological data into practical teaching programs for each student.

Tenet two pleas for an awareness of what has been alluded to as intraindividual variation of educable mentally retarded children. Congruent with the present investigation, intraindividual variation implies awareness of individual learning styles of individual strengths and weaknesses in areas of perceptual modality. Tenet two also suggests that mentally retarded children should be grouped on the basis of educational and behavioral dimensions. This could be construed to imply that the use of an individual intelligence scale by itself may be quite inadequate (Jordan, 1966). Thus, additional information is required to match the mentally retarded child's learning style with the appropriate teaching technique.

Tenet three indicates the need for a scale by which judgments concerning areas of perceptual strength and weakness could be made about educable mentally retarded children. Jordan (1966) and Cooley and Lohnes (1968) suggest the need to develop instruments or means of data analysis to obtain observations that have some psychological significance. Jordan claims that in any consideration of mental deficiency there comes a time when it seems appropriate to arrange the information into a meaningful pattern. As Cooley and Lohnes suggest, " . . . degrees of strength or weakness of a trait in different people are measurable from behavior samples, so that the trait profile which characterizes a particular personality can be represented by a set of scores."

Should an instrument be developed by which teachers could obtain reliable and valid information concerning individual perceptual modality characteristics of the children, it would allow for program planning commensurate with each child's learning style. As Jordan (1966) suggests, "the goal is to increase the accuracy of statements above the level which guessing or chance would reach." The strength of the proposed scale would lie in its ability to predict the best method of teaching reading skills to mentally retarded individuals. If the scale reflects a pattern of strength in the child's auditory area, perhaps the best approach for that child would be phonetic analysis instead of a visual approach.

Tenet four alludes to the fact that teachers of retarded children need to be more than *receivers* of diagnostic information. Being receivers of this diagnostic information implies, first of all, that all teachers will be presented with such information and, secondly, that they will have sufficient diagnostic skills to synthesize such information for program development for each child.

Such a situation implies the requirement of a scale simple enough to be administered by teachers, yet sophisticated enough to provide diagnostic information relevant to program-child matching. If special educators were to conduct such an investigation it should center around the above suggestion.

Tenet five has special relevance for such a proposed investigation. Given the previous documentation that IQ and mental age are often inefficient predictors of reading skill, and since most teachers are not licensed to administer intelligence assessments, they could be provided with a scale designed to help them predict reading skill areas and reading skill levels among exceptional children. Such a scale could give adequate information to determine modality patterns within and among exceptional children, resulting in better reading program assignments, i.e. phonics, word recognition, sight vocabulary, necessity for kinesthetic training, combining approaches, and developing observed areas of weakness.

The rationale for such a proposal can best be summarized by highlighting the need for perceptual testing in a thorough psychoeducational diagnostic evaluation and the functional value of perceptual testing in forecasting reading achievement of exceptional children.

Harrington and Durrell (1955) state "the use of intelligence tests for predicting reading achievement . . . are inferior to the use of tests that tap aspects of perceptual functioning." Barrett's (1965) study of predicting reading attainment adds further evidence to the views of Harrington and Durrell. The results of his investigation supported the position that perceptual functions should be included to account for more of the variance in reading achievement. It is becoming increasingly clear that, for handicapped children and children with learning and perceptual problems, instruction must be highly individualized, with educational planning based on a psychoeducational evaluation of strengths and deficits of the individual (Pope and Haklay, 1970).

In attempting to predict behaviors as complex as reading skills, more than one variable or perceptual area is suspected to be important. As Neale and Liebert (1973) indicate " . . . a best prediction of the criterion can often be made by combining the predictor variables . . . which tap somewhat different dimensions regarding the criterion." Predictor variables in this proposed evaluation procedure would be scores from tests which measure auditory, visual, tactile, and kinesthetic perception.

Auditory

At some point in formal reading instruction the child is taught that each individual symbol is associated with a sound or sounds and that a grouping of these sounds constitutes the sound of a word. The beginning reader must equate the visual symbol to the sound, then the sound to the meaning (Vernon, 1959). Thus, the order of acquiring language is from understanding the words (hearing) to speaking vocabulary to reading vocabulary (Kaluger and Kolson, 1969). It is at this point that auditory perception and the ability to discriminate sounds become proposed factors in reading achievement.

Flower (1965) notes that auditory processes have a great influence on the activities surrounding the task of learning to read. He further implies that, before learning to read, a child's language learning depends almost exclusively upon auditory channels. Therefore, the language foundations upon which reading skills are to be built rely on his auditory ability. Those reading skills which involve attacking new words are also directly dependent on auditory processes. Thus, auditory disorders may be a perceptually important factor among the problems underlying reading difficulties.

Flower (1968) further proposed the following hierarchy of auditory processes that may be related to the complex task of learning to read: auditory sensitivity, auditory attending, auditory discrimination, auditory memory, auditory integration, and auditory-visual integration. Observing children's responses on tests believed to assess these measures, Flower (1968) concluded that auditory discrimination, auditory memory, and auditory-visual integration are at least partly responsible for a child's reading difficulties.

A number of research investigations support Flower's conclusions in part, but propose auditory tracking and sequencing as a factor separate from auditory memory and stress its importance in relation to reading ability (Jansky and de Hirsch, 1972, Kaluger and Kolson, 1969, and Wepman, 1964). In addition to this proposed factor, sound blending, or auditory integration, has been suggested by various investigators as an important predictor of reading achievement (Chall and Roswell, 1963, Mulder and Curtin, 1955, and Roswell and Natchez, 1964).

Research in the area of auditory perceptual efficiency has been virtually neglected in favor of the visual modality (Kottler, 1972, Lerner, 1971, and Reynolds, 1953). There are very few standardized tests available for assessing auditory perceptual efficiency.

Most of the auditory measures on reading readiness tests are unable to detect the subtle deficiencies present in a child with auditory perceptual problems (Carpenter and Willis, 1972). Those tests which are ordinarily used to assess auditory perception require only discrimination abilities. Some researchers have recommended that tests of auditory memory, auditory sequencing, and auditory integration should be included with tests of discrimination to thoroughly assess a child's auditory perceptual level (Benger, 1968, and Rosner, 1971).

Visual

The idea that reading is basically a visual process is frequently used in behaviorally or operationally defining reading. This seemingly natural association has precipitated or motivated more research investigations concerned with visual perception than any other perceptual domain. An early study by Gates (1940) suggested that measures of visual discrimination were important indices in forecasting reading achievement. Along with mental age, Gates' five visual discrimination predictors resulted in a multiple correlation of .76 with reading achievement. An interesting result, however, was the effectiveness of the fine visual discrimination measures after they were statistically weighted. The statistical weighting resulted in a multiple correlation of .71 with reading achievement. The interpretation of this finding points out the functional value of visual perception as a predictor of reading achievement. Visual perceptual activities, especially those purporting to tap or increase visual discrimination competency, can be implemented into the school curricula with the goal of increasing the subjects' readiness to read.

Goins' (1959) conception of reading behavior in the learner is a process or a processing behavior. In order to systematically study reading behavior, teachers, and researchers must concern themselves with the basic nature of the process. He further indicates the most obvious basic processes in reading are visual perception and visual discrimination. Because of visual perception and visual discrimination, the reader can determine differences in letters and words. As far as the literature on reading achievement is concerned, one of the most frequently occurring predictors of reading success is the ability to differentiate between like and unlike words (Goins, 1959). Roberts and Coleman (1958) add that visual perceptual assessment is valuable in understanding reading failure. To some degree they suggest that visual perceptual assessment may be a discriminator of reading failure and reading success. Their findings appear to indicate that children with reading failures are less efficient than normal readers when learning by visual methods alone, and that children with reading failure score significantly lower on tests of visual perception.

Kinesthetic

The use of kinesthetic learning has been incorporated into several reading approaches (Freidus, 1964, Fernald, 1943, Cooper, 1947, and Gillingham and Stillman, 1956). Because of the frequency of Grace Fernald's approach to reading being mentioned in most texts on the teaching of reading, this method is recognized by most authorities as the major kinesthetic approach to reading (Myers and Hammill, 1969). Tracing, in Fernald's approach, uses both the tactile and kinesthetic avenues (Kaluger and Kolson, 1969). The use of kinesthetic learning in Fernald's approach to reading is in some way supplemental — that is, supplementing the auditory and visual modalities (Johnson, 1967).

Roberts' and Coleman's (1958) research investigation demonstrated the supplemental value of kinesthetic elements to visual methods of teaching reading. They found that the group designated as reading failures showed more efficient learning when kinesthetic elements are added than when a strictly visual method is used in teaching reading. The results of their investigation led them to conclude,

> The preceding experimental findings would seem to indicate that a proportion of reading failures may be due to the lack of visual perceptual acuity and that, for such cases, the present pragmatic use of the Fernald method of remedial reading programs would appear justified. ... these findings suggest even more strongly the value of adding kinesthetic cues to the visual learning situation for children with deficiencies in perceptual

acuity.

Further evidence for the supplemental value of kinesthetic learning in reading is given in Myers' and Hammill's (1969) interpretation of Rood's (1962) article: "The act of tracing a word several times prepares the mental coordinates for an important message and then follows through on a selective avenue of approach. Thus the auditory and visual pathways are being activated in the same manner as the child sees and says the word as he is tracing it."

Kirk's (1933) early study was one of the first research investigations using the kinesthetic reading approach with mentally handicapped subjects. His study compared the kinesthetic and visual methods of teaching word recognition skills to retarded children. Although he failed to find any significant differences after two weeks in initial learning, he did find that the kinesthetic method was favored in producing greater retention.

The relationship between kinesthetic perceptual efficiency and achievement has been studied, particularly within the past twenty years. Many of the investigations have attempted to identify the correlates of kinesthetic or physical abilities through correlational and multiple correlational techniques. Klausmeier et al. (1959) determined that subjects with a low level of physical development exhibited a tendency for their achievement in reading and arithmetic to be low. This finding was found to exist only for boys. Ismail's and Gruber's (1967) comments relative to the correlates of kinesthetic ability imply it is when the range of IQ is either above or below the average range that the predictive power of motor tests increases.

Gross (1969), in determining the predictive validity of a test of kinesio-perceptual abilities, found that the test items accounted for 57 percent of the variance in arithmetic and 37 percent of the variance in reading standard scores of educable mentally handicapped children.

The most consistent view concerning kinesthetic perception and reading achievement is the potential status it has as a predictor of reading and as a method of teaching reading. It should be pointed out, however, that measures of kinesthetic perception cannot stand alone as predictors of reading. Their utility lies in their supplementary role in the linear prediction of reading skills.

The authors feel that the proposed instruments by which teachers could obtain reliable and valid information concerning individual perceptual modality characteristics pertaining to reading could also be projected to language development, arithmetic, etc. There are many standardized tests on the market to determine at which level students are functioning in all the areas of language, but an information test which could be used by teachers is of utmost importance. The proposal made by the authors could be implemented, and if such a proposal is developed for reading, naturally the teacher would have a very important tool for the other areas of language.

Standardized and Informal Measurement of Language Processes

Standardized observations usually consist of formal tests which assess speech and language behavior, as well as various behaviors demonstrated in psychological tests. Table I catagorizes some of the commonly used standardized assessment tools.

Informal Tools

1. The appearance and behavior of the child
2. The child's grades in school
3. The child's work (themes, computations, art work, etc.)
4. Teacher observations
5. Parental observations
6. Peer group evaluation

Interpreting Test Data

After the consultant, psychologist, teacher, etc., have selected and administered a test battery they must formulate an interpretation of the language behavior of the child. Although this interpretation entails considerably more than merely determining intelligence quotients or mental ages, the intelligence test should be administered first. The consultant will seek some global

Table I

Selected Tests of Language Behavior to Assess
the Structure and Content of Language (Yoder, 1974)

LANGUAGE STRUCTURE		TESTS
Phonology — Speech Sounds	a.	Templin-Darley Screening and Diagnostic Tests of Articulation
	b.	Goldman-Fristoe Articulation Test
	c.	The Deep Test of Articulation (McDonald)
	d.	Developmental Articulation Test (Hejna)
	e.	Fisher-Logeman Test of Articulation
Morphology — Word forms, tenses, plurality, possessive, comparative pronoun changes, prefixes, suffixes	a.	Tests of English Morphology (Berko)
	b.	Exploratory Test of Grammar (Berry and Talbot)
	c.	Auditory Test for Language Comprehension (Carrow)
	d.	Northwestern Syntax Screening Test (Lee)
and	e.	Evaluation of Grammatical Capacity (Menyuk)
Syntax — Word order, phrase structure, transformations	f.	Grammatic Closure — subtest of ITPA (Kirk and McCarthy)
	g.	Grammatical Comprehension Test (Bellugi-Klima)
	h.	Analysis of spontaneous language samples
	i.	Selected items from Peabody Language Development Kits (Dunn and Smith)
Semantics — Word meaning, vocabulary (choice, variety and number), concepts (classifications, relational and logical)	a.	Peabody Picture Vocabulary Test (Dunn)
	b.	WISC-R: Vocabulary and Similarities subtest
	c.	Stanford-Binet: Vocabulary subtest
	d.	ITPA: Auditory reception (Kirk and McCarthy) Visual reception Verbal expression Manual expression Auditory vocal association Visual motor association
	e.	The basic concept inventory (Engelman)
	f.	Boehm Test of Basic Concepts
	g.	Analysis of spontaneous language samples
	h.	Selected items from Peabody Language Development Kits (Dunn and Smith)

pattern from the WISC-R, Stanford-Binet or WAIS that will pinpoint a learning problem. All of the tests administered should present a pattern that will help the teacher in a remedial program for each individual child. The authors would like to present the WISC-R first and indicate what this test measures. The subtests of the WISC-R should be presented as shown in Table II.

Table II

VERBAL	PERFORMANCE
1. Information	2. Picture Completion
3. Similarities	4. Picture Arrangement
5. Arithmetic	6. Block Design
7. Vocabulary	8. Object Assembly
9. Comprehension	10. Coding (or Mazes)

In Table III the subtests fo the WISC-R and the factors of measurement are presented.

Testing

At the child guidance clinic various psychological and educational tests are administered to the child. The complete Revised Wechsler Intelligence Scale for Children, the Bender Visual-Motor Gestalt, and a reading evaluation are necessary for the preliminary evaluation. This is one situation where psychological tests can be quite valuable.

Hanvik (1961) describes some of the psychological diagnostic tools used in a child guidance clinic. They included a test battery consisting of the following: (1) Wechsler Intelligence Scale for Children (2) Bender-Gestalt, (3) Goodenough Draw-A-Man, (4) Seguin Form Board, (5) Knox Cube Test, (6) Porteus Mazes, (7) Memory for Design Test, (8) Raven Progressive Matrices, (9) Cerebral Dominance Test, and (10) Jastak Wide-Range Reading Test. In addition to this battery, the individual child also received a behavior rating scale with ten items.

Table III*

WISC-R SUBTEST SCORES	MEASURE
Information	Range of information picked up through the years, memory (cultural milieu inferred), verbal comprehension
Picture Completion	Discrimination between essential and nonessential detail, memory
Similarities	Concept formation, abstract thinking vs. functional and concrete, verbal comprehension
Picture Arrangement	Social alertness, common sense, planning and anticipating, sequencing, ability to synthesize
Arithmetic	Arithmetical reasoning, concentration, memory, numerical fluency
Block Design	Perception, analysis, synthesis, reproduction of abstract designs (logic and reasoning applied to space relationships)
Vocabulary	Vocabulary, word meaning (cultural milieu inferred), verbal comprehension
Object Assembly	Perception, visual-motor coordination, visual imagery, synthesis of concrete forms, flexibility of working toward a goal, spatial relationships
Comprehension	Verbal comprehension, judgment, understanding
Coding	Psychomotor speed, eye-hand coordination, pencil manipulation
Mazes	Ability to plan in a new situation (problem solving), ability to delay action, visual-motor coordination

---

*This is a variation of a table which appeared in *Diagnosing Learning Disorders* by Waugh and Bush, 1971.

Clinical observations in a study by Temmer (1965) indicated that a subject's level of performance on the Bender-Gestalt designs corresponds roughly with the degree of general intelligence as measured by standard tests such as the Wechsler. The subjects were divided into two groups — those with known neurological involvement and those for whom no neurological involvement was recorded. Since the better the performance, the fewer the errors, there was an inverse relationship between the Bender-Gestalt and the intelligence quotient.

> In a neurologically damaged individual, the usual "general intelligence" interpretation of the Intelligence Quotient needs to be qualified. If, for instance, manipulative and perceptual functions are selectively impaired, not only the performance, but also the full Intelligence Quotient is lowered, although the person may be capable of performing verbally at a superior level. Similarly, the Bender-Gestalt score, in such a case, is lowered and therefore ceases to reflect "general intelligence" as it does in the case of neurologically intact subjects ... the overall inferiority of the brain damaged on drawing tasks is found quite consistently (Temmer, 1965).

Clements and Peters (1962) thus far have isolated three principal patterns in the Wechsler Intelligence Scale for Children. The most common pattern is *scatter* in either or both the verbal and performance scales (W.I.S.C. Pattern I). Low scores most frequently occur in arithmetic and digit span in the verbal scale and block design, object assembly, coding, and mazes in the performance scale.

The second most frequent pattern (W.I.S.C. Pattern II) is that in which the verbal intelligence quotient is fifteen to forty points higher than the performance quotient. The third and least frequent pattern (W.I.S.C. Pattern III) is the reverse of the W.I.S.C. Pattern II, i.e. the performance intelligence quotient is fifteen to forty points higher than the verbal intelligence quotient.

While the W.I.S.C. is an important diagnostic tool in measuring perceptual disorders, the Bender Visual-Motor Gestalt is used to measure the perception and the visual-motor coordination of the child with learning disabilities. There are several reading tests which can be used to measure the sight-reading ability and determine reading level, types of errors, and comprehension of material.

The child with learning disabilities can have many kinds of distortions in symbolic perception, expression, and thinking. Kirk and McCarthy (1961) have devised a test of psycholinguistic abilities for children whose ages range between two and nine.

The idea of the test is to determine which functions the child has developed and which ones he has not. For example, a child may be able to see and speak adequately but may not be able to follow directions. There are times when a child understands what he hears but cannot interpret what he sees. The nine subtests of the Illinois Test of Psycholinguistic Abilities attempt to determine abilities and disabilities in children so that remedial instruction can be programmed.

Bateman (1964) points out that assessment of both the level of performance and manner of performance over a period of time are necessary for an accurate picture of test results.

Scherer's (1961) investigation attempted to identify relevant variables which would significantly contribute to the long-range prediction of academic achievement in brain-injured children. More specifically, the investigation was designed to determine the intellectual, personality, and physical status variables which might predict successful academic achievement in these children. He felt the study was important because the psychologist is continually called upon to make predictions in this area.

There is reason to believe, however, that there are variables other than intellectual, personality, and physical status which are important and about which the information necessary for successful prediction is unavailable. Among these are (1) information concerning academic readiness programs to which the child will be exposed either at home or in a school situation, (2) the effect of future diseases and accidents, (3) the child's future social environment, and (4) the child's level of verbal and language functioning.

Goodstein (1970) states that language behaviors must be placed in a primary position in man's behavioral repertoire, and the acquisition and development of language are prerequisite to learning the complex skills that are necessary to compete in modern society. It was further implied by Oleron (1957) that language furthers intellectual habits — that is, language contributes to the individual's learning or acquiring the concept of abstraction.

Kessler (1970) reports that speech competencies should no longer be viewed as a unitary function but should be analyzed in a relationship to mental or cognitive function.

It has been recognized that a child's use of language is directly related to his intelligence. Indeed, if psychologists were suddenly (and against their better judgment) limited to measuring only one aspect of behavior, the majority would probably choose language development as the single best index of intelligence in most children and adults (Robinson and Robinson, 1965).

Furth (1970) proposes the idea that language does not influence intellectual development in a direct manner, but may indirectly influence and accelerate intellectual development through the abstraction of ideas and concepts.

In discussing diagnostic procedures, Clements and Peters (1962) recommend the use of the entire Wechsler-Intelligence Scale for Children. The Bender Visual-Motor Gestalt, Gray's or Gates' reading test, and a small amount of appropriate picture cards from the Michigan Picture Test are used for personality assessment. They feel that clues to personality are constantly being produced by the child and observed by the examiner during the work-up; therefore a standardized projective technique such as drawing persons or objects, long interviews, and the Rorchach are inadequate even as screening devices.

Clements (1963) has compiled a checklist of the discernible features of the child with learning disabilities. Not all symptoms are likely to appear in a given child:

> *Normal or Above General Intelligence* (as determined from either the Verbal or Performance Scale on the WISC) — The important consideration here is that results of intelligence evaluation clearly indicate that although achievement is variable depending on the nature of the task, the overall level of intellectual functioning is within normal limits and that we are *not* dealing with a child who is generally mentally retarded, that is, deficient in all areas of endeavor.
>
> *Specific Learning Deficits* — Child cannot read at grade or age level: a mildly stressful situation may bring forth typical dyslexic errors; spelling poor, difficulty with abstractions and whole-part relationships; difficulty in mastering tasks which are dependent upon intact visual-motor-perceptual integration.
>
> *Perceptual-Motor-Deficits* — Printing, writing, and drawing

poor; poor and erratic performance when copying geometric figures (Bender Visual-Motor Gestalt Test); often attempts to compensate for the latter by task-perseverance and/or innumerable and meticulous tiny strokes of the pencil; often has difficulty in reproducing geometric designs with blocks; difficulty with figure-ground and/or whole-part discrimination.

General Coordination Deficits — Child often described as awkward or clumsy; this may appear in either fine muscle performance or in overall coordination, or both.

Hyperkinesis (or less frequently, hypokinesis) — Child appears to be in constant motion, flitting from one object or activity to another, or may be merely restless and fidgety; we have considered that the child's "drivenness" may manifest also as voluble, uninhibited speech, or as disorganized thinking, even in the absence of outward hyperactivity. Some children with learning and behavior symptoms and one or more "equivocal" neurological signs do not show hyperkinesis, but instead can be described as "slow as molasses," since they move, think, and talk at a very reduced rate. Frequently, this slow-responding child will have an "asphasoid" quality in this speech.

Impulsivity — The child cannot keep from touching and handling objects, particularly in a strange or overstimulating environment; he frequently speaks without checking himself; he may curse, be insulting, or eagerly relate all the family secrets. His impulsivity easily leads him into conflict with the demands of conformity as established by family, school, and society. Some children may commit striking anti-social acts, to the point of fire-setting, stealing, and even murder, with only a medium of provocation.

Emotional Liability — The child may be "highstrung," irritable, aggressive, or easily moved to tears, he will have quick changes of emotional behavior from high temper to easy manageability and remorse; he may be panicked by what would appear to others as a minimally stressful situation; however, some are again at the opposite end of the continuum in that they are consistently sweet-and even-tempered, cooperative, diligent, and display a very high frustration tolerance.

Short Attention Span and/or Distractibility — The child is unable to concentrate on one thing for very long; he especially fades out when abstract material is being presented. Even with this symptom, some show a tendency to become locked in a simple repetitious motor activity or preoccupation with one verbal topic. Some children show fair attention span when their interest is aroused, but when not so engaged, display marked distractibility to casual stimuli.

"Equivocal" or "Soft" Neurological Signs — Among the most frequently seen of such signs are: transient strabismus; dysdiadochokinesis; poor coordination of fingers; mixed and/or confused laterality; speech defect, or a history of slow speech development or irregularity; and general awkardness.

Borderline Abnormal or Abnormal EEG — Although agreement in this area is not complete, the high frequency of borderline or abnormal brain wave test records reported is felt to be significant.

Use of the brain wave as a method of identifying the brain-injured is a highly controversial area. Some authorities feel that there is a possible disturbance of function of the diencephalon. The most frequent neurological signs found have been gross coordination irregularities, perceptual-motor difficulties, fine coordination defect, strabismus, reading difficulty, dysdiadochokinesis, mixed laterality, some degree of ambidexterity, and speech defect. Clements and Peters (1962) state that this type of comprehensive and time-consuming diagnostic procedure also includes EEG findings.

Neurologist Cohn (1964) points out that current neurological practice cannot determine with precision the correlation between minimal signs in EEG and learning disabilities.

Hanvik (1961), in a study of children with abnormal EEG's, found a difference in the Bender-Gestalt Test rating and coding subtest scores of the Wechsler Intelligence Scale for Children but not in other batteries of tests. In children with learning disabilities, Hanvik found medical and neurological findings were not significantly different between the normal EEG group and the abnormal EEG group.

According to research concerning the importance of the EEG, it should be stated that thousands more readings are needed with adequate controls using children who have no problem of hyperactivity, retarded children, hyperactive children, children with emotional problems, and those in other categories. Many of the studies have been useful, provocative, and pioneering, but very limited in scope. It would seem, then, that the opinion of the experts is not unanimous.

The Wechsler Preschool and Primary School Intelligence Scale (Wechsler, 1966)

The Wechsler Preschool and Primary School Intelligence Scale (W.P.P.S.I.) appeared in 1966. This scale is based on the W.I.S.C. but introduces some new scales such as animal houses and provides for assessing verbal performance and full scale IQ's. The test was devised for children four to six and one-half years old, thus extending downward the age limits of the Wechsler Scales. It is extremely valuable clinically, is interesting to young children, and has proved to be a useful tool in the intellectual assessment of young children.

Stanford-Binet Intelligence Scale (Terman and Merrill, 1960)

The Stanford-Binet was originally developed in 1916 by Lewis Terman at Stanford University from the earlier test devised by Binet in 1905. The Stanford-Binet was most recently revised in 1960, and this form of the test ranges from age two to the adult level, but is most commonly used with children. The majority of the items are oral, although a few require the subject to read, write, draw, or carry out simple manipulative tasks. The Stanford-Binet can be used for intelligence testing of course, but it is not as good as the WISC-R in assessing other areas of disability such as language. It is true, however, that individuals with a language handicap will score relatively low on such a test as the Stanford-Binet. It should also be pointed out when interpreting the IQ that the Stanford-Binet is primarily a scholastic aptitude test and heavily loaded with verbal functions.

Illinois Test of Psycholinguistic Abilities (McCarthy and Kirk, 1961)

Research indicates that cognitive ability includes factors which are often omitted from intelligence tests. One such measure in this respect is the Illinois Test of Psycholinguistic Abilities (I.T.P.A.). This test measures linguistic skills and has shown a great deal of promise in the last few years. This test not only presents normative data on several aspects of linguistic behavior, but it is based on very sound psycholinguistic theories which were developed by Osgood (1957), and it provides for a remedial teaching program in relationship to many of the assessed defects. Savage (1968) stated that Frostig (1967) uses the I.T.P.A. in conjunction with her own developmental visual-perception measures to considerable advantage. The complete test is made up of twelve subtests which evaluate abilities in two major channels of communication. These two major channels are the visual-motor and the auditory-vocal. There are three types of psycholinguistic processes — receptive, organizing, and expressive. There are two levels of organization which are the representational and the automatic.

The Psycholinguistic Abilities

The nine psycholinguistic abilities are defined below. Each definition is accompanied by a brief explanation of how the ability is tested ... .(I.T.P.A. Manual, 1968).
  I. Tests at the Representational Level
    Tests at this level have one thing in common. They all assess some aspect of the subject's ability to deal with meaningful symbols — to understand the meaning of symbols (decoding), to express meaningful ideas in symbols (encoding), or to relate symbols on a meaningful basis (association).
A. *The Decoding Tests.* Decoding is the ability to comprehend auditory and visual symbols — that is, the ability to comprehend spoken words, written words, or pictures.
  Test 1. *Auditory decoding* is the ability to comprehend the spoken word. It is assessed by a controlled vocabulary test in which the subject is asked to answer yes or no by voice or gesture to a series of graded questions.
  Test 2. *Visual decoding* is the ability to comprehend pictures and written words. It is assessed by a picture identification technique in which the subject selects from among a set of pictures the one which is most nearly identical, on a

meaningful basis, to a previously exposed stimulus picture.
B. *The Association Tests.* Association is the ability to relate
visual or auditory symbols (which stand for ideas) in a
meaningful way.
Test 3. *Auditory-vocal association* is the ability to relate
spoken words in a meaningful way. This ability is tested
with the familiar analogies test in which the subject must
complete a test statement by supplying an analogous word
(e.g., the examiner says, SOUP IS HOT; ICE CREAM IS —
——).
Test 4. *Visual-motor association* is the ability to relate
meaningful visual symbols. The present test requires the
subject to select from among a set of pictures the one which
most meaningfully relates to a given stimulus picture.
C. *The Encoding Tests.* Encoding is the ability to put ideas into
words or gestures.
Test 5. *Vocal encoding* is the ability to express one's ideas in
spoken words. It is assessed by asking the subject to describe
simple objects such as a block or ball.
Test 6. *Motor encoding* is the ability to express one's ideas in
gestures. The manual language of the deaf is an example of
motor encoding. This ability is tested by showing the subject
an object and asking him to supply the motion appropriate
for manipulating it (e.g., drinking from a cup or strumming
a guitar).
II. Tests at the Automatic-Sequential Level
Tests at this level deal with the nonmeaningful uses of
symbols, principally their long term retention and the short
term memory of symbol sequences.
Unlike the representational level tests, no attempt has been
made to subdivide the automatic-sequential level tests into their
decoding, association, and encoding aspects because of the lack
of theoretical clarity at this level.
A. *The Automatic Tests.* Our frequent use of a language and
the abundant redundancies of language lead to highly over-
learned or automatic habits for handling its syntactical and
inflectional aspects without conscious effort. So familiar are
we with linguistic structure that we come to expect or predict the grammatical structure of what will be said or read
from what has ready been seen or heard. In speaking or
writing, these automatic habits permit one to give conscious

attention to the content of a message, while the words with which to express that message seem to come automatically. Test 7. *Auditory-vocal automatic* ability permits one to predict future linguistic events from past experience. It is called "automatic" because it is usually done without conscious effort. In listening to a speech, for example, we develop an expectation for what will be said which is based on what has already been said. In the present test, the subject must supply the last word to a test statement, invariably a word requiring inflection (e.g., the examiner says, FATHER IS OPENING THE CAN. NOW THE CAN HAS BEEN ———).

No suitable visual-motor counterpart to this test could be designed. The ability to read incomplete sentences and supply the correctly inflected word in writing would seem an appropriate task, but obviously it is not suited for two-and-a-half-year-old children. After many unsuccessful attempts to design a picture substitute for the visual-motor channel, the effort was abandoned.

B. *The Sequencing Tests.* Sequencing, as used here, is the ability to correctly reproduce a sequence of symbols; it is largely dependent upon visual and/or auditory memory.

Test 8. *Auditory-vocal* sequencing is the ability to correctly repeat a sequence of symbols previously heard. It is assessed by a modified digit repetition test.

Test 9. *Visual-motor sequencing* is the ability to correctly reproduce a sequence of symbols previously seen. It is tested by requiring the subject to duplicate the order of a sequence of pictures or geometrical designs presented to the subject and then removed (McCarthy and Kirk, 1961).

Marianne Frostig Center
of Educational Therapy

Gearheart (1973) tells us that Dr. Marianne Frostig and her Developmental Test of Visual Perception (DTVP) have been known to workers in learning disabilities for years. Authorities in the field of learning disabilities recognize her for many other professional accomplishments, and in 1968 the Association for Children With Learning Disabilities awarded her the Learning Disabilities Award. She has contributed to the field greatly through the Marianne Frostig Center of Educational Therapy which is located in Los Angeles and through the Developmental Test of Visual Perception, which is often called the Frostig Test.

> The Marianne Frostig Center of Educational Therapy is part of the Foundation of Education Therapy for children, located in Los Angeles. It is a nonprofit organization and has three major functions — service, professional training, and research. The service is for children with unusual learning difficulties, and the training is for learning disability professionals. The research component is focused on Dr. Frostig's interest in learning disabilities, with specific emphasis on her interest in visual-perceptual problems (Gearheart, 1973).

Marianne Frostig's test (DTVP) was first published in 1961, but since that time it has had two revisions. This test may be administered to groups of students by a classroom teacher, and it takes less than an hour to administer. Five subtests are used to measure visual-perceptual skills in five different areas. The five subtests are (1) eye-motor coordination, (2) figure-ground, (3) form constancy, (4) position in space, and (5) spatial relations.

The Developmental Test of Visual Perception has not been without its share of criticism. Olson's (1968) criticism of the DTVP led him to conclude, "The consensus of opinion ... strongly suggests that the content validity of the Frostig DTVP should be seriously questioned."

This statement followed his speculation that the individual tests are not sufficiently different to assume that they are measuring separate visual perceptual abilities. The subtests, in other words, do not represent mutually exclusive perceptual abilities as proposed by Frostig and Horne (1964). It should be pointed out, however, that Olson does not discount the role of visual perception in reading achievement or its role in predicting reading success.

The Developmental Test of Visual Perception (Frostig, 1963) seems to have some possibility as a predictor of reading achievement. As pointed out above, however, caution should be used in interpreting or generalizing the results. Olson (1966), for example, found that although there was some relationship between total DTVP scores, paragraph reading and word recognition skills were not as high.

The use of the Bender Gestalt as a means of diagnosing reading performance and as a measurement tool to predict or forecast reading ability has been studied. Keogh (1965) evaluated the use of the Bender given in kindergarten as a predictor of third grade reading ability. The predictive quality of this tool seems to be relegated to predicting reading success with extremely good performances on the Bender at kindergarten level. As Keogh states, "Only good performance on the Bender was predictive of reading performance." Low or poor Bender scores seem to be nondefinitive for individual prediction. The Bender Gestalt is probably one of the most frequently used diagnostic tests of visual perceptual-motor behavior.

This chapter has dealt with many aspects of language processes, but the authors have not mentioned very much about written language. As a matter of fact, in most books very little attention is given to the systematical remediation of written expression deficits. Wallace and McLoughlin (1975) tell us that written expression is basically an extension of oral language development. The child who is deficient in oral language skills needs help in this area first. Written skills can be developed gradually after an adequate oral language base is built. The "Selected Readings" at the end of the chapter are several informal teaching procedures for the written language.

Summary

This chapter proposed the need for both standardized and informal assessment of exceptional children in order to delineate their interindividual and intraindividual variations. The role of the teacher in the evaluation of exceptional children was also stressed. Although most teachers do not have the necessary credentials to administer the traditional tests of intelligence, the authors proposed the necessity for teachers to be closely involved in the psychological evaluation of exceptional children. This chapter stressed the diagnostic role of teachers in the assessment of intraindividual differences within exceptional children. It was also proposed that teachers of exceptional children be *facilitators* rather than *receivers* of diagnostic information. Diagnostic information related to the perceptual learning styles of exceptional children was stressed as an important component of the total evaluation plan. The literature reflects a growing trend of educators using tests of perceptional functioning to account for or explain differences among children with specific language problems. The most frequently occurring language problem which tests of perceptual functioning have been used to account for is reading failure. Since reading can be more frequently monitored and assessed by teachers, it was suggested that they employ tests of auditory, visual, and kinesthetic perception to assess each child's perceptual strengths.

The traditional assessment tools such as standardized intelligence tests were also discussed in relation to the psychological evaluation of exceptional children. The chapter was intended to familiarize the reader with the content and use of such standardized tests as the Wechsler Scales, Stanford-Binet, Illinois Test of Psycholinguistic Abilities, Developmental Test of Visual Perception, and the Bender Visual-Motor Gestalt. These standardized tests were also discussed in relationship with the various language functions which directly and indirectly underlie their performance.

Suggested Reading

INFORMAL WRITTEN LANGUAGE
TEACHING PROCEDURES
(Wallace and McLoughlin, 1975)

Arena, J. I. (Ed.): *Building Handwriting Skills in Dyslexic Children*. San Rafael, Acad Ther Pub, 1970.

This is a compilation of articles describing different aspects of handwriting, including identification, diagnosis, remediation, cursive writing, manuscript writing, left-handed writing, and various remedial considerations. All of the articles are practical, and most of the suggestions are easily adaptable to teaching children how to write.

Arena, J. I. (Ed.): *Building Spelling Skills in Dyslexic Children.* San Rafael, Acad Ther Pub, 1968.

A wide variety of versatile approaches which develop academic skills necessary for competent spelling are included in this book. Many different creative approaches for teaching spelling are concisely described. Various methods for diagnosing spelling difficulties are also delineated.

Platts, M. E.: *Anchor: A Handbook of Vocabulary Discovery Techniques for the Classroom Teacher.* Stevensville, Educational Service, Inc., 1970.

Many different games, aids, and teaching methods for increasing vocabulary are described throughout this book. Speaking and writing vocabularies are developed through unusual and interesting methods and activities.

Platts, M. E., Marguerite, Sr. Rose, and Schumaker, E.: *Spice: A Handbook of Activities to Motivate the Teaching of Elementary Language Arts.* Stevensville, Educational Service, Inc., 1960.

One section of this book lists a variety of games, ideas, and independent activities for developing creative writing skills. Detailed directions for teachers and variations of each activitity are included for each suggestion.

Wallace, G., and Kauffman, J. M.: *Teaching Children With Learning Problems.* Columbus, Merrill, 1973, Chap. 9.

This chapter offers a number of teaching suggestions for remediating handwriting, spelling, and written expression problems. The activities are grouped according to specific skill deficiencies.

BIBLIOGRAPHY

Barrett, T. C.: Visual discrimination tasks as predictors of first grade reading achievement. *The Reading Teacher, 18*:276-282, 1965.

Bateman, Barbara: Learning disabilities — yesterday, today, tomorrow. *Except Child, 31*:167, 1964.

Benger, K.: The relationships of perception, personality, intelligence, and grade one reading achievement. In Smith, H. K. (Ed.): *Perception and Reading.* Newark, Intl Reading, 1968.

Bond, G. L., and Tinker, M. A.: *Reading difficulties: Their diagnosis and correction.* New York, Appleton, 1957.

Carpenter, R. L., and Willis, D. J.: Case study of an auditory dyslexic. *J Learning Disabilities, 5:*121-129, 1972.

Chall, J., Roswell, F. G., and Blumenthal, S. H.: Auditory blending ability: A factor in success in beginning reading. *The Reading Teacher, 17:*113-118, 1963.

Clements, Samuel D.: The child with minimal brain dysfunction — A profile. *Children with Minimal Brain Injury.* Chicago, National Society for Crippled Children and Adults, 1963.

Clements, Samuel D., and Peters, John E.: Minimal brain dysfunction in the school-age child. *Arch Gen Pyschiatry, 6:*12, 1962.

Cohn, Robert: The neurological study of children with learning disabilities. *Except Child 31:*179, 1964.

Cooley, W. W., and Lohnes, P. R.: *Project talent: Predicting Development of Young Adults.* U. S. Department of Health, Education and Welfare. OE-610-065, 1968.

Cooper, J.: A procedure for teaching non-readers, *Education, 8:*494-499, 1947.

Fernald, G. M.: *Remedial Techniques in Basic School Subjects.* New York, McGraw, 1943.

Flower, R. M.: Auditory disorders and reading disorders. In Flower, R. M., Gofman, H. F. and Lawson, L. I. (Eds.): *Reading Disorders: A Multi-Disciplinary Symposium.* Philadelphia, Davis, 1965.

Freidus, E.: Methodology for the classroom teacher. In Hellmuth, J. (Ed.): *The Special Child in Century 21.* Seattle, Spec Child, 1964.

Frostig, M.: *Developmental test of visual perception.* Palo Alto, Consulting Psychologists Pr, 1963.

Frostig, M.: Teaching reading to children with perceptual disturbances. In Flower, R. M., Gofman, H. F., and Lawson, L. I. (Eds.): *Reading Disorders: A Multi-Disciplinary Symposium.* Philadelphia, Davis, 1965.

Frostig, M., and Horne, D.: *The Frostig Program for the Development of Visual Perception.* Chicago, Follett, 1964.

Furth, H. G.: A review and perspective on the thinking of deaf people. As stated in Hellmuth (Ed.): *Cognitive Studies.* New York, Brunner-Mazel, 1970.

Gallant, R.: The development of a diagnostic instrument. In Farr, R. (Ed.): *Measurement and Evaluation of Reading.* New York, HarBrace, 1970.

Gates, A. I.: A further evaluation of reading readiness tests. *Elementary School J, 40:*571-577, 1940.

Gearheart, B. R.: *Learning Disabilities: Educational Strategies.* St. Louis, Mosby, 1973.

Gillingham, A., and Stillman, B.: *Remedial Reading Training for Children With Specific Disabilities in Reading, Spelling and Penmanship.* Bronxville, The Authors, 1956.

Goins, J. T.: Visual and auditory perception in reading. *The Reading Teacher, 7:*9-13, 1959.

Goodstein, H. A.: Performance of mentally handicapped and average IQ children on two modified cloze tasks for oral language. *Am J Ment Defic, 75*:290-297, 1970.

Gross, J. C.: "The Development and Validation of a Test of Kinesio-Perceptual Ability. Unpublished doctoral dissertation, Southern Illinois University, 1969.

Hanvik, Leo: Diagnosis of cerebral dysfunction in the child. *Am J Dis Child, 100*:71, 1961.

Harrington, J. J., and Durrell, D. D.: Mental maturity versus perception abilities in primary reading. *J Educ Psychol, 46*:375-380, 1955.

Harris, L. A., and Rosewell, F. G.: Clinical diagnosis of reading disability. In Natchez, G. (Ed.): *Children With Reading Problems: Classic and Contemporary Issues in Reading Disability.* New York, Basic, 1968.

Ismail, A. H., and Gruber, J. J.: *Motor Aptitude and Intellectual Performance.* Columbus, Merrill, 1967.

Jansky, J. J., and de Hirsch, L.: *Preventing Reading Failure: Prediction, Diagnosis, Intervention.* New York, HarRow, 1972.

Johnson, W. et al.: *Speech Handicapped School Children,* 3rd Ed. New York, HarRow, 1967.

Jordan, T. E.: *The Mentally Retarded,* 2nd Ed. Columbus, Merrill, 1966.

Kaluger, G., and Kolson, C. J.: *Reading and Learning Disabilities.* Columbus, Merrill, 1969.

Keogh, B. K.: The bender gestalt as a predictive and diagnostic test of reading performance. *J Consult Psychol, 29*:83-84, 1965.

Kessler, J. W.: Contributions of the mentally retarded toward a theory of cognitive development. In Hellmuth, J. (Ed.): *Cognitive Studies.* New York, Brunner-Mazel, 1970, vol. 1.

Kirk, S. A.: The influence of manual tracing on the learning of simple words in the case of subnormal boys. *J Educ Psychol, 24*:525-535, 1933.

Kirk, S. A.: *Educating Exceptional Children,* 2nd Ed. Boston. HM, 1972.

Kirk, S. A., and McCarthy, J. J.: The Illinois test of psycholinguistic abilities: An approach to differential diagnosis. *Am J Ment Defic, 66*:399-412, 1961.

Klausmeir, H. J., Leham, I. J., and Beeman, A.: Relationship among physical, mental and achievement measures in children of low, average, and high intelligence. *Am J Ment Defic, 63*:647-656, 1959.

Kottler, S. B.: The identification and remediation of auditory problems. *Acad Ther, 8*:73-86, 1972.

Lerner, J. W.: *Children With Learning Disabilities.* Boston, HM, 1971.

McCarthy, James J., and Kirk, Samuel A.: *Illinois Test of Psycholinguistic Abilities Examiner's Manual.* Urbana, U of Ill Instit for Res Except Child, 1961.

Mulder, R. L., and Curtin, J.: Vocal phonic ability and silent reading achievement: A first report. *Elementary School J 56*:121-123, 1955.

Myers, Patricia I., and Hammill, Donald D.: *Methods for Learning Disorders.* New York, Wiley, 1969.

Neale, J. M., and Liebert, R. M.: *Science and Behavior: An Introduction to Methods of Research*. Englewood Cliffs, P-H, 1973.

Oleron, P.: Recherches sur le developpement mental des sourds-muets. Paris, Centre National de la Recherche Schietific, 1957. As stated in Hellmuth, J. (Ed.): *Cognitive Studies*. New York, Brunner-Mazel, Inc., 1970, vol. I.

Olson, A.: The Frostig developmental test of visual perception as a predictor of specific reading abilities in second-grade children. *Elementary English, 43*:869-872, 1966.

Osgood, C. E.: Motivational dynamics of language behavior, *Nebraska Symposium on Motivation*. Lincoln, U of Nebr Pr, 1957.

Pope, L., and Haklay, A.: Reading disability. In Wortis, J. (Ed.): *Mental Retardation: An Annual Review*. New York, Grune, 1970, vol. II.

Reynolds, M. C.: A study of the relationships between auditory characteristics and specific silent reading abilities. *J Educ Res, 46*:439-449, 1953.

Roberts, R. W., and Coleman, J. C.: An investigation of the role of visual and kinesthetic factors in reading failure. *J Educ Res, 51*:445-451, 1958.

Robinson, H. B., and Robinson, N. M.: *The Mentally Retarded Child: A Psychological Approach*. New York, McGraw, 1965.

Rood, M.: The use of sensory-receptors to activate, facilitate and inhabit motor response, autonomic and somatic, in developmental sequence. In Stattley, C.: *Approaches to the Treatment of Patients With Neuromuscular Dysfunction*. Dubuque, Brown, 1962.

Rosner, J.: Perceptual skills: A concern of the classroom teacher? *The Reading Teacher, 24*:543-549, 1971.

Roswell, F., and Natchez, G.: *Reading Disability: Diagnosis and Treatment*. New York, Basic, 1964.

Savage, R. Douglass: *Psychometric Assessment of the Individual Child*. Baltimore, Penguin, 1968.

Scherer, Isidor W.: The prediction of academic achievement in brain-injured children. *Except Child, 28*:103, 1961.

Smith, R. M.: *Clinical Teaching: Methods of Instruction for the Retarded*. New York, McGraw, 1968.

Smith, R. M.: *An Introduction to Mental Retardation*. New York, McGraw, 1971.

Spache, G. D.: Estimating reading capacity. In Schell, L. M., and Burns, P. C. (Eds.): *Remedial Reading: An Anthology of Sources*. Boston, Allyn, 1968.

Temmer, Helena W.: Wechsler intelligence scores and Bender-Gestalt performance in adult male mental defectives. *Am J Ment Defic, 70*:86, 1965.

Terman, Lewis, M., and Merrill, Maud A.: *Stanford-Binet Intelligence Scale*. Boston, HM, 1962.

Vernon, M. D.: The perceptual process in reading. *Reading Teacher, 13*:2-8, 1959.

Wallace, Gerald, and McLoughlin, James A.: *Learning Disabilities: Concepts and Characteristics*. Columbus, Merrill, 1975.

Waugh, Kenneth W., and Bush, Wilma: *Diagnosing Learning Disorders.* Columbus, Merrill, 1971.

Wepman, J.: The perceptual basis for learning. In Robinson, H. A. (Ed.): *Meeting Individual Differences in Reading.* Chicago, U of Chicago Pr, 1964.

Wepman, J.: The modality concept. In Smith, H. K. (Ed.): *Perception and Reading.* Newark, Intl Reading, 1968.

Yoder, David E: Evaluation and assessment of children's language and speech behavior. In Wisland, Milton V. (Ed.): *Psychoeducational Diagnosis of Exceptional Children.* Springfield, Thomas, 1974.

Chapter 4

LANGUAGE DEVELOPMENT OF THE MULTIPLE HANDICAPPED

IN this chapter we shall deal with the blind child, the cerebral palsied blind, the cerebral palsied deaf, the deaf and blind, and the culturally deprived child. There are many other children who have more than one handicap, but they have been covered in other chapters. The visually handicapped child is included because he will have perceptual problems along with the blindness and because he is deprived of the sense which most children use to learn 80 to 90 percent of what they learn during the first six years of life.

The Blind and Visually Impaired

The incidence of mild visual defects is fairly high. It is estimated that about one out of every four children has some type of vision problem. However, recent studies indicate that a small proportion, approximately one in four hundred of the preschool and school population, have such marked visual difficulties that even with the best medical and optical care they cannot see well enough to profit by the educational facilities that are provided for children with normal vision. Kerby (1952) found that less than 30 percent of 7,310 children in partially sighted classes actually fell between 20/70 and 20/200 after correction. This leads one to believe that the lower limit of vision for educational purposes is indeed difficult to define.

According to a pamphlet published by the American Foundation for the Blind, Incorporated (1975) the following children should be classified as blind or partially seeing:

> Severe visual impairment may be called "blindness," "functional blindness," the inability to read newsprint, or "legal blindness," a definition used to determine eligibility for public

assistance. A person is said to be "legally blind" if his central visual acuity does not exceed 20/200 in the better eye with correcting lenses or his visual field is less than an angle of 20 degrees. In simpler terms, a person is considered "legally blind" if he can see no more at a distance of 20 feet than someone with normal sight can see at a distance of 200 feet.

There are many definitions of blindness, all referring to how well the individual can see even with the best corrective lenses. Actually, most so-called "blind" persons — over 75 percent of the blind persons in this country — do have some usable vision. How then can one decide when a person should be considered severely visually impaired? The primary concern should be how well the person can function with his limited vision. The individual is handicapped to the degree to which his visual impairment prevents him from living the life he wishes to lead. For example, the person who would like to be able to drive a car or do a lot of visual reading will find poor vision more of a handicap than the person whose life style does not include these activities. In other words, the person is severely handicapped when he considers himself to be severely handicapped.

The American Foundation for the Blind prefers that the term "blindness" be reserved for a complete loss of sight with all other degrees of visual loss considered as visual impairment which can accurately be determined by ophthalmic measurements. Therefore, anyone whose loss of vision affects his normal functioning and performance would be eligible for materials, services, and training to alleviate his loss as much as possible and to encourage fullest use of his remaining senses.

The person with normal vision can read the twenty-foot row at a distance of twenty feet. Thus 20/70 means that the person sees at twenty feet what the individual with normal vision could see at seventy feet.

Snellen's notation and percentage of visual efficiency follows:

20/20	100.00 percent
20/35	87.5 percent
20/70	64.0 percent
20/100	48.8 percent
20/200	20.0 percent

Causes

A large number of the partially sighted are affected by prenatal conditions, some of which are hereditary. Other causes may be diseases, accidents, or developmental anomalies (see Table IV.)

Table IV

CAUSES OF BLINDNESS

Heredity	15%
Infectious diseases	7%
Prenatal causes	50%
Injuries	3%
Poisoning	20%
Tumors	5%
	———
	100%

Kerby, in a national survey of the visual defects found in 600 classes for partially seeing children which was made by the National Society for the Prevention of Blindness, reports the following finds concerning types and percentage of defective vision (Kerby, 1952):

Refractive errors (myopia, hyperopia, etc.)	49 percent
Developmental anomalies of structure (cataracts, albinism, etc.)	22 percent
Defects of muscle function (strabismus, nystagmus, etc.)	17 percent
Disease or defects of the eye (due to infection, injuries, etc.)	11 percent
Others, causes undetermined	1 percent

In a study of 131 partially seeing children (see Table V), Bateman (1963) found a frequency and percentage of eye conditions which corresponds well with Kerby's findings.

Table V

FREQUENCY AND PERCENTAGE OF EYE CONDITIONS

Condition	Number of Cases	Percent %
Albinism (including albinism with nystagmus)	7	5
Cataracts (including bilateral, unilateral, congenital, and aphakia)	20	15
Myopia (including progressive, degenerative, myopic astigmatism)	32	24
Myopia with strabismus, esotropia, or nystagmus	7	5
Hyperopia (including hyperopic astigmatism, and with strabismus, nystagmus, or esotropia)	10	8
Retrolental fibroplasia	17	13
Esotropia (including esotropia with nystagmus, and including amblyopia ex anopsia)	11	9
Nystagmus	10	8
Other (optic atrophy, glaucoma, chorioretinitis, etc.)	17	13
Total	131	100

The Blind

Only about 20 percent of all legally blind children and adults are totally blind; therefore, for the purpose of language development in this chapter, we are discussing the child who has a visual acuity of 20/200 or less in the better eye after correction. After 20/200 on the continuum would be *counts fingers,* followed by *sees hand movement, light perception,* and *light projection.*

Definition

The legally blind have a vision acuity of 20/200 or less in the better eye after correction. It is possible for children who are legally blind to read large print and even function as partially sighted. Most of the blind persons in this country are in the sixty-five-and-older age group. The total number of blind persons in the United States is estimated to be about 400,000.

Unspecified prenatal causes account for approximately 50 percent of all blindness. Other causes include infectious diseases, accidents, poisoning, heredity, and tumors.

Characteristics

Myers (1930) found that, out of 2,860 blind children, 50.2 percent were boys and 49.8 percent were girls. As has already been mentioned in this chapter, mental retardation is not a necessary concomitant of blindness. Many studies are available which indicate that partially seeing children do not deviate to any great extent from seeing children as far as intelligence is concerned.

There is much controversy concerning the emotional adjustment of the blind and the partially seeing. Meyerson (1953) has pointed out the many discrepancies in the research concerning the adjustment of this group. Cowen (1961), in one of the most sophisticated studies, found no great difference beween the blind in residential schools, the blind in day schools, and a group of seeing students in comparable situations.

Education

The education of the blind and partially sighted, as with all persons, begins at birth and continues throughout life. The visually handicapped person has special educational needs which the sighted person does not have. These needs are met in varying ways. How these needs are fulfilled and how well they are fulfilled depends upon the degree of disability, the facilities available to the person, and upon the person himself.

The visually-handicapped child begins life with the basic needs of any child. Jones (1963) states, "The child who is handicapped by a visual loss or impairment must have the love and care of his parents just like his normally seeing brothers and sisters. He may have even greater need for their affection if he is to make a healthy adjustment to his defect."

Given a comfortable environment, a child whose only handicap is a visual one should acquire many skills at about the same age as a fully sighted child. He should learn to walk, talk, develop independent eating habits, and be toilet trained at about the same age as his sighted counterpart.

A blind or partially sighted child who is otherwise normal can be taught in preschool and early school years to begin to acquire educational aids such as nonvisual cues. Whitstock (1973) suggests the following nonvisual cues:

> A bakery with its characteristic odor serves to locate it as a landmark, or informs the blind person of its purpose. A trolley has a sound all its own. This sound identifies the street as a major thoroughfare, or points out the location of a possible means of transportation. The wind can give a great deal of information: it rustles through the leaves and sighs through pine branches. If constant, it can give a method of checking one's direction. If a person steps past the protection of a building, its unchecked gust identifies an open space adjacent to him. A driveway can act as a landmark and can be distinguished as a break in the sidewalk, or a gravel strip through concrete.

These and similar aids can greatly increase a blind child's orientation and mobility.

If possible, a blind or partially seeing child should have nursery school experience with seeing children. Pauline Moore, in her study (1952), found that the teacher of seeing children usually required some reassurance before accepting a blind or partially sighted child into his/her class. The teacher usually had fears concerning the child's safety, the adequacy of the size of the staff, and concern for the common good of the group. Certain standards of readiness were adopted, and most of the children in this study met them between three and one-half and five years of age. These standards were not too different from those set for seeing children. However, the children with visual disabilities were usually placed in a group of younger children. Moore concluded that the experiences of the children she followed were most worthwhile: "The independence stressed in a nursery school program was extremely important to all the blind children in helping them to develop initiative and to build confidence in themselves." She also found some carryover of learning from school to home and the development of many positive attitudes for all the children.

Language for the Blind

As explained earlier in this text, a child's ability to use language effectively is based upon his earlier reception or understanding of the language stimuli which surrounds him. The child who is born with a significant visual impairment has in essence been deprived of one avenue in which language stimuli could be received. Since much of a child's early receptive language learning is based on the association of words with the objects they represent, we necessarily find that the visually impaired child is deprived of many opportunities for association learning to take place. The research indicates that the initial vocabulary of young children is made up almost exclusively of nouns, i.e. names of objects in their environment. The learning of the symbolic names of objects can be clearly facilitated if the visual pathway operates efficiently. For example, consider the difficulties the totally blind child would have in acquiring the language symbol of car. Because of his visual impairment the child must rely on other sensory avenues that eventually can form the concept of car. The visually impaired child's learning of the concept of car must be attained through such avenues as tactile exploration, kinesthetic sensations, and auditory association.

Therefore, if one compares the visually normal child with the visually impaired child, it is quite possible that one would observe a difference in the level of receptive language development. It is predictable that the visually normal child would initially outdistance the visually impaired child in receptive language development. The deficiency of the receptive language vocabulary might have extensive generalizing effects on the blind child's symbolic language development.

Deaf-Blind

Current federal legislation defines the deaf-blind person as " . . . one who has both auditory and visual impairments, the combination of which causes such severe communication and other developmental and educational problems that he cannot properly be accommodated in special educational programs, either for the hearing handicapped child or for the visually handicapped child" (English, 1972).

This is a very broad definition and is not specific enough. The National Center for Deaf-Blind Youths and Adults has developed a definition of deaf-blind:

> Central visual acuity of 20/200 or less in the better eye, with correcting glasses, or central visual acuity of more than 20/200 if there is a field defect such that the peripheral field has been contracted to an extent that the widest diameter of visual field subtends an angular distance no greater than 20 degrees, and a chronic impairment of hearing so severe that speech cannot be understood, even with optimum amplification (English, 1972).

There is a regional center concept for the benefit of deaf-blind children in the United States. There are presently ten regional centers for services to deaf-blind children which encompass all fifty states. According to the most recent information there are over 5,000 deaf-blind children and adults presently living in the United States. The majority of these children are victims of the rubella epidemic of 1963-1965.

Language Development of the Deaf-Blind

Parents can do many things to help their deaf-blind child develop readiness for language. However, a child who is handicapped this severely will need the help of professionals in developing language. Parents of such children should give them a great deal of love, hug and kiss them a great deal, and encourage them in all areas of development. The parents should seek professional help and determine where the child can be sent for the best help and at which age he should be sent. There are many places throughout the United States now which have facilities for the deaf-blind, and most of the state institutions for the blind and deaf have programs for deaf-blind children.

A pamphlet published by the American Foundation for the Blind has this to say about speech development of the deaf-blind child:

> The question of speech is of primary importance and naturally is uppermost in the minds of parents. Although it is possible to give your child some preliminary training in speech by singing to him, letting him feel the vibrations in your body or in a musical instrument, there is the danger that you may allow yourself to focus your whole attention on this one phase at the expense of other much-needed training. It is not our thought here that speech and speech reading should be disregarded but rather, if you can give your child the foundation for physical and social self-reliance, he will be better prepared to acquire speech and language understanding in the hands of a trained specialist. Every experience you can give him will help to increase his mental curiosity, which in turn will speed up his learning process.

Cerebral Palsy

The condition now known as cerebral palsy has existed as far back as recorded history goes, as noted in biblical description of the lame and in ancient Egyptian hieroglyphics depicting the characteristic postures of the cerebral palsied. The earliest references to the relationship between intracranial hemorrhage at birth and the later development of cerebral palsy can be found in medical literature dated 1826 to 1835. In 1838 a London orthopedist, William John Little, described some of the consequences of birth lesions, and in 1869 gave the name *spastic paralysis* to the condition characterized by a crosslegged gait, drooling, speech difficulties, and mental retardation. The condition became known as *Little's disease,* and his belief that the prognosis was hopeless for those so afflicted persisted for many years.

In the early 1900's, during an epidemic of poliomyelitis, it was discovered that many children being brought to clinics diagnosed as victims of infantile paralysis actually had Little's disease. The problem was thus forced to the attention of the medical profession. Many doctors began to question Little's *hopeless* attitude and launched full-scale investigations into the problem. Among these pioneers were Bronson Crothers and one of his students, Winthrop Morgans Phelps, both physicians. Phelps is given credit for proposing the term *cerebral palsy*. *Cerebral* denotes that the causative lesion is in the brain; *palsy* indicates the consequences of such a lesion, which is a loss or impairment of motor functioning.

During the last ten years *cerebral palsy* has become an increasingly familiar term to many professions and the general public as a result of increased research, educational and fund-raising campaigns, and the active parent groups which have been organized in all parts of the country. We are told that there is one cerebral-palsied individual born per every 215 live births, or seven cerebral palsied births per 100,000 of our population, or one cerebral-palsied birth every fifty-three minutes. The medical profession is keeping these babies alive and promising them an increased life expectancy every day. But what happens to the families who must make room for a handicapped child, the schools which must educate them, the industries which will be asked to hire them, and the society which will be asked to accept them? Behind the statistics are human beings. Interest in the complexities of cerebral palsy and the details of its prevention and treatment must always be oriented toward the individual. In order that these individuals can learn to function to the highest level of their capacities, the combined efforts of the medical profession; the psychologists; the teachers; the speech, occupational, and vocational therapists; and many others are necessary.

Cerebral palsy has aroused public interest and concern in recent years; it is a major medical and sociological problem, but many people do not realize the complexity of this condition. Perlstein (1952) defines cerebral palsy as " ... a condition characterized by paralysis, paresis, incoordination, dyskinesia, or aberration of motor function that is due to involvement of the motor areas of the brain." In addition to the motor dysfunction there are usually coexisting conditions such as mental retardation, sensory loss, convulsions, and emotional disturbances. Crothers and Paine (1959) point out that two arbitrary criteria have been generally accepted: The lesion must occur in early life, and no progressive disease may exist at the time of the diagnosis.

Cerebral palsy has been defined in the United Cerebral Palsy Research and Educational Foundation Program for calendar year 1961 as follows:

> Cerebral palsy is the clinical picture, usually manifesting itself in childhood, with dysfunction of the brain in which one of the major components is motor disturbance.
>
> Thus, cerebral palsy may be described as a group of conditions, usually originating in childhood, characterized by paralysis, weakness, incoordination of any other aberration of motor function caused by pathology of the motor control centers of the brain. In addition to such motor dysfunction, cerebral palsy may include learning difficulties, psychological problems, sensory defects, convulsions and behavioral disorders of organic origin (Phelps, 1950).

Incidence

There are many different estimates on the number of cerebral palsy victims. Phelps (1950) reported that seven afflicted children were born each year per 100,000 population. He states that one of these children would die during infancy, which would change the estimate to six per 100,000 population. Recent figures given by the United Cerebral Palsy Association estimate the number of cerebral-palsied individuals at 550,000. This is an even larger number than the projected figures of Phelp's study. Cardwell (1956) suggests the increased birthrate may be the reason for the difference.

Types

The three main types of cerebral palsy consist of the *spastic* individual who moves stiffly and with difficulty, the *athetoid* who has involuntary and uncontrolled movements, and the *ataxic* whose sense of balance and depth perception are disturbed. Since cerebral palsy affects the muscle control centers of the brain, its most common effects are awkward, shambling gait, lack of balance, tremors, guttural speech and grimacing. Spasms and seizures in varying degrees, mental retardation and defects in vision and deafness are also commonly an integral part of the disorder.

Speech, Hearing, and Sight

Saltman (1964) tells us that speech is just one part of the communication process so vital to the development of a child. But learning to speak is so extremely complex, so closely bound up with other senses, and so necessary for the emotional expression and development of the child that it takes precedence over almost every other problem, even walking. Learning to speak presents many problems to the cerebral-palsied child. Coordinated movements of a large group of muscles in his lungs, throat, tongue, lips, and so on must be successfully accomplished. Later, he must learn to read — that is, to connect visual symbols to his heard and learned speech — and finally to connect all these to the motor activities of the hand so that he can write what he hears, speaks, and sees. All persons concerned with the child's care must be enlisted in the effort to encourage the child in his attempts to speak. It is important not to expect too much. Almost inevitably, his efforts will not sound entirely normal, but the ability to speak is so important that their progress should be grounds for great satisfaction. Other means of communication such as writing, typing, or even the use of signs are also important, but should not be allowed to interfere with the efforts to learn to speak.

The proportion of the cerebral palsied having hearing defects has been estimated at anywhere from one-tenth to one-third, but there is no doubt it is much more prevalent than in the normal population. The largest number of defects of hearing among cerebral-palsied children occur among those with a history of Rh incompatibility. A deaf or nearly deaf cerebral-palsied child can sometimes be helped by a hearing aid provided that he can safely wear one and that he can be trained in its mechanics and use.

Otherwise, lipreading and other substitute measures may have to be accepted.

Defects of vision are of special concern to the cerebral palsied — they may retard all his learning and set him apart even more sharply from the rest of the world, adding immeasurably to his emotional burden. Treatment of visual defects may include covering the good eye to strengthen the muscles of the weak one by forced use; glasses to improve vision, correct distortions, and overcome headaches; prism glasses and muscle-strengthening exercises; surgery to correct the same sort of muscle contractures that affect the limbs.

It goes without saying that the more handicaps a child has, the harder it will be for him to function properly in his environment. In the case of a cerebral palsied child who is deaf and/or blind, his problems in acquiring language are magnified a hundredfold. Many cerebral-palsied children have problems with communicating and acquiring language, and any additional handicap can only increase the problem. Any avenue used by a child to acquire language that is denied at birth makes the life of that child very hard and very difficult.

The Culturally Deprived Child

Blank and Soloman (1970) propose that when culturally deprived children are exposed to an infinite number of ostensibly enriching stimuli there is no assurance that deficits will be overcome. In other words, presentation alone does not insure that the child will learn the newly-available material. Active involvement refers, according to Blank and Soloman (1970), not to motor activity but rather to an internal mental manipulation of experiences. The experiences are skills which involve the ability to organize thoughts, to reflect on situations, to comprehend meaning, and to learn to choose among alternatives.

The two cited authors (Blank and Soloman) refer to an abstract attitude, and they state that failure to develop this attitude represents the most glaring deficiency of deprived children. They do not possess a symbolic system by which to organize the plentiful situation which surrounds them. The assumptions made by

Blank and Soloman (1970) follow:

1. Deprived preschool children do not have a firm language base for thinking. They will develop one only if they are given consistent guidance. This leads to the further assumption that the most effective teaching is based on individual tutoring.

2. Language acquisition, like any new complex skill, may be met with some resistance. To prevent resistance from becoming established, the child should not be permitted to leave a task unfinished. If necessary, the task can be simplified, but the child should still be required to fulfill the demands set by the teacher. Once these initial difficulties have been conquered, the child is able to experience great pleasure both in using this new tool and in knowing that he has this tool to use.

3. Young children have short attention spans and therefore need relatively brief but frequent reinforcement of new skills (i.e., 5 days a week for 15-20 minutes each day, resulting in a total of about 1½ hours of tutoring per week).

4. The new command of language will allow the child to cope more effectively with an otherwise debilitating environment. Therefore, marked improvement in many aspects of maladaptive behavior should occur.

What Does Culturally and Socially Disadvantaged Mean?

When children are labeled culturally and/or socially disadvantaged there is always the danger that they will be identified as inferior-type children from the lower class and thought of as lower-class human beings. We hear a lot about racial equality, civil rights, and the need for blacks and minority groups to occupy status positions in society. We also hear political candidates tell how they are going to help the culturally deprived and enable them to *pick themselves up by the boot straps.* Middle-class people in prestige positions preach the gospel about how we can help the blacks, the Indians, or the Puerto Ricans and Chicano people fit the mold of the *advantaged culture.* This would indicate, to this author at least, that professionals often look down on minority groups and play the role of the caretakers of the poor. As long as this is true the people from the lower class who have deprived children are not going to be able to improve the scholastic position of their children very much. The pecking order of the advantaged and disadvantaged society will be strongly reinforced. Teachers, more than any other group of people, should know and understand the culture of the socially disadvantaged child. Butts (1955) lists the meaning of culture as follows: "The whole way of life that is created, learned, held in common, and passed on from one generation to another by the members of a particular society. Culture is the sum total of ways of behaving that a group of people builds up and expects its members to acquire, share, and live by."

This author likes the definition that Robert Havighurst (1964) gives. He states that the socially disadvantaged child is one who has a disadvantage relative to some other child or some kind of social life. Therefore, this child is handicapped in growing up and will be prevented from leading a competent and satisfying life. Very often the handicaps are well defined within the family and in the psychosocial group in which the family operates. The socially disadvantaged have a host of language, learning, and background problems.

Intellectual Processes

There are many aspects of thinking, reading, language, intelligence, and academic achievement of the deprived child which must be discussed in order for improvements to be made in the teaching of the disadvantaged. If children are reared in the slum areas or in isolated rural districts, in all probability they will be deprived in one or all of the cognitive processes listed above. There are so many effects of being deprived that we can never say that there is a universal effect. Whenever deprived children are observed and examined for intelligence, language, or achievement one can always see that individual differences exist. Therefore, we can say that deprived children are not homogeneous when it comes to cognitive abilities. Naturally, the mental ability will vary in a group of disadvantaged youngsters. The teacher must be aware of this and treat these children as having limited experiences.

Thinking

Martin Deutsch (1964) and his associates at the Institute for Developmental Studies pinpointed the observation made by many teachers who have reported that socially disadvantaged children are inferior to children from the lower middle class and above in abstract functioning and in the classification of visual stimuli. William White (1964) has the following to say about the thinking process of socially disadvantaged children:

> Numerous research studies support the statement that the thinking patterns of deprived children are different from those of advantaged children. It should be clearly stated, however, that this does not mean that deprived children cannot think; it means only that they think in a different mode. If any characterization can be made of children born and raised in poverty, it must be the slowness with which they shift to abstract thinking levels. The transition to the use of signs and symbols in interpreting things perceived is much less frequent and less automatic in disadvantaged children than in children from homes where there is more stimulation from oral language, pictures, printed materials, tools, music, and toys. The total quantity and quality of concepts generated by deprived children appear to be lower than among their advantaged peers. The causes of the reduced number of concepts and the predominately concrete style of conceptualization in deprived children are still debatable. Probably the most significant contribution of educational psychology to our understanding of the conceptualization processes of deprived children has been Ausubel's (1964, 1965) conclusion that a delay in learning certain language forms by the disadvantaged slows down their passing from concrete to abstract modes of thinking. Ausubel has suggested that the transition "normally" begins during the junior high school period. Children passing through this "stage" are no longer limited to intuitive, concrete, and particularized thought processes but can formulate precise, abstract, and universal concepts.

The Puerto Rican in the New York City Schools

It is safe to say that there is an estimated ten million Spanish-speaking people in the United States, and a substantial number are of school age. The language abilities of these Spanish-speaking children vary along a continuum from Spanish/English bilingualism to multilanguage abilities determined by specific cultural and subcultural backgrounds.

Despite the things just said, Spanish-speaking children face certain general difficulties in their search for equal educational opportunities. It is estimated that there are 250,000 Puerto Rican school-age children enrolled in the New York City school system. A report by Fleishman (1973) found that 94,800 have significant language difficulties. Noel Rios (1973) states that approximately 4,418 of the Puerto Rican children were receiving special services in 1970. It is graphically clear that there is a huge discrepancy between those needing service and those receiving service.

The authors would like to point out some additional statistics which the readers might find startling. The Puerto Rican Forum (1969) tells us that 86 percent of all Puerto Rican children are below the normal reading level. Jenkins (1971), who had a great deal to do with the Puerto Rican Forum, states that the dropout rate for Puerto Rican children is extremely high. He estimates that 57 percent of these children drop out of school. Rios (1973) states that this statistic does not reflect the high incidence of students who leave the New York City school system and migrate back to Puerto Rico.

Educational Approaches

There are two approaches for the Puerto Rican children which are being used extensively. These two approaches are the English as a second language approach (ESL) and the bilingual approach. Noel Rios (1973) has the following to say about the ESL approach:

> In the ESL approach, all instruction is conducted in English (generally in integrated classrooms), and special English instruction is provided for those who need it. The difficulty with this approach surfaces when the number of students who need assistance far outnumber the personnel available to provide it. Thus, instruction in English for nonspeakers may be as limited

in the ESL approach as it is in the regular class.

In the bilingual approach, instruction is conducted in English and Spanish. As a student's fluency in English increases, the instruction time in the child's native tongue is decreased. This bilingual approach has been very successful in the Coral Way School in Miami, Florida. In 1973 the New York City school system had not implemented the bilingual approach. To end the discussion concerning the Puerto Rican and the New York City schools, the authors would like to quote a paragraph from a lecture by Noel Rios (1973):

> To suggest that the needs of the New York City school system are great is to grossly understate and oversimplify a socioethnic problem that is manifested in our schools. Attempts to assess the determination with which the system approaches the solution of this problem reveal a lack of commitment and a surprising amount of administrative negligence in terms of hiring and training staff to carry out these programs.
>
> The parents of the Puerto Rican student are a source of advocacy which has not been mobilized to any large extent. Perhaps a more militant stance on the part of the parents is needed before the educational system can be changed. It would appear that before this occurs, the educational community would do well to lead rather than follow the lay group.

Language, Cultural Contrasts, and the Black American

In America we have a multicultural population; therefore, an understanding of cultural distinctions between a certain population of children and so-called average children is crucial if educators are to have a clear perception of all of these students. Language is an excellent behavioral system to use for performing a contrasting analysis of a culture. It has been stated for years by many authorities that language is the vehicle through which most information is transmitted.

Very few people would deny that language is also an expression of a culture. Language also represents the concepts and underlying ideas of a culture. Language, therefore, can be easily recognized as a very important topic when discussing cultural variations in any moment in time. In recent years, though, minority-group children have been considered important enough to be of major academic interest and taken into consideration. Why has this come about?

We have had much civilian disorder, and the minority groups are no longer willing to be ignored. We have had a great deal of research and funds for a variety of programs for the disadvantaged members of our society. There has also been a sharp increase of scholarly and scientific interest in the language and culture of culturally different people.

Orlando Taylor (1973), in a paper presented in Las Vegas, Nevada, states that there is another reason for the upsurge in interest of the study of language and culture of the minority groups; that is because the central cities have moved from predominantly white to predominantly brown, black, yellow, and red. This change has given rise to the highly controversial issue of busing. An increasing number of blacks and other minorities have been elected to the various state, national, and local offices around the country.

Blacks now represent the nation's largest minority, and in many cities they are in the majority. Therefore, the current interest in the study of culture would naturally include black culture and language. Taylor (1973) had some interesting remarks to make concerning the new era of cultural pluralism:

> We are now approaching a new era. It is the era of cultural pluralism. Different strokes for different folks! After extensive study, many scholars have come to the conclusion that the United States was never a single culture; it was not and is not a melting pot. In reality, it is a country which allows a wide variety of people an opportunity to live together in a common geographical space, maintain most of their native culture, and at certain moments in time, interact with individuals from other cultures according to economic, social, or educational needs. Thus in New York, the presumed capital of the melting pot, we see bastions of cultural enclaves — China Town, Little Italy, Brownsville, Harlem, Spanish Harlem, etc. In other words, we see individuals maintaining their cultural patterns even though they interact with the larger society in a variety of ways. However, this maintenance of cultural patterns rarely carries over into our school systems. If one is different in the typical school

system, he is usually viewed as a special problem. And language, a major basis for cultural diversity, is a major basis for this "problem."

Minority Children Who are Gifted

Minority children have long suffered in the area of identification of giftedness. Actually the identification of gifted children in America has never been a top priority in spite of the tremendous potential contributions that could be made by these children. Often when these children are identified there is a resentment toward them and even feelings of hostility or apathy toward them.

The gifted child does not always excel, and the general public feels that this child will excel in spite of all the obstacles placed in his path. Too often, though, the gifted child is not identified, and he never reaches his potential. This is particularly true if he is from a minority group or from a lower socioeconomic family or even an isolated rural area. These children often do not develop language which will allow them to make high grades on our present assessment tools. Therefore, many children who are actually intellectually gifted are discriminated against by our tests, and we never really discover these children and thus lose the potential contributions they could make.

When children are non-English-speaking they are particularly discriminated against, and the gifted and talented among them may never be discovered or they may be placed at a disadvantage because of discriminatory practices.

Because of all the things stated above, it is very important to look beyond English language competency in classifying minority children as retarded or gifted. We should be especially skeptical of labeling children if the child has been reared in a language environment that is linguistically different from that of standard English.

The Mexican-American

The Mexican-American, or Chicano, is the second largest minority group in the United States. This group constitutes approximately three fifths of the ten million persons of Spanish origin in America. Naturally this group does not constitute a homogeneous cultural entity. We could say, as a matter of fact, that one of the most significant aspects of the Mexican-American population is its heterogeneity. Because these things are true, it makes the education of the Chicano children even more difficult.

There are other things which make education, social acceptance, and employment of the Chicano distinct. The average number of years of school completed by the Chicano is nine and a half, which is significantly lower than the national average of twelve years. In Texas alone one half of the Mexican-American children drop out of school before they reach the twelfth grade. In California less than two out of three Mexican-American children ever graduate from high school.

The Mexican-American Child has the same problems in language that other non-English-speaking children have. Viola Sierra (1973) told the following story in a speech delivered in Las Vegas, Nevada, concerning storytelling, which tells us something about the language of the Chicano child:

> The child from a traditional Mexican-American family is reared in a structured family environment where the roles of dominance and submission are fairly well defined. This apparently influences the types of relationships that the child seeks with other adults. This is shown by an analysis made on the types of relationships that the children preferred to have with the authority figures such as teachers and parents. The findings showed that Mexican-American children, more so than Anglo children, preferred relating with authority figures who took a personal interest in them and who were sincerely concerned for their welfare. This suggests that a more personalized style of teaching with substantial encouragement and support would be a more effective manner of dealing with these children.
> Further analysis of data in the same study indicates that the storytelling tradition of the Mexican-American has apparently resulted in an intellectual advantage for the Mexican-American child. Stories told by Mexican-American and Anglo children using stimulus cards were compared on the length and detail used in the story. It was found that the Chicano children had told longer stories and had included more characters than the

Anglo children.

This brings to mind an incident which demonstrates the strong storytelling tradition and the implication it carries for utilizing the valuable resources that the culturally diverse child presents. Just recently a doctoral student was trying to obtain some Spanish language samples of children residing in northern New Mexico. The student carefully selected magazine illustrations that he thought would elicit conversation from the children. He tried these with several of the children, receiving only minimal responses. However, when these children were asked to relate a story that they had heard their parents or grandparents tell, these children eagerly launched into stories of ghosts, folktales, and a variety of family episodes, inserting elaborate descriptions and detail. This occurrence is interesting, also, in view of the fact that many claim that Spanish-speaking children not only have a limited facility in English, but in Spanish as well.

The Asian American

To the average white American the Asians look basically alike and think alike; therefore it is generalized that they must be alike. Naturally this is not true. The diversity among Asian-Americans is as great as the diversity among white Americans, blacks, Chicanos, etc.

There are some things that make language and communication a problem for Asian-Americans if they are bilingual. For example, Filipinos have approximately eighty-seven major dialects. A Chinese who speaks only Cantonese cannot communicate very well verbally with another Chinese that speaks only Mandarin.

The marginal Asian-American exists between the margin of two cultures — that of his parents and that of the dominant culture in which he lives. If he sees the dominant culture as a power culture, he may become westernized and may even try to *out white* the whites with various maneuvers such as perfecting his speech until his English is flawless and has no trace of an accent.

The Asian-American who grows up in a home where two languages are taught will have the same trouble in communicating as any other child in a bilingual situation.

The American Indian

In modern America the American Indian in our society is in a miniminority group and is at the very bottom of the educational, economic, and social ladder. Because of his minority status, he does not have the opportunity of obtaining the cultural goals of the dominant group. Yet most Indians are conscious of their identity as native Americans even though this consciousness is often suppressed by the impact of the dominant culture.

In language the American Indian grows up in a bilingual culture, and when he begins school the English language is entirely foreign. Very often he survives in class only through rote learning and actually perceives little of what is taught.

In a class where the English language is the key to teaching and grading, the native American offers little competition. The Indian student will get C's, D's, and F's, and when he has collected several low grades, he becomes affected and looks for any reason to drop out. It is important to note that these same students can do well in classes which do not require the English language as the sole yardstick for success.

Indian students must be integrated into school systems with high-achieving students if they are to be successful. Segregated schools for an Indian will only perpetuate gross and misleading stereotypes. Also, for the Indian child to be successful in a school where there are English-speaking students and teachers, he must be exposed to the English language at a very early age.

Language is Symbolic

Research studies of children acquiring language demonstrate that a particular child takes advantage of a systematic aspect of language. Because language consists of patterns, it is indeed fortunate that we learn our native tongue in such a short period of time. Just think, though, of the child from lower socioeconomic levels who does not hear good English usage, and some of the problems he will have.

Because the past tense forms are normally formed in English

through the use of *ed*, the child is likely to extend this to the irregular past tense forms and create bringed for brought, comed for came, and goed for went. When it comes to the formation of plurals one often hears children say foots for feet, mouses for mice, and gooses for geese. If the child does not have a proper model to imitate and to tell him what is right and wrong, he is indeed fortunate if he gets to the first grade and is only one year behind the rest of the children.

A child's dialect is also a reflection of the social circumstances under which we all learn to speak. Thus, a black child who is reared with parents not speaking the standard variety of English will enter school speaking like his parents. A Spanish-speaking Chicano child will use the dialect his parents use and will enter school with this dialect. All of these aspects of language have to do with how our peers react to us.

Along the lines of how our peers act to us, in 1962 four researchers, Maslow, Kelly, Coombs, and Rogers, decided to get together and address the notion of emotional crippling. The findings of their study was printed in a book called *Perceiving, Behaving, Becoming*. It was published by the Association for Supervision and Curriculum Development as the Yearbook of 1962. These four researchers conclude that children perceive themselves as they think others perceive them. This is very frightening, because what these four researchers were saying was that children accept what other people think about them more readily than what they think about themselves. Therefore, when a child enters school with a language problem or any handicap, he will be influenced by what his peers think about his differentness.

BIBLIOGRAPHY

American Foundation for the Blind, Inc: *Facts About Blindness*. New York, American Foundation for the Blind, Inc., 1975.

Ausubel, D. P.: How reversible are the cognitive and motivational effects of cultural deprivation? Implications for teaching the culturally deprived child. *Urban Educ*, *1*:16-38, 1964.

———The effects of cultural deprivation on learning patterns. *Audio-visual Instruction*, *10*:10-12, 1965.

Bateman, Barbara Dee: Reading and psycholinguistic processes of partially seeing children. *CEC Research Monograph, No. 5.* Washington, Counc Exc Child, 1963.

Blank, Marion, and Soloman, Frances: A tutorial language program to develop abstract thinking in socially disadvantaged preschool children. In Mussen, Paul Henry, Conger, John Janeway, and Kagan, Jerome (Eds.): *Readings in Child Development and Personality.* New York, HarRow, 1965.

Butts, R. F. A.: *A Cultural History of Western Education.* New York, McGraw, 1955.

Cardwell, V. E.: *Cerebral Palsy, Advances in Understanding and Care.* New York, North River Pr, 1956.

Cowen, E. F. et al.: *Adjustment to Visual Disability in Adolescense.* New York, American Foundation of the Blind, 1961.

Crothers, B., and Paine, R. S.: *The Natural History of Cerebral Palsy.* Cambridge, Harvard Univ Pr, 1959.

Deutsch, Martin et al.: Communication of information in the elementary school classroom. *Cooperative Research Project 908.* Institute for Developmental Studies, Dept. of Psychiatry, New York Medical College, 1964.

English, Jack R.: *Adult Basic Education for Deaf-Blind Persons: Identifying the Need.* Paper presented at the National Conference of State Directors of Adult Basic Education. St. Louis, July, 1972.

Fleishman Commission Report: Children with English Language Difficulties. Albany, State Commission on the Cost, Quality, and Finance of Elementary and Second Schools, 1973, Part 3 of vol. 2.

Hathaway, Winifred: *Education and Health of the Partially Seeing Child,* 4th Ed. New York, Columbia Univ Pr, 1959.

Havighurst, Robert: Who are the socially disadvantaged? *Negro Education,* 9:210-217, 1964.

Jenkins, M.: *Bilingual education in New York City.* Prepared for the program of recruitment and training of Spanish-speaking teachers. Board of Education, New York City, 1971, pp. 1-72.

Jones, John Walker: *The Visually Handicapped Child.* U. S. Department of Health, Education, and Welfare, Bulletin 39, 1963.

Kerby, Edith C.: A report on visual handicaps of partially seeing children. *J Except Child, 18*:110, 1952.

Meyerson, L.: The visually handicapped. *Rev Educ Res, 23*:65, 1953.

Moore, Pauline, M.: *A Blind Child, Too, Can Go To Nursery School.* American Foundation for the Blind, Pre-School Series No. 1, 1952.

Myers, Edward T.: A survey of sight-saving classes in the public school of the United States. *The Sight-Saving Class Exchange.* New York, National Society for the Prevention of Blindness, 1930.

Perlstein, M. A.: Infantile cerebral palsy, classification and correction. *JAMA, 149*:310, 1952.

Phelps, W. M.: The cerebral palsied. In Newlson, W. E. (Ed.): *Mitchell Nelson*

Textbook of Pediatrics. Philadelphia, Saunders, 1950.

Rios, Noel: The Puerto Rican in the New York City schools. In Bransford, Louis A.; Baca, Leonard, and Lane, Karen. *Cultural Diversity and the Exceptional Child.* Reston, Counc Exc Child, 1973.

Saltman, J.: Meeting the challenge of cerebral palsy. *Public Affairs Pamphlet No. 158B.* New York, January, 1964.

Sierra, Viola: Learning style of the Mexican American. In Bransford, Louis A., Baca, Leonard, and Lane, Karen (Eds.): *Cultural Diversity and the Exceptional Child.* Reston, Counc Exc Child, 1973.

Taylor, Orlando: Language, cultural contrasts and the black American. In Bransford, Louis, Baca, Leonard, and Lane, Karen (Eds.): *Cultural Diversity and the Exceptional Child.* Reston, Counc Exc Child, 1973.

White, William: *Tactics for Teaching the Disadvantaged.* New York, McGraw, 1971.

Whitstock, Robert H.: *Orientation and Mobility for Blind Children.* Commission for the Blind, New York State Booklet No. 204.

Chapter 5

LANGUAGE DEVELOPMENT OF
THE MENTALLY RETARDED

ONE of the current problems in the field of special education is the area of language and the mentally retarded. Language is espoused to be one of man's greatest achievements. It is an acquisition that is unique to man and sets him apart from other forms of life. Enumerable writers in many areas have continually emphasized the major importance of language. McGrady (1968) states that language is what makes man man. Lerner (1971) says that man's language is a more important achievement than all of man's physical inventions in the last two thousand years. Langer (1958) describes language as the most momentous and, at the same time, the most mysterious product of the human mind. Lenneberg (1967) argues that language is one of man's most impressive accomplishments.

It would appear that language serves several purposes for man — it provides for a means of communication and socialization, it allows for the transmission of man's culture from generation to generation, and it becomes a vehicle for thought (Lerner, 1971). Myklebust (1965) proposes that language encompasses the ability to abstract, to attach meaning to words, and to utilize words as symbols for thought. Kolstoe (1972) describes in depth the qualities and functions of man's language:

> ... foremost of the requirements is the existence of a symbol system. Not only must the language enable an individual to use convenient symbol substitutes for real things, but it must be flexible enough to allow one to manipulate time so past, present, and future can provide some perspectives for evaluating events. It must also allow for some method of information reduction so that thousands of sense stimuli can be synthesized into managable units for grouping, classifying, sequencing and associating. Finally, it must be conventional so that the symbols will have the same meaning to others that they have to oneself; it must allow for communication.

In the light of the aforementioned requirements and functions of language, what then is the plight of the individual with a language deficit in today's society? This question would appear to be the crux of the problem of language and the mentally retarded.

Vast tracts of literature document the irregularities, lags, and general inefficiencies of the language of the mentally retarded, but this research has primarily been concerned with the incidence of speech impairments and the relation of these impairments to organicity and/or to delays in intelligence among the retarded (Schiefelbusch, Copeland, and Smith, 1967). Spradlin (1963) states that systematic studies of the gestures or the comprehension of language in mental defectives are, for the most part, absent. It is due to this absence that so much attention has been given to the speech of mental defectives while references to other language events are sparse. Thus, it appears that there has been a definite neglect of research concerning language and the mentally retarded, and the central role language plays in an adequate formulation of mental retardation.

Jordan (1966) reported that Binet and Simon first called attention to the importance of language in their formulation of mental retardation, but due to the technical problem of measurement, higher order considerations, e.g. language of the mentally retarded, have been neglected for over fifty years.

Myklebust (1965) points out a paucity of research concerning language in general and states that despite the importance of language in the history of mankind and its relationship to learning and adjustment, science has given only limited attention to it.

The lack of language quantification and research in the area of the mentally retarded has created definite problems in providing these individuals with adequate speech and language services. The volume of these services has increased somewhat in the past few years, but the total available resources are still relatively small (Leach and Rolland, 1964, and Schiefelbush et al., 1967).

One of the major reasons for the scarcity of language services for the retarded seems to be due to a lack of an organized body of information on which to base highly developed programs. Those programs now in existence for speech and language training of the retarded presuppose information which is not yet available (Schiefelbusch et al., 1967).

Recently there seems to be a developing trend in the study of language as it is related to cognitive processes. Jordan (1967) points out that a desirable development in this area would be the infusion of contemporary ideas about learning into the development of language. The specification of what a learner is would allow researchers to categorize criterion measures and interject ideas from one behavioral discipline into another. Through this type of attention the study of language processes would aid in refinement of the concept of mental retardation.

Recent developmental formulations of mental retardation may aid in determining the role of language in the mentally retarded. Kolstoe (1972) espouses a new definition of mental retardation based on the developmental works of Piaget. He states,

> The careful work of Piaget has demonstrated that thinking at succeeding stages of development is qualitatively different than at lower levels. If Piaget is correct, then intelligence is not a continuum of abilities which cumulate as a baby grows to become an adult. Rather, intelligence is represented by the ability of an individual to develop new systems of thinking. At succeeding stages of growth, he is able to use different and more complex systems of data processing.

Based on this information he goes on to define the mentally retarded:

> As a corollary, if intelligence is the capacity to develop new ways of thinking even though the research to substantiate this is quite limited, the fact that no investigator (has) found the retarded able to demonstrate hypothetical thought would indicate that mental retardation can now be defined as *a condition of intellectual arrest at some level below Piaget's level of formal thought.*

This definition of mental retardation is substantiated in the research of Sweeter (1968) and Clausen (1967). Farber (1968) also proposes that the mentally retarded adult may never reach Piaget's level of formal thought.

Langer (1958) alludes to language and conceptual attainment in stating that through language the individual acquires the free use of symbolization and the record of articulate conceptual thinking, and that without language there seems to be nothing like explicit thought whatever.

If this is the function of language at the level of hypothetical thought, and if even the most able of the retarded (mildly retarded) do not demonstrate ability beyond the concrete operational stage of Piaget, then there is the distinct possibility that the language utilized by the mentally retarded is also arrested at a point somewhere below the level of formal thought. Thus, the mildly retarded individual will be inefficient in language, especially at an abstract level. The question then arises concerning the extent and ways in which the language of the retarded differs from that of the normal individual. The answer to this question then becomes one of the main goals in understanding the language of the retarded and provides some direction for research in this area.

Vast tracts of literature point to the inefficiency with which the retarded learn and the poverty in their language use. In addition, it now appears that even the most able of the retarded do not utilize much skill in hypothetical thought, and the lower level retardate may not progress beyond the level of intuitive thought (Kolstoe, 1972). If the goal is to prepare the retarded for placement in society and for effective communication in that society, then more information about the variables that affect communication is needed. If this can be accomplished, the development of systematic programs for language training of retardates will no longer proceed by assumption, and satisfactory adjustment of the mentally retarded in the various situations they will be placed can be better achieved.

A few researchers have investigated mean length of response and the relationship between this and certain other measures of the language of the retarded.

Meacham (1955) utilized the length of verbal productions as a measure of language. Tests were administered to three groups of mentally defective children. The experimental group, consisting of twenty-one children (CA range of 9 to 18 years and IQ range of 41-75) was given a pre- and posttest following an eight-week period of speech therapy. The other two control groups of mentally defective children received no therapy. Results demonstrated that the experimental group showed a significant increase in average sentence length among other things.

Schlanger (1953) attempted to study articulation, word-count measures of mean lengths of sentences, number of words per minute, and sound discrimination in the speech of mentally defective children. Subjects consisted of seventy-four children between the ages of eight and sixteen with IQ's of 40 or above. The author used past studies of sentence length to establish procedures for measuring length of production. Each subject was tested approximately one hour in order to collect a sufficient number of sentences for quantification. Results revealed that the mean number of sentences for the group was 88.8 with no subject having fewer than fifty sentences. The mean sentence length was 3.96 words. The greatest individual mean score was 8.14, and the lowest, 1.3. Results of these measures showed that mentally retarded children demonstrate a significantly shorter mean length of sentence than do normals. Twenty-one percent of the sentences consisted of only one word which stemmed from naming objects and people. The retarded utilized a large number of concrete nouns as complete sentences.

In measuring verbal output or total number of words spoken per unit of time, this study utilized the timing of total verbal output in words per minute. Results indicated that mean number of words for all subjects was 50 with a standard deviation of 26.

Another study which demonstrates the deficiency of retardates in mean length of response was done by Siegel (1962). In a study to determine interexaminer reliability for mean length of responses, tape recordings were made of the responses of fifteen boys and fifteen girls from the Parsons (Kansas) State Hospital and Training Center for the retarded. No IQ range was given for the subjects, but they ranged in CA from eleven to seventeen years. Results demonstrated that the average mean length of response for the retarded subjects was considerably shorter than that of normal eight-year-olds studied by another investigator. The retarded group had a mean sentence length of 6.4 words. The author compared his work with Templin's (1957) results on normal children with a mean age of eight and a mean sentence length of 7.6 words. After the comparison, the retardates were judged to be more retarded in language development than the normal group.

Goda and Griffith (1962) conducted research on the spoken language of retardates to ascertain articulation errors; mean sentence length in words; and percentage of incomplete, simple, complicated, and elaborated sentences. Subjects for this study were 106 mildly retarded, institutionalized individuals with a median IQ of 60 and a median MA of 9.5 years. The authors concluded that the language achievement of the retarded group was comparable to a group of normals with an MA of seven to eight years.

Language behavior of lower level retardates was measured by Graham and Graham (1971). In this study, language samples from nine mentally retarded subjects with a CA range from ten to eighteen years and a MA range of three years, six months. Results indicated, among other things, that mean sentence length of these subjects appeared to follow an orderly progression corresponding to MA.

Milgram, Shore, and Malasky (1971) conducted research concerning language productivity with disadvantaged children. This study measured the linguistic and thematic categories of the oral productions of both disadvantaged and advantaged children. Advantaged subjects were twenty boys and twenty-nine girls, all of whom were white. The disadvantaged group numbered twenty-four boys and twenty-six girls of both black and white subjects. The mean CA for all subjects was 6.75 years.

Their study utilized the reading of an illustrated story to all subjects, who were later asked to retell the story in their own words. The subjects' oral productions were then analyzed in terms of linguistic categories (number of words and sentences) and thematic categories (story-relevant sentences and essential themes).

Results of the study indicated that the disadvantaged group was surpassed on all measures by the advantaged group. The advantaged group employed more words, more sentences, more relevant sentences, and more essential themes than did the disadvantaged group. Significance was found between groups on all measures. Results also demonstrated that disadvantaged children were more deficient in linguistic measures than in thematic measures.

Studies concerning abstract-concrete measures in the language of the retarded are, in the main, absent. Those studies which do deal with this aspect utilize it primarily as a secondary portion of the research.

A number of studies have demonstrated that the quality of language produced by the retarded is inferior to that of normal or nonretarded individuals.

Abstraction is definitely less common in the language of the retarded as demonstrated in a study by Badt (1958). In this study sixty mildly retarded, institutionalized individuals between the chronological age range of seven and fifteen years were utilized. Subjects were administered the vocabulary list of the Stanford-Binet Intelligence Scale (Form L) to assess their abilities to give abstract definitions. Results of the study showed that the retarded subjects were inferior in using abstractions but that the length of time spent by subjects in an institution affected the level at which they defined words and manipulated concepts.

Another study employing the qualitative analysis of Binet vocabulary responses of retardates was done by Papania (1954). In analyzing the responses of 250 institutionalized, *endogenous* mentally retarded children and one hundred normal children the author discovered

> When compared to "normal" groups of like MA, the retarded groups differed significantly in the following ways: They gave (a) fewer "abstract" definitions, and (b) more "concrete" definitions to the Binet vocabulary words. There were no differences between these groups in the proportion of correct definitions. Thus, while the number of acceptable definitions seems to be directly related to MA, the qualitative level of the responses does not.

A study to determine the relationship between abstraction and word meaning in retarded adolescents was done by Griffith and Spitz (1958). A verbal abstractions test consisting of twenty-four groups of three nouns each was administered to a group of twenty-six mildly retarded boys (IQ range 48-83). A vocabulary test, in which eighteen of the words were drawn from the verbal abstractions test, was also administered to the subjects. Results indicated that high-grade retardates were most likely to achieve verbal abstraction when they could define at least two of the three words in the noun triad. If only one or two of the three words could be defined by the subject, the more likely he would fail in attaining the abstraction. Abstractions in meaning were facilitated by previous use of the same process.

Another study to determine levels of concept formation and availability of mediators was done by Griffith, Spitz, and Lipman (1959). This was a continuation of a prior study. A group of retarded subjects, an equal MA group of nine-year normals and a group of seven-year normals, were administered an abstraction task. In the task, subjects were to discover a similarity among three words. Analysis of the data revealed an increase in the percentage of abstractions as the number of defined words common to a possible abstraction increased. The retarded and normal seven-year groups were not very successful in concept attainment unless they could define at least two words of the three-word groups. The normal nine-year group was relatively successful if they could define only one word in terms of an abstraction.

Feifel and Lorge (1950) also demonstrated that abstraction is less common in the language of the retarded. They tested 900 school children with IQ's slightly above 100. The subjects were white, male and female, between the CA range of six to fourteen. One hundred subjects at each one-year level or interval were tested with the vocabulary section of the Form L Stanford-Binet and the responses of each subject were analyzed. Results showed significant differences between the qualitative responses given by younger children when compared with older children. Younger subjects employed more often the use, description, illustration, repetition, and inferior explanation types of response.

Another finding of this study was that characteristic differences exist in the thinking of younger children when compared to older children of similar background. Younger children perceived words as *concrete* ideas with a tendency to emphasize the particular or isolated aspects whereas older children stressed the abstract or *class* features of the word meanings.

This study also revealed a strong similarity between the qualitative responses given by younger children and abnormals. The authors stated that the research supported the findings of Piaget and the belief that there are changes in the conceptual levels of children as they grow older.

Furth and Milgram (1965) demonstrated that educable mentally retarded children performed as well in conceptual classification tasks as matched MA normals when the tasks permitted them to demonstrate conceptual knowledge by a nonverbal response. In a similar task which required a verbal response the retarded subjects performed more poorly than normals at MA nine years. At the MA six level there was no difference between normals and retardates in verbal formulation of conceptual activity. The authors noted that this was due to the meager level of verbal formulation by all children at this age level. The results of this study also seem compatible with the conclusions of Piaget and his developmental formulations.

A further investigation of the aforementioned study was done by Milgram (1966). This study measured the relation between conceptual classification and verbal formulation in trainable retarded children. Subjects used in the study were fifteen trainable retardates with an MA range of 3.5 to 6.8 years. The educable retardate group numbered sixteen individuals with an MA range of 5.5 to 6.5 years. The normal group consisted of sixteen children from kindergarten and first grade classes with a mean MA of 6.1 years. Results of the study showed that the trainable group was deficient in verbal formulation when compared to educable retardates and normals of the same MA. In the nonverbal conceptual tasks there was no difference between groups, thus the author concluded that the greater the severity of mental retardation, the more limited the ability to formulate verbally the conceptual classifications which they were successful in recognizing in a nonverbal situation. The author admittedly states a tenuous assumption that the groups were equally matched on MA in this study.

Myklebust (1965) indicates that when comparing the written language of normals and the mentally retarded (EMR's) on the Picture Story Language Test that the retardates are markedly inferior in measures of total words, total sentences, words per sentence and in syntax, with the greater limitation being productivity, not correctness.

In discussing written versus spoken language, Myklebust also indicates that language in the written form requires more intelligence than in the spoken form.

In summation of the research the author was able to make some general conclusions regarding the areas of productivity and levels of abstract-concreteness in the language of the retarded. It would appear that in complex verbal tasks retardates are generally behind their normal MA controls but seem equivalent to them in simpler tasks. The retardate's language facility also seems to depend primarily on his MA. In productivity the retarded groups seem to lag behind the normal groups in most studies.

In reviewing the relevant research the author noted a definite inconsistency in criterion measures, modes of language quantification, control of variables, and sample selection. Most of the studies failed to look at different age levels in measuring language variables which, in itself, would justify a study of language of the retarded at different age levels.

Language Therapy: A Reinforcement Approach

Special education is undergoing many transitions, and education of the mentally retarded has become a major issue. Until recently, scientific experimentation of behavioral techniques with the retarded have been limited.

Traditional approaches and content may be reviewed in several books (Kephart, 1960, Kirk, 1972, Kirk and Johnson, 1951, and Mainord and Love, 1973). Numerous publications have appeared describing behavioral approaches to education (Asham and Poser, 1973, Cohen, Filipczak, and Bis, 1967, Gardner, 1971, Neisworth and Smith, 1973, Thompson and Grabowski, 1972, Walker and Buckley, 1974 and Winters and Cox, 1972), and most recent books which review the literature involving the education of the mentally retarded have included articles on operant learning, reinforcement principles and/or behavioral techniques (Ellis, 1966, 1968, Johnson and Blank, 1968, Kirk and Weiner, 1963, Madsen and Madsen, 1970, Stevens and Heber, 1964). In addition, most volumes regarding behavior modification in education have devoted a section to the mentally retarded (Becher, 1971, Buckley and Walker, 1970, Fargo, Behrns, and Nolen, 1970, Krasner and

Ullman, 1965, MacMillan, 1973a, O'Leary and O'Leary, 1972, Sulzer and Mayer, 1972, Ullman and Krasner, 1966, and Ulrich, Stachnik, and Mabry, 1966, 1970, 1974).

Many authorities have defined behavior modification, and most agree that it is the systematic application of learning principles to change behavior in a desired direction. O'Leary and O'Leary (1972) generally define it as "a process in which some observable behavior is changed by the systematic application of techniques that are based on learning theory and experimental research." This definition does not take into consideration the type of behavior to be changed.

Emphasis has recently been placed on classroom structure and the use of behavior modification techniques to enhance learning. Ross (1967) refers to "a *therapeutic educator* with training in the application of behavioral principles that can be brought to bear on the teaching of children with psychological problems." Haring (1968) speaks of "maximizing conditions for learning," and Birnbrauer (1971) suggests the notion of a "socialization teacher," an individual who teaches social skills through the use of reinforcement principles.

A broad range of behaviors, mediators, environments, and subjects have been involved in behavioral theory research. Operant conditioning techniques have been successfully applied to behaviors ranging from the precise and easily definable, such as reading and spelling achievement (Campbell and Sulzer, 1971), to the broader category of managing classroom behavior (Osborne, 1967). The behaviors may be verbal (Broden and Hall, 1968), motor (Patterson, 1966), creative (Lovano-Kerr and Savage, 1972, and Miller and Geller, 1972), or a combination of behaviors as in the development of social interaction skills (Harris and Miksovic, 1972).

In either case (changing unacceptable behavior or enhancing the learning of acceptable behaviors) there are several common assumptions. Virtually all behavior is learned, behavior is a function of its consequences and behavior can be altered through the systematic application of learning principles (Ross, 1967 and R. A. Sherman, 1973). Other assumptions include the necessity and ability to objectively observe and measure behavior, the power of individuals to plan and control antecedent and consequent events, and therein the power to change behavior in a desired direction (Haring, 1968, Neisworth and Smith, 1973, O'Leary and O'Leary, 1972, and Thompson and Grabowski, 1972).

Several studies conducted in the school environment have dealt with the effects of positive reinforcement on language and verbal behavior of retarded children (Butz and Hasazi, 1973, Straughn, Potter, and Hamilton, 1965, Stremel, 1972, and Striefel, 1972). Butz and Hasazi used differential reinforcement (DRO) in the form of pennies and praise to eliminate perseverative speech in a seven-year-old mildly retarded boy.

In the study by Straughn et al., a fourteen-year-old elective mute received reinforcement in the form of a light and candy for verbal responses to questions. Vocal responses to peers also increased.

Stremel developed a program to train three moderately to severely retarded students to produce the basic grammar relations using positive reinforcement to increase appropriate responses.

Programmed instruction has been used as an approach to teaching reading, writing, and arithmetic to retarded children (Bijou, Birnbrauer, Kidder, and Tague, 1966, Birnbrauer, Bijou, Wolf, and Kidder, 1965a, and Birnbrauer, Wolf, Kidder, and Tague, 1965b). Generally they obtained increased productivity and accuracy with a decrease in amount of time out. However, the student/teacher ratio was frequently as low as 1/1.

Birnbrauer and Lawler (1964) appear to be responsible for the first published investigation of the use of token reinforcers in a special education classroom. They found that teachers could administer the program without aides and effectively modify the children's behavior; however, in many cases the improved behavioral change did not generalize to situations outside the classroom. With his associates, Birnbrauer (1965a) and Birnbrauer et al. (1966) reported extensive research on several aspects of token systems used with the mentally retarded. They employed a token system in conjunction with programmed instruction materials to teach various school subjects and practical skills (Birnbrauer et al., 1965a). A subsequent study indicated that token reinforcement procedures rather than teacher attention accounted for the behavioral changes) Birnbrauer et al., 1965b). Check marks were used as tokens and could be exchanged for candy or prizes after the student completed his work. A detailed description of the token system is included.

Using token reinforcement for giving a complete sentence description of a picture, Wheeler and Sulzer (1970) increased the frequency of correct responses to cards in the Peabody Language Kit, and Guess (1969) used tokens to train two retardates in the correct use of plurals.

A matched group design was used to demonstrate the effectiveness of a token economy system in producing improvement in the academic performance of children with Down's Syndrome (Dalton, Rubino, and Hislop, 1973). Token reinforcement for correct responses produced significant improvement in arithmetic and language while verbal praise to the same materials showed significant gains in language only. The token group maintained its gains in both subjects a year later, but the no-token group showed a significant decline in language performance.

Ross and Ross (1972) combined several techniques to teach listening skills to ten-year-old educable mentally retarded children. Peer modeling and tangible social and token reinforcers were included in the procedure. The posttraining total score was below that of an average group, but on one subtest they surpassed the average group and on three subtests they equaled it. A control group showed no improvement, suggesting that the traditional special education class program effects little or no improvement in listening skills.

Research Concerning Language Development of the Retarded

Since the 1950's, research associated with language of the mentally retarded individual has escalated at an astonishing rate. Smith (1968) indicates this research has been precipitated by the view that levels of language performance are directly related to performance levels of other areas. As emphasized in his test, "Clinical Teaching Methods of Instruction for the Retarded," Smith expresses a dissatisfaction with the traditional disability categories obtained through intelligence measures. He proposes the premise that a clinical approach in teaching the retarded will result in the occurrence of learning at a level and rate which are more consistent with the capabilities of the retarded.

According to the findings of Karlin and Strazzula (1952) regarding developmental data of the mentally retarded, intelligence measures are apparently related to attainment of developmental milestones in children. Their findings indicated that low performances on tests of intelligence were related to delays in learning to sit, walk, and talk. It is interesting to note, however, that there was a greater delay in the onset of the higher level of symbolic activities such as speech than in the onset of predominately motor activities such as sitting and walking. One may postulate that regardless of the final intellectual endowment of the mentally deficient child, his maturation process for one reason or another is proceeding at a much slower rate, and this is especially pronounced in spheres that are concerned with higher intellectual functions. This view was reflected earlier by Tredgold (1937), who indicated that the lack of speech at four years of age is of particular significance in the diagnosis of mental retardation.

Another study which demonstrates the deficiency of retardates in language development was done by Papania (1954). He conducted a quantitative analysis of the vocabulary responses of institutionalized, mentally retarded children and concluded that abstract definitions generally increased with an increase in mental age; concrete definitions decreased with an increase in mental age. The retarded groups gave fewer abstract definitions and more concrete definitions to the Binet vocabulary cards, again illustrating language deficiencies among retardates.

The inefficiency of normal language development among mentally deficient children of a nonpathological origin is also of importance to this study. These children belong to a group known as cultural-familial, the largest single group of mildly retarded children in institutions and by far the majority of retarded children living in the community. They exhibit a fairly uncomplicated picture of borderline to mild subnormality. By and large, these children do tend to come from the lower socioeconomic segments of society. This might suggest that causation is

due to a complex interaction of both environmental and hereditary factors. Dunn (1973) proposes there is a predisposition to
intellectual subnormality among the cultural-familial group.
According to Zigler (1967), cultural-familial children have the
same developmental patterns as normal children and represent
the lower tail of the normal probability curve of intelligence.
Since their developmental patterns evolve at a slower rate, one can
conclude that their language develops at a slower rate than that of
normals. However, further studies will illustrate that the language patterns of the cultural-familial are not as delayed as that of
mentally deficient of an organic nature.

Schlanger (1957) studied the expressive language skill of the
training school population in Vineland, New Jersey, through
generalized placement of each subject in an oral language-ability
group based on three levels of language functioning. Linguistic
skills of the various etiological groups were also ascertained. In
estimating the oral communication behavior of the mentally deficient, Schlanger concludes that the oral language of the Mon-
goloid would be least developed while the cultural-familial
would be most like normal speakers. Greater variations in language abilities are most apt to be found among the organic because normal maturation of motor function, perceptual integration, and symbolization are often hampered by brain damage.

As stated previously, language is directly related to general
intelligence (Robinson and Robinson, 1965). Language behavior
and word recognition have for this reason served as the basis of a
number of specialized tests. A few of these assessment tools have
been suggested as having special utility with mentally retarded
children. One, the Illinois Test of Psycholinguistic Abilities
(ITPA) (Kirk and McCarthy, 1961), was based on a clinical model
of aphasic behavior and Osgood's (1957) theoretical construct of
linguistic functioning. This battery of nine subtests was developed to measure three behavioral functions of communication
referred to as decoding, association, and encoding. It also assesses
the different levels of language organization and the channels of
input and output.

The reliability of the total score on the ITPA with a group of
sixty-nine children ages six years to six years, nine months, was

shown to be .70. The various subtests yielded reliability coefficients of only .18 to .72, thus caution must be exercised in interpreting differences between subtests scores and retest scores. Therefore, the practical reliability of this test appears to be substantial (Robinson and Robinson, 1965).

One compromising approach to the problem of indexing the mental abilities of the mentally subnormal has been the *picture vocabulary test* technique. Research has shown that vocabulary is one of the best single indicators of general intellectual ability (Terman and Merrill, 1937, Wechsler, 1949, and Dale and Reichert, 1957).

The Peabody Picture Vocabulary Test (PPVT) (Dunn, 1959) was constructed especially for use with retarded children although its levels of difficulty range up to a superior adult level. It consists of 150 plates, each composed of four pictures. The plates are arranged in increasing levels of difficulty from one year, nine months, to eighteen years. A number of studies have shown that Peabody MA's below four or five years tend to be significantly lower than MA's on the Stanford-Binet (Budoff and Purseglove, 1963, and Tobias and Gorelick, 1961). This is an especially serious fault when the test is to be used with young retarded children or severely retarded adults, and restandardization of the scale may be desirable (Robinson and Robinson, 1965).

Dunn and Hottel (1961) conducted an investigation of the Peabody Picture Vocabulary Test's reliability and validity in a study involving 200 trainable children enrolled in special day classes in Tennessee. PPVT scores were compared with Revised Stanford-Binet (R S-B) mental age scores.

The PPVT was found to exhibit high alternate form reliability. The predictive validity for the PPVT was less than that for the R S-B in terms of language arts achievement, and the meager accomplishments of the subtests leave broad generalizations.

A number of studies have demonstrated that the quality of language produced by the mentally deficient is inferior to that of normal or nonretarded individuals. Milgram, Shore, and Malasky (1971) conducted research concerning language productivity with disadvantaged children. This study measured the linguistic and thematic categories of the oral productions of both disadvantaged and advantaged children. Their study utilized the reading of an illustrated story to all subjects, who were later asked to retell the story in their own words. The subject's oral productions were then analyzed in terms of linguistic categories (number of words and sentences) and thematic categories (story-relevant sentences and essential themes).

Results of the study indicate that the disadvantaged group was surpassed on all measures by the advantaged group. Results also demonstrated that disadvantaged children were more deficient in linguistic measures than in thematic measures.

Abstraction is definitely less common in the language of the retarded as demonstrated in a study by Badt (1958). In this study subjects were administered the vocabulary list of the Stanford-Binet Intelligence Scale (Form L) to assess their ability to give abstract definitions. Results of the study showed that the retarded subjects were inferior in using abstractions but that the length of time spent by subjects in an institution affects the level at which they defined words and manipulated concepts.

Myklebust (1965) indicates that when comparing the written language of the normals and the mentally retarded (EMR's) on the Picture Story Language Test that the retardates are markedly inferior in measures of total words, total sentences, words per sentence, and syntax, with the greater limitation being productivity, not correctness.

Naylor (1972), in a study utilizing a revised form of the Myklebust PSLT, found that normal subjects did significantly better than retarded subjects on all measures of abstract-concreteness. The stories of normal groups exhibited a continuous pattern of growth from concreteness to abstraction as chronological age increased, while retarded groups, at their highest level of performance, were unable to deal with abstraction and were confined to a concrete level. The story-telling ability of retarded groups resembled the ability of younger normal groups. These findings seem to be consistent with the developmental theory of Piaget and the definition of mental retardation espoused by Kolstoe (1972):

> ... if intelligence is the capacity to develop new ways of thinking even though the research to substantiate this is quite limited, the fact that no investigation (has) found the retarded

able to demonstrate hypothetical thought would indicate that mental retardation can now be defined: A condition of intellectual arrest at some level below Piaget's level of formal thought.

Research in language development of the mentally retarded child has been accomplished primarily in terms of incidence and classification of speech defects, instruments designed for the evaluation of language skills, description of therapeutic programs and results, and functional language measurements such as extent of vocabulary, sentence length, and frequency of use of grammatical parts of speech.

In summarizing the status of relevant research in language behaviors this investigator is able to make some conclusions regarding competencies of mentally-deficient populations in verbal productivity and overall language usage. It appears that in complex verbal tasks the retardate is markedly inferior to the nonretardate but seems equivalent to him in simpler tasks. Retardates also appear delayed in productivity when compared with normal groups. However, most of the studies have not concentrated on the role of language factors in explaining the variance in mental age among the mentally deficient and normals.

Issues for Speech and Language Training

It can be generally stated that the mentally retarded are delayed in developing linguistic functions such as generalizations, associations, discrimination, and manipulation of verbal concepts. Copeland, Schiefelbusch, and Smith (1967) state that additional observations of the retarded drawn from the literature and from experience reveal a number of negative characteristics which presumably affect language functioning of the retarded. These characteristics include:

1. Poor auditory retention span (auditory memory)
2. Short attention span developed through negative training and/or inherent in the biological mechanism
3. Linguistic ability deficient as demonstrated by poor grammar and minimal content
4. Perseverance in oral expression
5. Minimal creative or imaginative pursuits

6. Inability to transfer meanings
7. Absence of self-criticism
8. Poor evelution and organization of perceptual clues
9. Frustration in communication activities leading to withdrawal and lowered thresholds of frustration

Many of the above observations are concerned with receptive communication, and some of the above observations can be attributed to learned expressive communication behavior. The mentally retarded can present inappropriate social responses because of their limited communication skills. This same linguistic deficiency also adds to the inadequate speech and language that the mentally retarded have. It can be stated that the mentally retarded are treated as a minority group, and therefore they are subjected to prejudices and discriminations. Many people, for example, assume that defective communication skills result from mental retardation. Actually there is the possibility that the poor communication ability of the retarded results from the way his peers feel about him. Although the learning ability may be there, poor learned habits may further depress the communication abilities. For the mentally retarded in a communication training program the attitude of the therapist may be as important and in need of reorganization as the communication habits of the retarded child.

Copeland, Schiefelbusch, and Smith (1967) list the following broad principles for a therapy program for speech and language training for the mentally retarded:

1. Start at the subject's level of language development — that is, where he is in terms of listening and expressive behavior.
2. Use a reward as a reinforcer.
3. Since learning is slow and considerable repetition is necessary, variety within a structured program is needed.
4. Activities should be meaningful.
5. Therapy needs forward progress and action.
6. There must be some understanding by the subject of what he is expected to learn.
7. Direct therapy on sound for the more able.

BIBLIOGRAPHY

Asham, B. A., and Poser, E. G.: *Adaptive Learning: Behavior Modification With*

Children. New York, Pergamon, 1973.

Badt, M. L.: Abstraction in vocabulary definitions of mentally retarded school children. *Am J Ment Defic, 63*:241-246, 1958.

Becker, W. C.: *An Empirical Basis for Change in Education.* Chicago, Sci Res Assoc, 1971.

Bijou, S. W., Birnbrauer, J. S., Kidder, J. D., and Tague, C.: Programmed instruction as an approach to teaching of reading, writing, and arithmetic to retarded children. *Psychol Rec, 16*:505-522, 1966.

Birnbrauer, J. S.: Preparing "uncontrollable" retarded children for group instruction. In Becker, W. C. (Ed.): *An Empirical Basis for Change in Education.* Chicago, Sci Res Assoc, 1971, pp. 213-218.

Birnbrauer, J. S., Bijou, S. W., Wolf, M. M., and Kidder, J. D.: Programmed instruction in the classroom. In Ullman, L. P. and Krasner, L. (Eds): *Case Studies in Behavior Modification.* New York, HR&W, 1965a, pp. 358-363.

Birnbrauer, J. S., and Lawler, J.: Token reinforcement for learning. *Men Retard, 2*:275-279, 1964.

Birnbrauer, J. S., Wolf, M. M., Kidder, J. D., and Tague, C. E.: Classroom behavior of retarded pupils with token reinforcement. *J Exp Child Psychol, 2*:219-235, 1965b.

Broden, M., and Hall, R. V.: Effects of teacher attention on the verbal behavior of two junior high school pupils. Paper presented at CEC Convention, New York, 1968.

Buckley, N. K., and Walker, H. M.: *Modifying classroom behavior.* Champaign, Res Press, 1970.

Budoff, M., and Purseglove, E. M.: Peabody picture vocabulary test: Performance of institutionalized mentally retarded adolescents. *Am J Ment Defic, 67*:756-760, 1963.

Butz, R. A., and Hasazi, J. E.: The effects of reinforcement on perseverative speech in a mildly retarded boy. *J Behav Ther Exp Psychiatry, 4(2)*:167-170, 1973.

Campbell, A., and Sulzer, B.: Natural available reinforcers as motivators towards reading and spelling achievement by educable mentally handicapped students. Paper presented at the American Educational Research Association meeting, New York, February, 1971.

Clausen, J.: Mental deficiency — Development of a concept. *Am J Ment Defic, 71*:727-745, 1967.

Cohen, H. L., Filipczak, J., and Bis, J. S.: *Case I: An Initial Study of Contingencies Applicable to Special Education.* Silver Springs, Educ Facility Pr, 1967.

Dale, E., Reichert, D.: *Bibliography of Vocabulary Studies.* Columbus, Ohio State University, Bureau of Educational Research, 1957.

Dalton, A. J., Rubino, C. A., and Hislop, M. W.: Some effects of token rewards on school achievement of children with Down's Syndrome. *J Appl Behav Anal, 6*:251-259, 1973.

Dunn, L. M.: *Peabody Picture Vocabulary Test Manual*. Minneapolis, American Guidance Service, 1959.

Dunn, L. M. (Ed.): *Exceptional Children in the Schools*, 2nd Ed. New York, HR&W, 1973.

Dunn, L. M., and Hottell, J. V.: Peabody picture vocabulary test performance of trainable mentally retarded children. *Am J Ment Defic*, *65*:448-452, 1961.

Ellis, N. R. (Ed.): *International Review of Research in Mental Retardation*. New York, Acad Pr, 1966-68, 3 vols.

Farber, B.: *Mental Retardation: Its Social Context and Social Consequences*. Boston, H-M, 1968.

Fargo, G. A., Behrns, C., and Nolen, P. (Eds.): *Behavior Modification in the Classroom*. Belmont, Wadsworth Pub, 1970.

Feifel, H., and Lorge, I.: Qualitative differences in the vocabulary responses of children. *J Educ Psychol*, *41*:1-18, 1950.

Furth, H. G., and Milgram, N. A.: The influence of language on classification: A theoretical model applied to normal, retarded, and deaf children. *Genet Psychol Monogr*, *72*:317-351, 1965.

Gardner, W. I.: *Behavior Modification in Mental Retardation*. Chicago, Aldine, 1971.

Goda, S., and Griffith, B. C.: Spoken language of adolescent retardates and its relation to intelligence, age, and anxiety. *Child Devel*, *33*:489-498, 1962.

Graham, J. T., and Graham, L. W.: Language behavior of the Mentally Retarded: Syntactic Characteristics. *Am J Ment Defic*, *75*:623-629, 1971.

Griffith, B. C., and Spitz, H.: Some relationships between abstraction and word meaning in retarded adolescents. *Am J Ment Defic*, *12*:247-251, 1958.

Griffith, B. C., Spitz, H., and Lipman, R. S.: Verbal mediation and concept formation in retarded and normal subjects. *J Exp Psychol*, *58*(3):247-251, 1959.

Guess, D. A.: A functional analysis of receptive language and productive speech acquisition of the plural morpheme. *J Appl Behav Anal*, *2*:55-64, 1969.

Haring, N. G.: Behavior Principles in Special Education. Paper presented at 17th Annual Series of Lectures in Special Education and Rehabilitation, University of Southern California, July, 1968. In Klein, Roger D. *et al.* (Eds.): *Behavior Modification in Educational Settings*. Springfield, Thomas, 1973.

Harris, M. B., and Miksovic, R. S.: Operant conditioning of social interaction in preschool retarded children. In Harris, M. B.: *Classroom Uses of Behavior Modification*. Columbus, Merrill, 1972.

Johnson, G. O., and Blank, H. D. (Ed.): *Exceptional Children Research Review*. Washington, Counc Exc Child, 1968.

Jordan, T. E.: *The Mentally Retarded*. Columbus, Merrill, 1966.

Jordan, T. E.: Language and mental retardation: A review of the literature. In Schiefelbusch, R., Copeland, R., and Smith, J. (Eds.): *Language and Mental Retardation*. New York, HR&W, 1967.

Karlin, I. W., and Strazzulla, M.: Speech and language problems of mentally deficient children. *J Speech Hear Disord*, *3*:17, 1952.

Kephart, N. C.: *The Slow Learner in the Classroom*. Columbus, Merrill, 1960.

Kirk, S. A.: *Educating Exceptional Children*. Boston, HM, 1972.

Kirk, S. A., and Johnson, G. U.: *Educating the Retarded Child*. Boston, HM, 1951.

Kirk, S. A., and Weiner, B. B. (Eds.): *Behavioral Research on Exceptional Children*. Washington, Coun Exc Child, 1963.

Kolstoe, O. P.: *Mental Retardation: An Educational Approach*. New York, HR&W, 1972.

Krasner, L., and Ullmann, L. l. (Eds.): *Research in Behavior Modification*. New York, HR&W, 1965.

Langer, S. K.: *Philosophy in a New Key*. New York, Ment. NAL, 1958.

Leach, E., and Rolland, J.: National speech and hearing survey of state and residential hospitals and/or institutions for the mentally retarded. Parsons, Parsons State Hospital and Training Center, 1964.

Lenneberg, E.: *Biological Foundations of Language*. New York, Wiley, 1967.

Lerner, J. W.: *Children With Learning Disabilities: Theories, Diagnosis, and Teaching Strategies*. New York, HM, 1971.

Lovano-Kerr, J., and Savage, S.: Incremental art curriculum modification for the mentally retarded. *Except Child*, *39* (3):193-199, 1972.

MacMillan, D. L.: *Behavior Modification in Education*. New York, MacMillan, 1973a.

Madsen, C. H., Jr., and Madsen, C. K.: *Teaching/Discipline: Behavioral Principles Toward a Positive Approach*. Boston, Allyn, 1970.

Mainord, J. C., and Love, H. D.: *Teaching Educable Mentally Retarded Children*. Springfield, Thomas, 1973.

McCarthy, James, J., and Kirk, Samuel A.: Illinois Test of Psycholinguistic Abilities Examiner's Manual. Institute for Research on Exceptional Children, University of Illinois, Urbana, 1961.

McGrady, H. J.: Language pathology and learning disabilities. In Myklebust, H. R. (Ed.): *Progress in Learning Disorders*, New York, Grune, 1968, vol. 1.

Meacham, M. J.: The development and application of procedures for measuring speech improvement in mentally defective children. *Am J Ment Defic*, *60*: 301-306, 1955.

Milgram, M. J.: The development and application of procedures for measuring speech improvement in mentally retarded children. *Am J Ment Defic*, *60*: 301-306, 1955.

Milgram, N. A., Shore, M. F., and Malesky, C.: Linguistic and thematic variables in recall of a story by disadvantaged children. *Child Devel*, *42*:637-640, 1971.

Miller, M. B., and Geller, D.: Curiosity in retarded children: Sensitivity to intrinsic and extrinsic reinforcement. *Am J Ment Defic*, *76* (6):668-679, 1972.

Myklebust, H. R.: *Development and Disorders of Written Language*. New York,

Grune, 1965, vol. I.

Naylor, David Lynn: A Comparison of Productivity and Levels of Abstract-Concreteness in the Spoken Language of Normal and Mentally Retarded Individuals. Unpublished doctoral dissertation, University of Northern Colorado, 1972.

Neisworth, J. T., and Smith, R. M.: *Modifying Retarded Behavior.* Boston, HM, 1973.

O'Leary, K. D., and O'Leary, S. G. (Eds.): *Classroom Management: The Successful Use of Behavior Modification.* New York, Pergamon, 1972b.

Osgood, C. E.: Motivational dynamics of language behavior, *Nebraska Symposium on Motivation.* Lincoln, U of Nebr Pr, 1957.

Papania, N. A.: Qualitative analysis of vocabulary responses of institutionalized mentally retarded children. *J Clin Psychol, 10*:361-365, 1954.

Patterson, G. R.: An application of conditioning techniques to the control of a hyperactive child. In Ullmann, L. P., and Krasner, L. (Eds.): *Case Studies in Behavior Modification.* New York, HR&W, 1966.

Robinson, H. B., and Robinson, N. M.: *The Mentally Retarded Child: A Psychological Approach.* New York, McGraw, 1965.

Ross, A. O.: The application of behavior principles in therapeutic education. *J Spec Educ, 1*:275-286, 1967.

Ross, D., and Ross, S. A.: The efficacy of listening training for educable mentally retarded children. *Am J Ment Defic, 77*(2):137-142, 1972.

Schiefelbusch, R. L., Copeland, R. H., and Smith, J. O. (Eds.): *Language and Mental Retardation.* New York, HR&W, 1967.

Schlanger, B. B.: Speech measurements of institutionalized mentally handicapped children. *Am J Ment Defic, 58*:114-122, 1953.

Schlanger, B. B.: Oral language classification of the training school residents. *The Training School Bulletin, 52*:243-247, January, 1957.

Sherman, R. A., and Sherman, L. H.: Individual and group behavior modification in the school setting. In Sherman, R. A.: *Behavior Modification: Theory and Practice.* Belmont, Brooks-Cole, 1973.

Smith, R. M.: *Clinical Teaching: Methods of Instruction for the Retarded.* New York, McGraw, 1968.

Spradlin, J. E.: Language and communication of mental defectives. In Ellis, N. (Ed.): *Handbook of Mental Deficiency.* New York, McGraw, 1963.

Stevens, H. S., and Heber, R. (Eds.): *Mental Retardation: A Review of Research.* Chicago, U of Ohio Pr, 1964.

Straught, J. H., Potter, W. L., Jr., and Hamilton, S. H., Jr.: The behavioral treatment of an elective mute. *J Child Psychol Psychiatry, 6*(2):125-130, 1965.

Stremel, K.: Language training: A program for retarded children. *Ment Retard, 10*(2):47-49, 1972.

Striefel, S.: Television as a language training media with retarded children. *Ment Retard, 10*(2):27-29, 1972.

Sulzer, B., and Mayer, G. R.: *Behavior Modification Procedures for School*

Personnel. Hinsdale, Dryden Pr, 1972.

Sweeter, R.: Discovery Oriented Instruction in Science Skills for Educable Mentally Retarded Children. Unpublished doctoral dissertation, Colorado State College, 1968.

Templin, M. C.: *Certain Language Skills in Children, Their Development and Interrelationship.* Minneapolis, U of Minn Pr, 1957.

Terman, L. M., and Merrill, M.: *Measuring Intelligence.* Boston, HM, 1937.

Thompson, T., and Grabowski, Jr.: *Behavior Modification of the Mentally Retarded.* New York, Oxford U Pr, 1972.

Tobias, J., and Gorelick, J.: The validity of the Peabody Picture Vocabulary test as a measure of intelligence of retarded adults. *The Training School Bulletin,* 58:92-98, 1961.

Tredgold, A. L.: *A Textbook of Mental Deficiency.* Baltimore, Williams & Wilkins, 1937.

Ullmann, L., and Krasner, L. (Eds.): *Case Studies in Behavior Modification.* New York, HR&W, 1966.

Ulrich, R., Stachnik, T., and Mabry, J. (Eds.): *Control of Human Behavior.* Glenview, Scott F, 1966-1974, 3 Vols.

Walker, H. M., and Buckley, N. K.: *Token Reinforcement Techniques: Classroom Application for the Hard-to-Teach Child.* Eugene, E-B Pr, 1974.

Wechsler, David: Wechsler Intelligence Scale for Children Manual. New York, The Psychological Corporation, 1949.

Wheeler, A. J., and Sulzer, B.: Operant training and generalization of a verbal response form in a speech-deficient child. *J Appl Behav Anal,* 3:139-147, 1970.

Winters, S. A., and Cox, E. (Eds.): *Behavior Modification Techniques for the Special Educator.* New York, MSS Information Corp., 1972.

Zigler, E.: Familial retardation: A continuing dilemma. *Science,* 2:155, 1967.

Chapter 6

LANGUAGE DEVELOPMENT OF
THE HEARING IMPAIRED

In a recent article by William C. Greer (1975) we are reminded that an aspect of Indian culture astonished the colonists was the belief that the gods had a special feeling and concern for mentally and physically handicapped people, and all the creatures of the earth were expected to share this concern.

The colonists were more accustomed to the feelings held over from the middle ages that if any help were offered the mentally and physically handicapped it would be placement in an *asylum*.

The colonists learned from the Indians, and people in general developed a better attitude toward the handicapped in our society. Such an individual was Thomas Hopkins Gallaudet, a teacher and a teacher of teachers. He became extremely interested in the communication problems of the deaf and hard of hearing, and because of this interest he went to Paris to visit a school for the deaf. The school had been started by a young priest by the name of Abbe' de l'Eppe' and was being operated by his successor, Sicard. When Mr. Gallaudet returned to the United States he brought with him a young deaf man who had trained at the Paris school. In 1817 the young deaf man, Laurent Clerc, and Mr. Gallaudet established the first formal school for the deaf — the American Asylum for the Deaf located in West Hartford, Connecticut. Later in the chapter we shall discuss Mr. Gallaudet, Sicard and Abbe' de l'Eppe' in greater detail.

The partially hearing child has always been a member of the regular classroom or placed in an institution. Until the development of the pure-tone audiometer and the hearing aid, however, he was usually classified as a trouble-maker because of his inability to hear the teacher or the recitation of his classmates. In recent years there has been a spurt of interest and a positive movement toward better education for the deaf and hard-of-hearing.

Wooden (1963) describes the partially hearing as those for

126

whom the loss of hearing is educationally significant, but whose residual hearing is sufficient for interpreting speech with or without the use of a hearing aid. The educationally hard-of-hearing possess hearing levels of 30 to 59 decibels or a little higher.

Hearing loss refers to all degrees of hearing beyond 15 decibels. (The decibel is a unit of measure used to express the magnitude of sound power or sound pressure.) The deaf have a hearing loss that is very severe, and the use of residual hearing is nonfunctional for discrimination of speech.

Early Education

The early education of the deaf child is very important. Of the children currently enrolled in schools for the deaf in the United States, 10 percent are under six years of age. The private and residential schools for the deaf also have a large number of pre-school children enrolled.

Most deaf children are deaf from birth or before they have developed speech sufficiently to have obtained a permanent mastery of it. This means that most deaf children are deaf before reaching school age. About two fifths of all deafness is congenital, and the remaining is accounted for by diseases and accidents, but more often by diseases. The diseases primarily responsible are meningitis, scarlet fever, measles, whooping cough, and abcesses of the ear and head.

Most parents have a difficult time accepting the fact that they have a deaf child and tend to hope that the child is just slow in developing. But because the infant cannot hear, he becomes handicapped very early; this handicapping process starts at the age of about three months. Naturally infants receive enjoyment from vocalizing. Normal babies have started babbling by the age of six months. The deaf child babbles too, and his tones and sounds are very much like those of a normal child. If one did not know, it would be impossible to tell the differences between the two. However, the deaf child is not imitating the voices of others; he is merely engaging in chance vocalizations. Ewing (1958) states that at about the ninth month the hearing child will probably look up when he hears his name and respond to a few other words. It is here that the deaf child really begins to fall behind in his development. The hearing child begins to understand words and obey them, but the deaf child can only imitate gestures.

A deaf child's parents need not wait until the child fails to talk to discover that he is deaf. There are many other ways to discover this. The parents can talk or make noises at different distances behind the child to see if he responds. If they suspect that the child does have impaired hearing they should take him to an otologist. The otologist can test the child for hearing loss as early as seven months of age. It is stated by Ewing (1958) that in severely deaf children, research has found that most of them drag their feet and are very clumsy. They tend to sit up and walk later than other children do.

When parents discover they have a deaf child, they must accept the fact that the child is to be treated as much like a normal child as possible. Perhaps the only good thing about the parents not discovering their child's deafness at an early age is that they treat him as normal when they think that he is normal. The more normally the child is treated, the better adjusted he and his family will be. It is difficult for the parents to accept the fact that only in a very few cases can the child's deficiency be cured.

Special procedures have been developed to teach deaf children to speak using the senses of touch, sight, and sound, but usually the child is two years old before he can be admitted to special schools. As soon as a parent discovers that his baby is deaf, he should immediately try to find out what can be done to help. Usually the parents can do a great deal to prepare the child for education, and in some cities the deaf schools provide two-week courses for the parents of deaf children. If the parents do not live near such a school, home courses are available. Most parents need to overteach their children and forget that all the learning must take place in normal family-like situations. The teaching should be fun and the desire to communicate must be promoted. One of the best things that a parent can do is talk to the child in a pleasant tone, using animated facial expressions.

The otologist, a medical doctor specializing in ear problems, can discover if the child has residual hearing. If he has, a hearing aid should be obtained as soon as possible and he should be taught how to use it to the fullest advantage. Frampton and Gall (1955) tell us that when talking to a deaf child a person should always get the child's attention, then talk directly facing him. The more the child is spoken to, the more he will want to respond in speech. Deaf children are more dependent upon their parents than hearing children, and because of this the parents have extra responsibilities.

Preschool Education

Most authorities believe that if the deaf child learns to speak by parental training, he should be placed in an ordinary nursery or kindergarten. If he does not, he should be placed in a special nursery or day school for deaf children as soon as possible. By the time a deaf child finishes one of these schools, say Ewing and Ewing (1958), he should be able to enter an elementary school at about the same level of development as a hearing child. If the parents live in a rural district or small town, the child should be sent to a residential or boarding school for the deaf.

Authorities such as Ewing and Ewing (1958) tell us that the main aim of education for the deaf child is to give him words to think with, to understand the expressed thoughts of others, and to enable him to express his thoughts. They should be reached very early, and during these impressionable years their beginnings in communications must be established. Therefore, they should be admitted to school at the earliest possible age.

In the nurseries, deaf children have routines similar to normal children except that special emphasis is placed on lipreading. We are told that after the child becomes familiar with the activities of the school, it becomes easy for him to recognize that certain movements of the teacher's lips must mean "Take off your coat," or "We're going out to play," because these are the things that have always happened at this time of the day. Thus, we have the beginning of the child's lipreading. Now, with residual hearing, a hearing aid may be introduced. At first the child should wear it just a few minutes each day in order to hear a sound.

Priorities

The young hearing-impaired child should be given every opportunity to learn to communicate with his fellow human beings. The task of early education in the skills of communication must be the number one priority. The learning tasks of hearing-impaired children cannot develop on a continuum expected of hearing children. The process of true language development cannot be separated from the total developmental picture, and the environment of the child is very important in all areas of development. Millichamp (1970) makes the following statements concerning the order of tasks presented in childhood: The order of tasks as presented by Child Study specialists are, in brief: "(1) human relationship and learning in human interaction; (2) self-identity and discovery of self as a person; (3) emotional learning; (4) learning the skills of learning; (5) cognitive learning and intellectual endeavor."

Concerning language as a priority, Harris (1971) has the following to say: "Language is learned, and in the beginning, is learned auditorially. A child, if not physically restricted, will one day learn to walk on his own. Language, however, is not learned in any such predestined way. It is understandable, therefore, that the infant or young child with a hearing loss will not develop language skills without special attention."

To further paraphrase Harris (1971), the hearing child with average intelligence produces his first word at approximately one year of age, although he probably understands a great deal more than he expresses. During the first two years of life, symbolic language expression, which is referred to as speech, is so minimal that language acquisition cannot be considered established. After the age of two the hearing child progresses rather fast and readily responds with spoken language to everyone and everything in his environment. The hearing-impaired child begins to rapidly fall behind his hearing peer in all areas of language, and at this point the hearing-impaired child desperately needs auditory stimulation and aural training.

Many people tend to associate the absence of hearing with the lack of spoken speech. Therefore, as Harris (1971) tells us, potential absence of speech often causes parents to act in a most unnatural way toward the child. Naturally, this can be very damaging to the child and can heighten his frustration and conflicts.

Speech is extremely important; therefore we should stress other forms of communication skills but not at the expense of spoken language. Harris (1971) states, "No matter how we may sidetrack the importance of spoken language, understood and used, and although we may use the excuse that language is just one form of communication, any attempts to use, and to deliberately restrict people who have severe hearing impairments to other symbolisms will only result in hiding ignorance in obscurity."

Identification

The school faces a great problem in trying to locate those children with hearing losses severe enough to warrant special help. The children are usually referred by the teacher. A group audiometric test is then given to those suspected of having a hearing loss. Another and better way is to give a group audiometric test to all children in the school system and refer those found to have a hearing loss to an otologist who will administer medical treatment if necessary.

Classification

The system of classification generally applied to the deaf is as follows:
1. The congenitally deaf — those born deaf
2. The adventitiously deaf — those individuals who were born with normal hearing but became deaf or nonfunctional later in life
3. The hard-of-hearing — those individuals who have a functional sense of hearing with or without a hearing aid
4. The profoundly deaf — those children who have a hearing loss greater than 75 decibels and who require intensive care and instruction without the use of a hearing aid
5. The severely deaf — those children who have a hearing loss

between 40 and 60 decibels and who need amplification of sounds for educational instruction

6. Marginally deaf — those children having a 30 to 40-decibel loss in the better ear.

Prevalence

There is much conflict concerning prevalence, but according to Silverman (1957) 5 percent of school-age children have a hearing malfunction and roughly five in a thousand will require special attention educationally.

Measuring Hearing Loss

Although there are several crude, informal methods of testing hearing, including the whisper test, the conversational test, the coin-click test, the watch-tick test, and the tuning-fork tests, the most accurate is made with a pure-tone audiometer.

Pure-Tone Audiometer

The pure-tone audiometer creates sounds of controlled intensity and frequency. *Frequency* is the number of vibrations per second of a given sound wave. *Intensity* is the loudness of the sound.

The individual responds when he hears a tone, and the degree of hearing loss is recorded on an audiogram. The audiogram is marked by the examiner — 10 to 100 decibels, and the hearing in each ear is tested and plotted separately.

Signs of Deafness in Children

If you answer yes to five of the following questions, then you, as a teacher or parent, should have the child tested, using a pure-tone audiometer, and refer him to an otologist if necessary.

1. Does he hear better when he is looking at you?
2. Does he turn the TV up louder than you do?
3. Does he withdraw from people?

4. Does he respond to noises as opposed to words?
5. Does his voice have a monotonal quality?
6. Does he often have tantrums to get attention?
7. Does he yell or scream to express pleasure?
8. Do his answers not make sense?

To Help the Child

The following is a list of ways in which parents and teachers can help the hearing-impaired child:
1. Face him as you talk to him.
2. Have the child sit near the front of the room.
3. Talk naturally.
4. Ask the child to repeat directions.
5. Write out difficult and unusual words.
6. Place the child with his back to the light.

Types of Defects

There are three main types of defects:
1. Conductive hearing loss — the intensity of sound reaching the middle ear is reduced
2. Sensory-neural-defect — defect of the inner ear and of the transmitting auditory nerve
3. Central deafness — hearing malfunction due to injury or abnormality of the central nervous system

How We Hear

Although this is oversimplified, sound waves strike the eardrum and operate the three smallest bones of the body — the ossicles, known as the hammer, anvil, and stirrup.

The stirrup, in turn, vibrates the oval window, a thin membrane stretched across the entrance of the inner ear. Movement of the oval window is passed on to the cochlea, the organ of hearing which *feels* the mechanical movements caused by the sound waves. This vibrating membrane, containing 25,000 tiny hair-like cells, analyzes the vibrations received and sends the results to the brain via the eighth or hearing nerve.

Education of the Deaf

The two methods commonly used for the education of the deaf in institutions and special schools are referred to as oralism and manualism. The oral method does not use signs or gestures in developing speech but only uses speech and lipreading. The manual method uses gestures and the manual alphabet to achieve communication.

Recently, many special educators working with the hearing-impaired children have developed a total communications program. These special educators use all methods and tools available to help hearing-impaired children in the language area. In other words, lipreading would be one skill. Others would be finger spelling using the manual alphabet, gesturing, and using the tactile sense. The theory behind the total communication program is that every available skill should be utilized to help hearing-impaired people.

There is much controversy concerning the education of the deaf. People involved usually classify themselves in one of the two stated categories, oralism and manualism. This controversy between the two factions has been raging for many years, however there is evidence to indicate a gradual shift toward the total communication program.

History

As was mentioned earlier in this chapter, Abbe' Charles Michel de l'Eppé founded the first public school for the deaf in 1775 in Paris. Abbe' de l'Eppé believed that only by means of signs could the deaf be taught. A German contemporary, Samuel Heinicke, believed the deaf could learn to read lips and be taught to speak. Thomas Braidwood of the British Isles opened a school for the deaf in 1760 and used the oral method. As previously reported, the American, Thomas Hopkins Gallaudet, went to England to study the successful oral approach of Braidwood, but because of the secretive attitude of the Englishman he had to go to France to study educational methods for the deaf. Gallaudet studied in France under Sicard, l'Eppé's successor, and brought the manual approach to America.

First American School

When Gallaudet opened the first school for instruction, the first seven pupils were taught by the manual method. Gallaudet's work was later carried on by his son, Edward Minor Gallaudet, and today the federally sponsored college for the deaf in Washington, D.C., bears the name of the Gallaudets.

Gallaudet College offers the B.A., B.S., and M.S.E. degrees and allows only deaf youth to enter. Riverside City College in California offers deaf students a two-year program with emphasis in vocational subjects but includes other college subjects such as English, psychology, history, etc. In 1966 the first Catholic institution for the deaf, St. Joseph College for the Deaf, was opened in Buffalo, New York. Massachusetts has always been a leader in elementary, secondary, and higher education for the hearing-impaired.

Characteristics of the Hearing-Impaired

Many authorities believe that the Binet Intelligence Scale is unsuited for testing the deaf because of the language deficiency of these people. Therefore, men like Pintner (1941) surveyed the results of other tests and concluded that the average IQ among the deaf individuals is not quite 90. Myklebust (1960) bases his decisions and discussions concerning the deaf on more than twenty years of study. He found that the deaf, as a group, score higher on certain intelligence-test tasks than normal children and lower on certain others. Myklebust (1960) concludes that deafness affects intelligence more in the verbal areas than in the others.

Achievement

Pintner, Eisenson, and Stanton (1941), in their research, found no difference in the achievement of children who lost their hearing between two and five and those who lost it before the age of two. However, it is stated by Myklebust (1960) that children who lose their hearing after age six have a better concept of language than those losing it before six.

Fusfield (1954) studied the scores of the applicants to Gallaudet College on the Stanford Achievement Test and concluded that students did better in punctuation, capitalization, and grammar than in word and paragraph meaning.

A vocabulary study was conducted by Young and McConnell (1957), and they found that the hard-of-hearing child does not measure up to his intellectual capacity. In other words, his scholastic achievement does not keep pace with his mental ability.

Adjustment

The impact of an impairment such as deafness depends upon the degree of deafness and the age of onset. If a child does not lose his hearing until age twelve or thirteen, he has acquired speech, and the effect upon his development would not be as great as it would be upon the child born deaf or the child who loses his hearing before learning to talk. The prelanguage deaf child will not have normal experiences and is very limited in communications and social experiences. Pintner and Brunschwig (1963) found that deaf children who come from families with no other deaf members are less well adjusted than deaf children from families with other deaf members.

If the schools and homes make unrealistic demands on the deaf children, the experience can lead to very disturbing problems for the children. Most authorities agree that if we do not try to make deaf children perform beyond their capacity, they, as a group, are fairly well adjusted individuals.

Educational Provisions

Both the oral and manual methods are used in the education of the deaf in the United States today. In some schools a combined oral and manual approach is used, and the program is fitted to the needs of the child.

In the *day school* the child remains at home with his parents but attends the day school for instruction. All the children at the school are deaf. A *residential school* is a total program of training with cottage parents and education for the child. In *special classes,* children are grouped together according to age, ability, and interests. In *regular classes,* the hearing-impaired child attends a regular school and his special problems are handled by a regular class teacher.

The child should go to a regular class, special class, or day school if adequate provisions exist in the community. In many instances, the community does not have adequate facilities; therefore the child should go to a residential school.

There are several factors which influence whether a child can be educated in a regular class or a special facility. Naturally, intelligence is a factor as is the degree of deafness and the age of onset of deafness. The hard-of-hearing child of average or above-average intelligence should be able to function adequately in the regular classroom. The child who loses his hearing at age six or seven is far advanced in language development when compared to the child who is born deaf; nevertheless, if he is profoundly deaf he may need institutional education.

Authorities in the field of education for the deaf emphasize acquisition of language as the greatest problem. The deaf child cannot acquire language from the spoken word as does the normal child. He is born in a society which was formed and fashioned by the influence of the spoken word through ages of development. The spoken word is the main influence from which the normal course of mental and social development stems. The normal child acquires language with ease, and it becomes his passport into the society of which he is a part. As he becomes proficient in the use of language, he finds it increasingly easy to break through barriers that have separated him from other minds.

The deaf child does not acquire his passport to meaningful communications with others in this spontaneous way or with the ease of the normal child. Language acquisition must be slowly and carefully structured by sequential steps before the deaf child can learn it and incorporate it into his intellectual frame of reference. Henry Ward Beecher said,

Thinking cannot be clear till it has had expression.

We must write, or speak, or act our thoughts, or they will remain in a half torpid form.

Our feelings must have expression, or they will be as clouds, which till they descend in rain, will never bring up fruit or flowers.

So it is with all the inward feelings: expression gives them development.

Thought is the blossom; language, the opening bud; action, the fruit behind it (Brown, 1965).

Myklebust clearly described how a sensory deprivation such as deafness could limit the world of experience:

It deprives the organism of some of the material resources from which the mind develops. Because total experience is reduced, there is an imposition on the balances and equilibrium of all psychologic processes. A lack of one type of sensation alters the integration and function of all other types. Experience is therefore constituted differently; the world of perception, conception, imagination and thought has an altered foundation, a new configuration (McHugh, 1964).

A recent report by the Advisory Committee on the Deaf to the Secretary of Health, Education, and Welfare (1965) outlines some of the shortcomings in the field of deaf education:

The American people have no reason to be satisfied with their limited success in educating deaf children and preparing them for full participation in our society.

Less than half of the deaf children needing specialized preschool instruction are receiving it.

The average graduate of a public residential school for the deaf — the closest we have to generally available "high schools" for the deaf — has an eighth grade education.

Seniors at Gallaudet College, the nation's only college for the deaf, rank close to the bottom in performance on the Graduate Record Examination.

Five sixths of the deaf adults work in manual jobs, as contrasted to only one half of our hearing population.

This lack of development of the intellectual potential of the deaf is attributed to the lack of adequacy in the use of language. This problem is summed up editorially by an authority in the field of education of the deaf:

> As educators of the deaf, we must never cease to seek and try new methods. We must be equally ruthless at discarding methods that do not stand the test. The test? Does it impart language to the deaf child? If it does not, it is not doing the job. No amount of bombast or argument can go around this basic problem, and language. Give the deaf the ability to communicate intelligently and he will take it from there — the jet age, the space age, or any "you name it" are yet to come, notwithstanding (Fusfield, 1966).

As proof that other authorities in the area of education of the deaf are aware of acquisition of language as the crucial problem in educating the deaf child, the following is a thought on this theme that cuts through the basic structure of traditional education of the deaf:

> The history of the education of the deaf is full of sporadic suggestions to solve the problems. Let's face it — a real problem is lack of language. The persons with good language, communicative skill, is having no problems of receiving adequate training and placement. Very seldom he or she has need of counseling and guidance.
>
> Given a well trained teacher for every deaf child, we face a problem of time distribution. Perhaps it would be wiser to devote more time to language — communicative skill — oral and written and less time to vocational work. This would mean a change of thinking on the part of administrators, teachers, parents, and the general public. The residential schools have been looked upon as terminal. This would no longer be true if we changed the emphasis to academic rather than a combination of academic and vocational. If we were to accept the concept of change in emphasis, we would need to make provision for vocational training on a postgraduate level, or dropout level (Fusfield, 1966).

Clearly, language is crucial in the development of the intellectual growth of a child with deafness as a disability. Language, like amber, embalms and preserves the history and ancient wisdom of the world into which the deaf child is born. His socialization and ultimate self-actualization depend to a great degree upon his acquisition of language. He must become as competent in the use of language as his potentialities permit if he is to achieve a high degree of self-realization.

The Changing Population

On the changing population of the residential schools for the deaf that implied curriculum revision, Brill (1963) stated that there was a larger population of children identified as congenitally deaf. In addition to this, Weir (1963) noted the sharp increase in the number of multihandicapped children in residential schools.

Another factor in the changing population of the residential school for the deaf is the emphasis on nursery and preschool programs. Statistics compiled by the *American Annals of the Deaf* (Doctor, 1960, 1964) revealed an average minimum age of admittance of 3.9 in 1960 and 3.5 in 1964. This shift in population calls for decisive curriculum in order to meet the needs of the children.

Another trend revealed in current literature is the area of vocational education. Williams (Ott, 1964) felt that vocational training, as such, is neither desirable nor possible in the present schools for the deaf. This, he feels, is because vocational education is highly specific and terminal.

Teaching Machines

Teaching machines to aid the deaf have been studied by researchers. Birch and Stuckless (1962) compared experimental and control groups of deaf children on a programmed approach to written language. They reported no difference between the groups in language learned, but stated that the experimental group learned the material in half the time. Fehr (1962) found favorable results in an experiment involving the teaching of language principles by a programmed approach.

New and improved training equipment available since World War II and the research involving such equipment is of importance to those in charge of curriculum planning. A recent development is a unisensory approach to auditory training known as *acoupedics*, which appears to be of importance. Pollack (1964) described an acoupedics program as one which emphasized listening as a continuous activity which keeps an individual in constant contact with the world about him. This program departed from the multisensory approach by avoiding lipreading. Pollack reported that vocabulary is built more rapidly than for the visually oriented child; the voice quality is more pleasing; and speech patterns are more normal. This approach is limited to children with at least limited hearing ability.

The need for continued research to improve education for all children and for encouragement of the classroom teacher to try new ways of doing old things was expressed recently by a teacher in the field of special education. She emphasized the use of all that has been successful in education since the dawn of history but warned that among educators there is too much of a tendency to "follow the beaten path." She stated that mankind is only seeing the dawn of the new day that could come in the education of deaf children. She warned against too much conformity in schools in general and special education in particular. She suggested that education for exceptional children might be made better if educators got out of the rut of educational conformity and security in the familiar, and gave much thought to new methods and ideas that might help children learn. She recalled the comment of Thoreau in *Walden* in which he said, "If a man does not keep pace with his companions, perhaps it is because he hears a different drummer. Let him step to the music that he hears however measured and far away." It might be in this way, she said, that the greatest advances would be made in the education of all children, and particularly the deaf child.

Legislation for the Deaf

Parents of deaf children will be interested in the following information from Hoag (1965):

> On June 8, 1965, President Johnson signed into law an act to provide for the establishment and operation of a National Technical Institute for the Deaf (Public Law 89-36). The legislation authorizes the Secretary of Health, Education, and Welfare to

enter into an agreement with an institution of higher education for the establishment, construction, equipment, and operation of a post-secondary technical training facility for young deaf adults. A 12-member ad hoc National Advisory Board on the establishment of the National Technical Institute for the Deaf will be appointed by the Secretary of Health, Education, and Welfare to review proposals from institutions of higher education and to advise him on location of the institute.

Early Guidance for the Parents

In an effort to secure positive attitudes in the parents it is good to begin working with and guiding them while the child is still very young. It is obvious that attitudes can best be influenced while they are in the making.

There are three reasons why special problems exist for the deaf child. These special problems create a need for special services and help. The first reason is that parents, like others, have preconceived ideas about deafness which, unfortunately, are for the most part quite negative. People think that loss of hearing incapacitates the individual and makes him helpless and dependent.

The second reason is that all parents expect their child to be at least normal and hope that he will be superior. If the body image of the child differs so radically from the one expected by the parents, they have to make a very painful and difficult adjustment. It is natural that they will blame themselves for the child's deafness, regardless of the truth. They feel that they have failed their child physically and will look for reasons for the imagined failure. Religious influences and naive concepts of justice as well as superstitions explain deafness as retribution for the sins committed by the parents. Thus, many parents feel that deafness in their child is a punishment imposed upon them and are ashamed of their handicapped offspring.

The third and final reason is that as the child grows up, parents will be confronted with the effects of deafness on the child, most frequently in terms of slowing down his development and rate of learning. Parents expect their child to perform according to the standards set forth for other children. It is only natural that a deaf child will, in many instances, be unable to fulfill this expectation and will demand of the parents adjustments in treatment and techniques which are sometimes quite difficult.

When we consider that the above-mentioned things are true and that they greatly affect the handicapped child's functioning ability in society, then we understand that early guidance and counseling for the parent is a must. Many parents who are confronted with a hearing-impaired child are overwhelmed by lack of understanding concerning what they can and should do. The John Tracy Clinic offers two means by which parents can learn about their hard-of-hearing child. This clinic offers a correspondence course and has films available for parents.

The Alexander Graham Bell Association for the Deaf issues kits of literature dealing with the problems and needs of hearing-impaired children. The Conference of Executives of American Schools for the Deaf issues the same kind of kits mentioned above. Also, the American Hearing Society offers help to parents of hearing-impaired children through its local societies.

Resource Rooms

The hearing-impaired child needs the help of a resource teacher to help with certain academic subjects. In small towns, though, the resource room is out of the question. Many people must work together if the hearing-impaired child is to function adequately in the regular classroom. Parents, teachers, administrators, and other agencies must correlate their efforts in the best educational interests of the child.

This chapter does not deal with the child who is born deaf. If one is profoundly deaf he must have special treatment and special placement in order to develop his maximum potential. In mentioning above that this chapter does not deal with the child who is born profoundly deaf, it is meant so far as educational placement in a regular classroom is concerned.

The hearing-impaired child faces many tasks and many conflicts. If he is to survive in the regular classroom he must have a great deal of help, but he can be educated adequately there.

THE DEAF ADULT

Henkels (1972) states that when a young deaf person completes secondary school, he probably has achieved to the point of being ready to pass the entrance examinations to Gallaudet College or he faces a world that is hostile to him. There are few agencies like the Vocational Rehabilitation Administration which attempt to place him on a job, but the difficult-to-place young deaf adult is often relegated to the welfare rolls.

It is further stated concerning the young deaf worker (Henkels, 1972):

> The adult deaf worker, even with a college degree, is often faced with the fact that he may have desires and skills which are not marketable for a deaf person in a hearing world. He may have to work at menial tasks which, although providing a livelihood, are far from satisfying or appropriate in relation to his capabilities. The vocational spectrum needs to be aggressively and systematically explored for possibilities of placement for deaf workers. There are a great many skills possessed by the deaf which the world needs, but the hearing world has not been educated about the potential of the deaf worker and the hearing employers are unwilling to "take a chance." Many employers who finally have employed a skilled deaf worker have been so highly pleased that they have looked further to employ the deaf.

Developmental Stages in Speech

The normal child goes through several stages in developing speech. The hearing-impaired child must go through the same stages but needs a great deal of help in understanding spoken language and the development of receptive language. The normal speech development that a hearing child follows is (1) birth cry, (2) cries that express needs and desires, (3) laughing, (4) babbling (vowel sounds first), (5) understanding of spoken language, (6) imitation of speech, (7) invented words, (8) speech to achieve something, (9) first one-word sentences — nouns and verbs; prepositions, pronouns, conjunctions, etc., much later, (10) sentences and phrases in haphazard order, (11) correct sentences (Harris, 1971, Gesell, 1940, and Moulton, 1966).

The Greatest Deprivation

Dr. Samuel Rosen, writing in his autobiography, tells us that Helen Keller delighted in showing off her garden. While relying entirely on the sense of smell she would point out the flowers. Miss Keller spoke in a harsh, gutteral voice, which at first had the appearance of animal-like sounds. Naturally she could not hear her voice, and this accounted for the sound of it. Dr. Rosen stated in his book that the sound of Miss Keller's voice added to the strangeness one felt about her, but one soon became accustomed to her way of speaking. When Dr. Rosen's wife, Helen, got to know Miss Keller rather well, she asked whether she felt the loss of sight was worse than the loss of hearing. "My dear," Miss Keller said, "you can touch a rose. You can smell it. You do not have to see or hear it to know it. But not to hear a fellow human being's voice is the greatest of deprivations" (Rosen, 1973).

BIBLIOGRAPHY

Advisory Committee on the Education of the Deaf: *Education of the Deaf: A Report to the Secretary of Health, Education, and Welfare.* U.S. Department of Health, Education, and Welfare, 1965.

Birch, Jack, and Stuckless, E. Ross: *The Development and Evaluation of Programmed Instruction in Language for Children with Auditory Disorders.* Pittsburgh, U of Pittsburgh Pr, 1962.

Brill, Richard, G.: Deafness and the genetic factor. *Am Ann Deaf, 108*:4, 1963.

Brown, Ralph Emerson (Ed.): *The New Dictionary of Thoughts.* New York, Standard Book Company, 1965.

Doctor, Powrie, V. (Ed.): *Am Ann Deaf, 105*:867, 1960.

Doctor, Powrie, V. (Ed.): *Am Ann Deaf, 108*:935, 1964.

Ewing, Irene, R., and Ewing, Alex, W. G.: *New Opportunities for Deaf Children.* Springfield, Thomas, 1958.

Fehr, Joann D.: Programming language for deaf children. *Volta Rev, 64*:319, 1962.

Frampton, Merle, E., and Gall, Elena D.: *Special Education for the Exceptional.* Boston, Porter Sargent, 1955, vol. I.

Fusfield, Irving S.: A Cross Section Evaluation of the Academic Program of Schools for the Deaf. *Gallaudet College Bulletin*, 1954.

Fusfield, Irving S.: Guidelines for the language teaching program. *Report of the Proceedings of the Forty-Second Meeting of American Instructors of the*

Deaf. U.S. Government Printing Office, Document 7, 1966.

Gesell, A.: *The First Five Years of Life.* New York, MacMillan, 1940.

Greer, William C.: New era for special education. *Am Educ,* June, 1975.

Harris, Grace M.: *Language for the Preschool Deaf Child,* 3rd Ed. New York, Grune, 1971.

Henkels, Milo P.: The deaf and the hard of hearing. *Education of the Exceptional Child.* Scranton, Intext, 1972.

Hoag, Ralph L.: National technical institute for the deaf. *Except Child, 32:*167, 1965.

McHugh, Hollie: Sensori-neural deafness in children. *Report of the Proceedings of the Forty-First International Congress on Education of the Deaf.* U.S. Government Printing Office, Document 106, 1964.

Millichamp, D.: *Priorities in Preschool Education.* Toronto, The Brora Center, 1970.

Moulton, W.: *A Linguistic Guide to Language Learning.* New York, Modern Lang, 1966.

Myklebust, Helmer R.: *The Psychology of Deafness.* New York, Grune, 1960.

Ott, Joseph T. (Ed.): *Proceedings of a National Workshop on Improved Vocational Opportunities for the Deaf.* Knoxville, U Tennessee, 1964.

Pintner, R., and Brunschwig, H.: Some personality adjustments of deaf children in relation to two different factors. *J Genet Psychol, 49* 187, 1963.

Pintner, R., Eisenson, Jon, and Stanton, Mildred: *The Psychology of the Physically Handicapped.* New York, F. S. Crofts and Company, 1941.

Pollack, Doreen: Acoupedics: A uni-sensory approach to auditory training. *Volta Rev, 66:*425, 1964.

Rosen, Samuel: *The Autobiography of Dr. Samuel Rosen.* New York, Knopf, 1973.

Sapir, E.: *Language.* New York, HarBrace Jovanovich, 1949.

Weir, R. C.: The impact of the multiple handicapped on special education. *Volta Rev, 65:*6, 1963.

Wooden, Harley Z.: Deaf and hard of hearing children. In Dunn, Lloyd M.: *Exceptional Children in the Schools.* New York, HR&W, 1963.

Young, C., and McConnell, F.: Retardation of vocabulary development in hard of hearing children. *Except Child, 23:*117, 1957.

Chapter 7

LANGUAGE DEVELOPMENT
OF CHILDREN WITH
LEARNING DISABILITIES

LEARNING disabilities (LD) is a term used to describe children who have significant deficits in essential learning processes which require special educational techniques for remediation. The term has been applied in two ways: First, it has been applied in a limited sense in setting up programs for children with low-average, average, or above-average intelligence who are significantly retarded in basic academic skills and, secondly, in a broad sense in reference to children in other special education programs and in the regular classroom who have discrepant areas of functioning, for example those children having significantly less skill in one or more areas of functioning than in others. It should be pointed out that the child we are talking about (LD) is not mentally retarded. A mentally retarded child may be working three years below his chronological age, but still is working at his mental age capacity. This type child is not classified as one having learning disabilities.

During the past five decades increasing emphasis has been placed on providing remedial instruction for students who have not achieved as well as expected in the basic academic subjects. Among students in such remedial programs who have apparent average or above-average intelligence are some who have not responded to usual instruction and/or remedial instruction. Analysis of their problems have revealed deficiencies in their receptive and expressive behaviors associated with listening, reading, and writing. Naturally, these deficiencies affect their use of language and symbolization. In reading and listening, for example, these children may be having difficulty in remembering words learned by sight, hearing the differences between sounds in words, moving the eyes smoothly from left to right along a line of

147

print, associating meaning with words, etc. In speaking, writing, and other motor expressive behavior, they often have problems in the choice of appropriate words, the arrangement of the words in appropriate order and with proper grammatical structure, coordinating eye and hand in writing or drawing, blending sounds represented by letters in a word, in developing number concepts — counting by one-to-one matching, orientation in space or time, and the list is endless.

In the past the explanation often given for the lack of progress of these children was that they were emotionally maladjusted or that they were brain injured. Such terms as *dyslexia, minimal brain dysfunction, perceptual handicaps,* and *aphasia* have also been used to identify these children. The terms *brain injured* or *brain damaged* are not considered acceptable by many authorities because neurological impairment cannot always be clearly established. The presence of a neurological dysfunction, however, may be inferred from behavioral characteristics.

A term which is now widely used to identify these children is *learning disabilities.* Organizations of special educators and parents have promoted interest in this area. Two such organizations are the Association for Children with Learning Disabilities (ACLD) and the Division for Children with Learning Disabilities (DCLD) within the Council for Exceptional Children. Much attention has been directed toward finding ways of impoving the education of LD children through a more careful diagnosis of their specific strengths and weaknesses and a prescriptive program designed accordingly.

The authors wish to present a definition of children having learning disabilities:

> Children with learning disabilities may exhibit disorders of visual, auditory and haptic perception which interferes or impedes the acquisition and utilization of receptive and expressive symbolic language. Such children reveal a significant discrepancy between their capacity for symbolic language learning and their observed level of language ability.

The foremost distinguishing characteristic of children with learning disabilities is the marked retardation in basic academic skills, and special services will be required individually or in small groups. If the child qualifies in this regard, he may be admitted to the program without consideration of central nervous system dysfunction. In other words, if he is far enough behind his classmates in reading, writing, spelling, or calculating that the regular teacher cannot deal with the problem in the classroom, he qualifies for special remedial help. Among students so qualified, many will manifest characteristics which may indicate neurological dysfunction. They have specific disabilities and many contrasts in their diagnostic profile which indicate a significant impairment of learning efficiency.

A Broad Interpretation of Learning Disabilities

In other special education programs for handicapped children, learning disabilities are seen in the extreme when compared to normal children. Mentally retarded children are characterized by severe learning deficiencies in most academic areas, but this does not imply that they suffer from LD according to the premise established in this chapter. Emotionally disturbed children also exhibit extreme educational difficulty. Children having sensory deficits in hearing and vision may also have learning impairment because of their inability to receive the incoming learning stimuli. Cerebral palsied children have motor difficulties which interfere with the expression of reaction or response to the stimuli they receive.

Among these groups with serious defects are some children who appear to have discrepancies in several areas of functioning in that they perform well on some learning tasks but poorly on others. Also, a sizable number of children with learning discrepancies in areas of academic functioning are found in the regular classroom. They may be receiving instruction in a special education program for part of the school day, or they may not be included in special programs because the quota is filled or because they are marginally qualified or they are above average in their performance in some academic areas or skills. It is in the sense of the presence of lows as contrasted with highs on a diagnostic profile, or *scatter,* in the various areas of intellectual functioning, that a broad interpretation is given to the term *learning disabilities.*

Learning Disabilities and Communication Disorders

As has been indicated above, a major characteristic which is common to all children who are given special educational assistance is that of learning difficulty. A companion characteristic which almost always accompanies learning disability is that of communication difficulty. For example, children with sensory difficulty do not receive accurately the communicated message from others — that is, they do not receive the learning stimulus accurately.

Children with deficits in the processes of comprehension, formulation of ideas, perception of sensory stimuli, etc., may also be said to have basic communication difficulties. In fact, the functions of perception, conceptualization, expression, reception, etc., may be described as parts of the communication process which are involved in learning and which, when disordered, contribute to impairment of learning. The following definition of learning disabilities proposed by the National Advisory Committee on Handicapped Children (1968) highlights language development as an important consideration in the identification of children with such learning difficulties:

> Children with special learning disabilities exhibit a disorder in one or more of the basic psychological processes involved in understanding or using spoken or written languages. These may be manifested in disorders of listening, thinking, talking, reading, writing, spelling or arithmetic. They include conditions which have been referred to as perceptual handicaps, brain injury, minimal brain dysfunction, dyslexia, developmental aphasia, etc. They do not include learning problems which are due primarily to visual, hearing, or motor handicaps, to mental retardation, emotional disturbance, or to environmental disadvantage.

The initial section of the definition suggests a breakdown or dysfunction of the processes associated with the reception (decoding) and expression (encoding) of the various forms of language. By including within the definition children who were previously labeled *developmental aphasia*, the significance of language inadequacy was stressed as a formidable characteristic of these children.

Because of this coincidence of learning disabilities and communication disabilities, principles and techniques described in this chapter emphasize the improvement of learning and communication as simultaneous goals of special education.

It is hoped that classroom teachers, teachers of the mentally retarded, speech and hearing clinicians, psychologists, school nurses, social workers, and others who serve children with learning problems will find this chapter useful as they note disabilities in motor coordination, perception, conceptualization, or expression among the clients they serve.

Historical Viewpoint

Children with learning disabilities may be viewed as either a somewhat old or a fairly new exceptionality in special education. The book, *Visual Perception: The Nineteenth Century*, described the children of this field of study as early as 1801. However, *learning disabilities* is relatively new when viewed as a total area of special education. The *Journal of Learning Disabilities* was published in January, 1968. The first two full-length textbooks utilizing the term *learning disabilities* were published in 1967 by Johnson and Myklebust and Frierson and Barbe. That same year a looseleaf handbook for teachers was published using the label *learning disabilities*. During the 1960's several states passed legislation concerning the provision of services for learning-disabled children.

The Bureau for the Handicapped (United States Office of Education) became active in promoting college programs to train students in teaching the learning-disabled. Finally, Public Law 91-230, was signed by President Nixon on April 13, 1970, containing provisions for research, training, and model centers for children with learning disabilities (Gearheart, 1972).

It was in 1895 that James Hinshelwood, a Scottish ophthalmologist, wrote a report concerned with "word blindness" and included some tentative hypotheses. A British physician, James

Kerr, and a British ophthalmologist, W. P. Morgan, reported in 1896 on two separate cases of specific learning disabilities in children who had normal intelligence. In 1917, Hinshelwood published a monograph on word blindness which received considerable attention in medical circles. In 1918 Babinski reported on a different aspect of learning disabilities related to "agnosognosia," or the inability to correctly perceive and recognize body parts.

In 1947, The Cove Schools were organized to provide an educational program for *brain-injured* children, following the philosophy of one of the pioneers in the field, Dr. Alfred A. Strauss. Dr. Strauss's first work concerned the reeducation of brain-injured war veterans in Germany. Dr. Strauss's approach has been characterized as relating educational methods and procedures to medical and psychological knowledge and techniques. Today the Cove Schools still operate in Evanston, Illinois. The four major areas of learning which are emphasized in the Cove Schools at present include academic skills concerned with reading, spelling, arithmetic, and so on. Second, the improvement of motor and perceptual functions and language and conceptual abilities are stressed. The third and fourth areas are development of skills needed for daily life activities and growth in the skills necessary for social and group living (Gearheart, 1972).

Alfred Strauss, collaborating with Hans Wenrer, a child psychologist, and Laura Lehtinen, a teacher, researched and organized programs for children thought to have suffered brain damage. Strauss contended that children with brain injuries incurred before, during, or after birth are subject to major disorders in perception, thinking, and behavior, and that these disorders affect the child's ability to learn all academic subjects. The diagnosis of brain injury was primarily assumed because of the presence of behavioral manifestations or disorders and was not based solely on traditional neurological diagnosis. Strauss's educational methods consisted of instructional procedures and environmental changes that would correct or alleviate the disturbances in perception, thinking, and behavior, and integrate these techniques with procedures in teaching the academic subjects. Many subsequent developments in learning disabilities were stimulated by Strauss and Lehtinen's work. Among these developments are the perceptual motor approaches of William Cruickshank, Newell Kephart, Raymond Barsch, and Gerald Getman.

Cruickshank (1961) tested Strauss' hypothesis that a nonstimulating classroom with specially designed instructional materials will improve the functioning level of LD children. He used forty brain-damaged children and divided them into two experimental groups; he also had two control groups whereby he used a nonstimulating special class and a special class with a traditional program. However, Cruickshank's experiment did not demonstrate that hyperactive children can profit more significantly from a nonstimulating classroom than a traditional special class. The experiment did show that special education can produce academic progress in such children. It may also be true that for some individual children who are hyperactive, the procedure of decreasing the environmental stimuli is very beneficial. Group results, as cited above, do not always determine what is most beneficial for a particular child (Kirk, 1972).

Theoretical Approaches

There are many different approaches used in working with learning-disabled children. Many of the authorities disagree as to just what *learning disabilities* means and which approach is best in dealing with children having this handicap. There is no one method found to be best since every learning-disabled child is an individual and has a different type of learning problem. Following are a few major approaches used and the authorities who follow each method or approach. Naturally, many of the authorities could be listed as proponents of several of the approaches.

Neurological Approaches

Hughlings Jackson, although not the first neurologist who contributed to knowledge in this area, is probably the best known. The theory of cerebral dominance as related to speech and other behavioral disorders probably had its true begining with Jackson. In 1928 Jackson indicated that there are various degrees of aphasia, and that aphasia, agraphia, and alexia are defects in the use of symbols and in organized thinking. Jackson formulated his brain theories on studies of brain-damaged adults and epileptics. His writings and case descriptions had a tremendous influence on the later work of Henry Head in England and Samuel T. Orton in the United States. Orton, who was a neuropathologist, studied the effects of brain injury on the language function of adults and applied his findings to children having developmental language disorders. Orton was especially concerned with the specific disorder of alexia that puts stress on individuality.

Perceptual-Motor Approaches

Although there is a lack of conclusive empirical research to determine the efficacy of the perceptual-motor approach, it has been widely accepted as having beneficial results. This approach is applicable to certain children with specific learning disabilities, and children not having visual-motor perceptual problems may require different kinds of remediation.

Newell Kephart, late director of the Glen Haven Achievement Center in Colorado, was an outstanding and well-known contributor to the field of learning disabilities. In earlier days, Kephart was a co-worker of Strauss and conducted several research investigations with this authority. It was in 1960 that Kephart developed a system of diagnosis and remediation along somewhat different theoretical lines concerning learning disabilities. He relied less on brain dysfunction and more upon developmental psychology, which was more in keeping with his own background in child psychology. Kephart's basic thesis was that a child's first encounter with his environment was through motor activities which influenced muscle behavior, and these two became prerequisites for later learning. The child acquired motor generalizations through pattern of movement, and therefore perceptual cognitive structure was organized. It was Kephart's belief that as the child matures he is able to generalize and objectify the relationships of objects in time and space without using himself as a focal point.

Kephart's development of the Purdue Perceptual Motor Survey

has been used as an aid in diagnosing the child's level of perceptual-motor development prior to organizing a training program for the child. Kephart's theory was organized into stages of learning development. He called the three stages practical, subjective, and objective, and all four stages were based on four motor generalizations. The four motor generalizations are posture and the maintenance of balance, contact, locomotion, and receipt and propulsion.

Ray Barsch also worked with Strauss and is presently concerned with the world of space and movement within that space. Earlier in his career Barsch was primarily concerned with the brain-damaged child and parental counseling, the concept of regression, and methods of classification and evaluation. In recent times Barsch has directed his efforts toward the development of a conceptual scheme which describes the child as a learner and provides an approach to education he designed called "the physiologic approach." Barsch refers to his curriculum as "movigenics" and says that it was the "study of the origin and development of movement patterns which leads to learning efficiency." Barsch utilizes twelve dimensions which pertain to human learning and which serve as the areas constituting the educational curriculum.

Gerald Getman approached visual perception from a developmental position, and through his research has developed a learning readiness program designed to prepare children for school learning using motor and visual perception exercises. Getman not only presented six stages of visual-motor development but suggested a collection of activities to train the child at each stage.

Elizabeth Freidus has been associated for many years with the Lexington School for the Deaf in New York. She has conducted special courses and seminars in the area of learning disabilities and has primarily a developmental orientation to this field. Freidus drew upon and modified the ideas of Kephart, Strauss, and Lehtinen, Piaget, Bruner, and many other outstanding people. Freidus has developed a servosystem which includes the information being received and compares this with information already stored, the rise of response patterns, the response proper, and the feedback of part of the response to the input side of the model. This input side of the model insures that the process is self-correcting. Freidus's model has seven stages. She stated that she was not entirely concerned with the cause of the learning problem because etiology has little educational significance; however, the important consideration as far as she was concerned was the stage of the learning process where the child demonstrated his difficulty.

Multisensory Systems

The multisensory system is an eclectic approach which permits close-modality stimulation in most of its training activities. The tasks emphasized in this approach used visual-auditory-kinesthetic-tactile inputs, and these inputs permitted the child to capitalize on several areas of strength and, hopefully, constituted an improvement in these areas. This approach is often referred to as the V-A-K-T method of instruction.

It was Laura Lehtinen who developed a method or a teaching procedure based on Strauss's research and Strauss's theory of cortical damage. Lehtinen and Strauss both believed that emphasis should be placed on a child's weaknesses rather than building up his strengths. Many authorities, however, believe that there is evidence that when a child's strengths are neglected, they are likely to deteriorate. Strauss and Lehtinen utilized two approaches to remedial education for problems caused by distractibility, hyperactivity, disinhibition, and the emotional consequences of these three things. They believed that the environment of the child should be structured and, secondly, the child utilizes controls from within to help in the educational process.

Under the above-mentioned approach we can subsume William Cruickshank as one of the proponents. Cruickshank believed that behavior should be treated as a symptom of, or associated with, the frustration of failure which resulted from specific learning disabilities. Cruickshank modified the plan of education of Strauss and Lehtinen's concepts which were based on four principles, the four principles being the reduction of unessential visual and auditory environmental stimuli, the reduction of environmental space, a highly structured program, and the increase of the stimulus value of the educational methods. His program also involved the extensive and concentrated use of color in the teaching techniques and materials for all the areas. Cruickshank's program also involved suggestions and detailed teaching teachniques which were borrowed from Montessori to improve visual-motor perception, and also some of Kirk's principles were utilized regarding reading readiness.

Many years ago it was Grace Fernald who maintained that in order to make satisfactory adjustment to the environment a child needed successful experiences. She advocated that whenever possible the application of remedial techniques should be used before the child met extreme failure. Her case histories indicated that the children with whom she worked did have learning disabilities but had no serious emotional problems before entering school. Fernald's two general methods were called the *analytical method* and the *reconditioning method*. She also developed the kinesthetic method of teaching remedial reading. She had the child draw the words in sand, thereby using not only the kinesthetic approach, but the tactile approach in overcoming reading difficulty.

Language Development Systems

Three widely used systems which emphasize language development are the systems of Myklebust, Barry, and McGinnis. These three men were primarily concerned with the communication problems of children who had been diagnosed as having aphasia.

Helmer R. Myklebust, along with Johnson, identified five major types of learning disabilities — auditory-language, arithmetic, reading, writing, and nonverbal. They also made recommendations for the diagnosis and remediation of these problems. Myklebust is best known for his development and popularization of various terms to describe learning-disabled children. Among these terms are *psychoneurological learning disability, learning quotient,* and *developmental aphasia.*

Hortense Barry's approach was primarily based upon the principles set forth by Montessori. These principles encompassed the concepts of inner, receptive, and expressive language. Also, the need for presenting language in the same sequence in which normal children learn language is stressed. She was also concerned with the language disorders exemplified in receptive and expressive aphasia. Barry believed, however, that before a diagnosis of aphasia was made the diagnostician should look for other causes for the lack of normal verbal communication. She believed that there are two important considerations in training the aphasic child. First, there is the physical group which consists of corrective techniques for psychomotor dysfunction and impaired function. Secondly, she believed in a structured program in the development of language and used various other skills related to learning languge.

Mildred A. McGinnis believed that there were many nonlanguage children having multiple handicaps who responded to what she called the *associated method*. She believed that the children would respond to the associated method if their primary problem was aphasia. The associated method develops and associates systematically each of several specific skills which must be coordinated for the development of the ability to understand and the ability to use oral communication in language.

Phonics Systems

The methods under phonics systems include programs developed by Gillingham and Stillman in 1965 and Spalding (1957) and were primarily auditory due to the emphasis placed upon the teaching of sound-letter associations. Even though the system relied primarily upon the auditory modality, this did not mean that no other sensory channels were employed.

Katrina de Hirsch's theory would also be included under this system. Her theoretical position was that disorders of speech in children can be placed on a continuum of language dysfunctions. She is credited with starting the first clinic for language disorders in this country. Like Orton and Myklebust, she should be considered as a language pathology theorist (Kirk, 1972).

It was Anna Gillingham, who worked closely with Orton and Stillman, who tried to devise and refine teaching techniques for children who were learning-disabled. Gillingham and Stillman based their work upon Orton's theory of hemispheric dominance.

Romalda Spalding used a phonic approach in teaching reading, which she called the *unified phonics method*. Her program was different in that she did not start with reading, but advocated the writing of sounds of the spoken language, using the letters which represent the sounds. Her method was not exclusively a remedial method because it was intended to be used in the regular classroom, beginning in the first grade.

A Structured System

Barry, Lehtinen, and Cruickshank and others noted that some children with specific learning disorders have need for structure in their educational environment (Hammill and Myers, 1969).

Edith Fitzgerald maintained that deaf children required a visual guide to follow in structuring sentences because they were usually unable to hear their errors in construction. Her method was probably suitable for hearing children who also had difficulty in monitoring or structuring their sentences and who would profit from the visual reinforcement.

Valett Programs

Dr. Robert Valett, an educational psychologist and former director of the Learning Resource Center for Exceptional Children in Sacramento, California, has made a considerable contribution in attempting to integrate important components and aspects of various approaches to the education of children with learning disabilities. Gearheart (1973) indicated that Valett has organized the program so the classroom teacher can play a major role in establishing the specific learning skills that are needed when the children are provided a starting point for remediation. Valett used a language development scheme in one of the approaches toward remediating learning disabilities. In his language development approach he listed the following subtitles which should be diagnosed and remediated:

Language Development

1. Vocabulary
2. Fluency and encoding
3. Articulation
4. Word attack skills
5. Reading comprehsnion
6. Writing
7. Spelling

Test-Related Systems

Test-related systems are directly related to the diagnostic assessment instruments associated with them. Marianne Frostig designed a widely used test of visual perception. Along with the assessment of visual perceptual efficiency, her main interest centers around the development of perceptual skills rather than in providing specific skills in reading, spelling, and writing (Myers and Hammill, 1969).

The Frostig test measures five areas of visual perception and provides a training program for remediation purposes. The test includes visual perceptual skills and the program is basically a verbal-perceptual one. The materials, which are worksheets and activities, etc., comprise the training program which is easy to understand and motivates most of the children. The Frostig approach is a very usable one if the child's problem is mainly one of visual perception. Gearheart (1973) states that although Marianne Frostig uses the Illinois Test of Psycholinguistic Abilities and the Wepman tests in her center, these facets of language ability diagnosis in auditory discrimination are not a part of her published training program. Therefore, according to Gearheart (1973), the Frostig training program coordinated with the Developmental Test of Visual Perception is of limited value for children experiencing problems in the auditory channel; it seems to be insufficient as the only program of remediation.

Another program under this system is the Preschool Diagnostic Language Program, developed for culturally disadvantaged children and based upon the clinical model of the Illinois Test of

Psycholinguistic Abilities.

The last system which must be included is the *neurological organizational system* (Myers and Hammill, 1969) arising from the work of Delacato and Doman. The concept of this organization was that individual human neurological development repeats or recapitulates the pattern of man's evolutionary development of the nervous system. Delacato's basic premise was that if man did not follow the sequential continuum of phylogentic neurological development, he would exhibit problems of mobility and/or communication. The reader is directed to Chapter 1 for a more detailed study of the Delacato and Doman system.

Characteristics of
Learning — Communication Disabilities

Learning and Communication

It is widely recognized that the processes of human learning and human communication are interdependent. Therefore, it is unreasonable to expect one to occur without the other. One can say with assurance that learning the significant knowledge of one's heritage requires adequate facility in the communication processes of reading, listening, speaking, and writing. On the other hand, adequate communication skills are developed only through appropriate learning experiences.

This important interdependence of learning and communication is implied repeatedly in Mowrer's (1960) book, *Learning Theory and the Symbolic Processes,* in which the author describes learning as dependent upon symbolic behavior, the most intricate of which may be called language. Mowrer also suggests this interdependence in the introduction to one of his chapters on language and learning in which he says, "... we shall explore the way, or ways, in which language, once mastered as a tool, may then function as a means of producing the special kinds of learning that we call communication."

This close relationship of learning and communication leads to a variety of useful constructs and principles in the understanding of (1) normal and disordered learning and (2) normal and disordered communication, neither of which can be fully understood without reference to the other.

Definition of Learning

Learning is described as the acquisition of new behavior other than through means of physiological maturation. It is sometimes described as a change in behavior as a result of experiences or behavior modifications or response habituations, etc. Naturally, these brief statements do not explain the process of learning in detail, but only the behavioral result of learning.

Learning as a process has been explained in numerous ways for many, many years. It has been analyzed in terms of conditioning, stimulus-response bonds, contiguity and association, cause and effect and reinforcement, motivation and drive reduction, instrumental conditioning, etc., to the point that today's learning theorists speak of three or four major elements of learning and many facilitating conditions.

Major Elements and Conditions of Learning

The major elements of learning are generally defined as (1) stimulus, (2) motivation, (3) response and (4) reinforcement. The process involved is typically described as (1) the provision of certain stimulus conditions, (2) some of which may be internal drives or motivations, following which a person (3) makes a response which is then (4) reinforced through punishment or reward so that the response may be either eliminated or expected to occur under similar conditions in the future.

Many authorities state that, in addition to the major elements of learning, a number of conditions which facilitate learning have been described. Among them are (1) immediacy of reinforcement, (2) small increments toward or successive approximations of the desired cues or stimuli in the learning situation, (3) employing language as a mediator or facilitator of learning, (4) use of various types of reinforcers, (5) providing learning tasks at a level where the learner can succeed, (6) arranging whole-part-whole instead of part-part-whole sequences of learning tasks, (7) emphasis on reward as reinforcement instead of punishment, (8) providing the student with knowledge of the correctness of his responses, (9) active rather than passive participation of the learner, and (10) ensuring that the response (task) to be learned is meaningful to the individual learner, (Thurman, 1974).

The Emotionally Involved Child

There are many authorities who maintain that children classified as learning-disabled are also emotionally handicapped. These authorities maintain that if a child fails repeatedly in many of the tasks in life the environmental rejection and other trauma is enough to cause emotional and/or social maladjustment. Other authorities and special educators maintain that the emotional maladjustment came first and caused the learning disability. This concern leads psychologists and special educators to investigate the impact behavior modification has on the child who has an emotional problem or learning disabilities or both.

Educational Engineering

Concerning models in the local public schools for educational programs for emotionally disturbed children who also have learning disabilities, Hewett (1970) has this to say:

> There is the psychotherapeutic model with a psychodynamic, interpersonal emphasis; the pathological or medical model, which focuses on brain pathology and treatment of measured or inferred organic causal factors; and the pedagogical model, concerned with intellectual development, remedial techniques, and academic goals. Each model has influenced school programs for emotionally disturbed children, and depending on the intuitive, diagnostic, and curriculum skill of the teacher, has been useful to some degree.

Hewett (1970) describes a model called behavior modification which has been useful with emotionally disturbed children. This approach concentrates on bringing the overt behavior of the child into lines required for standards of learning: "Such standards may include development of an adequate attention span; orderly response in the classroom; the ability to follow directions; tolerance for limits of time, space, and activity; approval and avoidance of disapproval."

In Hewett's article he states that according to Ullman and Krasner (1965) the behavior modifier has three main concerns — (1) defining maladaptive behavior, (2) determining the environmental events which support this behavior, and (3) manipulating the environment in order to alter maladaptive behavior.

The Engineered Classroom

In this type of classroom, Hewett (1970) tells us that the teacher is assigned the role of a behavioral engineer. In this role she attempts to define appropriate task assignments for students and to provide meaningful rewards for learning. She maintains well-defined limits in order to reduce and hopefully eliminate the occurrence of maladaptive behavior.

The engineered classroom which was investigated by Hewett (1966) was introduced in the public schools by a teacher who had no previous experience with behavior modification theory. She attempted a transfer of this theory not rigidly but pragmatically to the school setting. The teacher organized the behavior modification principle in terms of a learning triangle. The sides of the triangle represent the three essential ingredients for effective teaching. These ingredients are (1) the selection of a suitable educational task for the child, (2) provision of a meaningful reward following accomplishment of that task, and (3) maintenance of a degree of structure under the control of the teacher.

Hewett (1970) comments on the students:

> Two types of students have been enrolled in experimental engineered classrooms to date: public school children with essentially normal intelligence from Santa Monica and Tulare in California and the Palolo School district in Oahu, Hawaii, identified as educationally handicapped (underachieving due to emotional, neurological, or learning disability factors); and emotionally disturbed children hospitalized on the Children's Service of the UCLA Neuropsychiatric Institute and enrolled in

the Neuropsychiatric Institute School. The public school population consisted mostly of boys with conduct disturbances, neurotic traits including long-standing school phobias, psychosomatic and borderline psychotic problems, as well as minimal neurological impairment. The hospitalized group represented more serious emotional problems and included grossly psychotic and more markedly neurologically impaired individuals. All students were in the age group from 8 to 12.

At the time of Hewett's investigation of engineered classroom design, it had been observed in four public school systems for two years, and despite the requirements for teacher aids it appeared to be a feasible design for the public school setting. At that time Hewett (1970) had this to say about the design:

> The engineered class design is not viewed as an end in itself. Observations suggest that the value of checkmarks and tangible exchange items soon gives way to the satisfaction of succeeding in school and receiving recognition as a student from peers, teachers, and parents. Transition programs have been worked out where children started in the engineered classroom have gradually been reintroduced into regular classes. While this stage is not wholly developed, it appears to be a natural evolutionary development in the program.

The treatment of fear or anxiety within an engineered classroom indicates that desensitization is a behavior modification technique used with considerable success (Lazarus and Abramovitz, 1962, Bandura, 1969, and Patterson, 1965). Systematic application of desensitization has traditionally been restricted to a clinical setting. Kravetz and Forness (1971) report the results of the work they did with a first grade boy who would not talk while in the classroom. Medical investigation revealed no hearing problem, and the origin of the elective mutism was unknown. Achievement testing indicated that the boy was working at grade placement in most subjects.

This child's only means of communication while in the classroom was tugging at the teacher's sleeve or occasionally whispering in her ear. The authors (Kravetz and Forness, 1971) placed the boy in an engineered classroom (Hewett, 1968). The child worked on individual assignments and received checkmarks for working and following behavioral rules of the classroom. The checkmarks were exchanged for candy or small toys at the end of the day.

For this child, twelve sessions, two per week, were devoted to the desensitization treatment. According to the authors (Kravetz and Forness, 1971) the investigator began by asking the child about favorite heroes and talking about folk heroes. The young boy at first was reluctant to talk, but the investigator verbally reinforced the child's expressed interest in Paul Bunyan. This type of hero talk was maintained as supportive treatment throughout the rest of the treatment period. The investigator arrived at a hierarchy of fearful situations (Kravetz and Forness, 1971):

1. Reading alone to investigator
2. Reading alone to roommate
3. Reading to two classroom aides (repeated)
4. Reading to teacher and classroom aides (repeated)
5. Reading to teacher, classroom aides, and small group of classroom peers (repeated)
6. Reading to entire class
7. Asking questions or making comment at weekly ward meeting when all patients, teacher, and staff were present.

Each time the young boy had trouble with any of the sessions the emotive image of Paul Bunyan was introduced into the imaginary situation to overcome unassertive response tendencies. Six weeks after the study was begun the boy was able to raise his hand and make audible comments on two separate occasions.

When the article was written (Kravetz and Forness, 1971), the boy had been discharged from the hospital and was reportedly functioning well in a regular public school classroom. It should be pointed out that reinforcement techniques, when used alone, did little to resolve the fear the boy had of speaking. Combined use of desensitization and reinforcement as outlined by Bandura (1969) was used and, according to the authors (Kravetz and Forness, 1970), appeared to be necessary for maximum generalization to natural settings. It is also pointed out that another important aspect of the treatment centered around classroom routine. By studying events in the life of Paul Bunyan and drawing pictures of him as academic tasks similar to those found in classrooms, this served as a focal point of a unit of academic instruction. Paul Bunyan's image provoked characteristics such as *strong, big,* and *unafraid.* This seemed to help the boy a great deal.

This study (Kravetz and Forness, 1971) indicated to this writer that desensitization could also be done in a resource-type room in the regular classroom building. An emotionally-disturbed child could go to the resource room periodically for reinforcement and desensitization, then go back to the regular classroom for academic work and socialization with other children.

Summary

In this chapter the authors have discussed language development of children with learning disabilities. A definition has been presented and a broad interpretation of learning disabilities has been discussed. It has been pointed out that a major characteristic of children with learning disabilities is that they also have communication disorders. The authors have presented a short historical viewpoint, and theoretical approaches have been discussed. Although behavior modification is discussed more extensively in another chapter, it has been mentioned in this chapter as it pertains to learning disabilities.

BIBLIOGRAPHY

Bandura, A.: *Principles of Behavior Modification.* New York, HR&W, 1969.

Cruickshank, W., Bentzen, F., Ratzburg, F., and Tannhauser, M.: *A Teaching Method for Brain-Injured and Hyperactive Children.* Syracus, Syracuse U Pr, 1961.

Frierson, E., and Barbe, W. (Eds.): *Educating Children With Learning Disabilities.* New York, Appleton, 1967.

Gearheart, B. R.: *Education of the Exceptional Child: History, Present Practices and Trends.* Scranton, Intext, 1972.

———*Learning Disabilities: Education Strategies.* St. Louis, Mosby, 1973.

Hewett, Frank M.: A hierarchy of educational tasks for children with learning disorders. *Except Child, 33:*7-11, 1966.

———*The Emotionally Disturbed Child in the Classroom.* Boston, Allyn, 1968.

———*The Emotionally Disturbed Child in the Classroom.* Boston, Allyn, 1970.

Johnson, D. C., and Myklebust, H. R.: *Learning Disabilities: Educational Principles and Practices.* New York, Grune, 1967.

Kirk, S. A.: *Educating Exceptional Children,* 2nd Ed. Boston, HM, 1972.

Krasner, Leonard, and Ullman, Leonard P.: *Research in Behavior Modification: New Developments and Implications.* New York, HR&W, 1965.

Kravetz, Richard J., and Forness, Steven R.: The special classroom as a desensitization setting. *Except Child, 37*:210, 1971.

Lazarus, A. A., and Abramovitz, A.: The use of "emotive imagery" in the treatment of children's phobias. *J Ment Sci, 108*:191-195, 1962.

Mowrer, O. H.: *Learning Theory and the Symbolic Processes.* New York, Wiley, 1960.

Myers, P. I., and Hammill, D. D.: *Methods for Learning Disorders.* New York, Wiley, 1969.

Myklebust, H.: *Development and Disorders of Written Language.* New York, Grune, 1969.

National Advisory Committee on Handicapped Children, 1968.

Patterson, G.: An application of conditioning techniques to the control of a hyperactive child. In Ullman, L., and Krasner, L. (Eds.) *Case Studies in Behavior Modification.* New York, HR&W, 1965.

Thurman, James E.: *Teaching Children With Learning Disabilities.* Unpublished pamphlet, 1974.

Chapter 8

LANGUAGE DEVELOPMENT OF
EMOTIONALLY-DISTURBED CHILDREN

BECAUSE of the rare frequency of this condition, little is known about the causes of this unusual mental disorder. The etiology of autism has been made up mostly of theories. Some writers defend that autism can be caused by complications during pregnancy (early bleeding in the first trimester of pregnancy); others believe that the condition is manifested by extreme maternal or parental deprivation.

The morbid self-absorption symptoms of psychotic children who manifest their psychoses very early in development were identified and first described by Kanner (1944) as being autistic. Early infantile autism represents one of the most serious, debilitating, and bizarre pediatric disorders found among children who exhibit varying degrees of personality disturbances. Early infantile autism, as a variant of childhood psychosis, was initially perceived as being a new subtype of subcategorization of schizophrenia. Kanner's original conceptualization of autism attempted to postulate the etiology of this condition as being innately determined. Due to the early establishment of symtomology, autism was considered to be a congenital rather than an acquired inability to establish functional relationships with the environment and normal intercourse with the surroundings. Autism was originally considered as a congenital personality disorder because the bizarre symptoms appeared before the environment had ample time to produce the autistic child. Later, however, Kanner and his associates extended the theoretical cause of autism to include the possible deleterious effects of the environment. Although Kanner extended the etiological explanation of autism to include environmental impacts, his suspicions of the psychosis being innately determined were not abandoned. Kanner and his followers later adopted the position of an

169

interaction of the two theoretical causes. This later extension attributed the development of early infantile autism to the inter-action of the innate and environmental factors.

Since Kanner's original description of the autistic child, several authorities have attempted to further define, characterize, and explain the symptomology of early infantile autism (O'Gorman, 1967, Senn and Solnit, 1968, Bettelheim, 1967, Rimland, 1965, and Ferster, 1961).

O'Gorman attempted to describe this condition occurring be-cause a "vulnerable child" was born into an extremely stressing environment or, as he states, "this condition could possibly be an attempt by a normal brain to adapts itself defensively against an excessively stressful environment."

Bettelheim (1967), in his text on autism, alludes to the autistic anlage which ". . . is the conviction that one's own efforts have no power to influence the world, because of the earlier conviction that the world is insensitive to one's reactions." He emphasizes the role of the parent in relation to "critical stages" in the devel-opment of the child. Weiland and Rudnik (1961) similarly point out ". . . the symptom (referring to autism) may be created by a lack of exposure to or absence of crucial experience in the first six months of infancy."

The official nomenclature of the American Psychiatric Asso-ciation defines functional psychoses as those "disorders of psy-chogenic origin or without clearly defined physical cause or structural change in the brain." The functional psychoses of adults are at best only partly understood, but they are better recog-nized and studied than the functional psychoses of children. Even so, the absence of a clearly defined physical cause or structural change in the brain may only mean that as yet we are unable to detect any changes. Some children and adults develop functional psychoses without evidence of exaggerated pathogenic factors of an emotional nature. Future research will undoubtedly clarify the roles of emotions, constitution, heredity, endocrines, and auton-omics. However, at the present time we only know that there is a group of psychotic children whose mental aberrations do not stem from any demonstrable physical malfunction of the central nervous system.

Description

The description of the autistic child is held by most writers and diagnosticians as an empty child, or a very sensitive individual, or a child with an inability to relate to his environment, or a disoriented child. Earl describes autism as "... individuals who are not interested in their surroundings; and are often solitary, sometimes morose, refuse to mix with others and tend to conceal themselves under tables or in corners. The head is often bowed, or the coat pulled over the face; or the child may sit in the intrauterine position."

It is important for one to remember that there are different levels of autism. Most of the characteristics of the child who is autistic are clearly observable but will vary in degree. Some of the most common characteristics are listed below.

Observable Characteristics of the Autistic Child

1. No anticipatory posture at nursing
2. No reaching out gestures
3. Mother not perceived by the child
4. No smiling responses
5. Show hyperactivity and hypermobility
6. Lack of normal language development
7. Intense isolation, withdrawal and confusion
8. Self-sufficient and content if left alone
9. Dancing, spinning and twirling movements
10. Little sense of physical danger
11. Fascinated with rhythmic and music patterns
12. Temper tantrums
13. Good motor coordination
14. Little sex-oriented interest
15. Child is usually attractive and hard to please

The diagnosis of autism can sometimes be readily recognized. The autistic child will exhibit failure to relate to parents and others, deficiencies in speech development, a history of normal development, and an obsession to maintain the same environment. These individuals have sometimes been associated with being mentally retarded, which is usually not true. The autistic child does not have the facial characteristics of a retarded individual, but rather a look of deep meditation and intelligence (Bakwin and Bakwin, 1963).

Some symptoms and characteristics remain unilaterally accepted among professional disciplines. Such characteristics exhibit the inability to relate to people and to different situations in their immediate and vicarious environments. This child shows extreme aloneness and withdrawal, language disturbance, obsessiveness, eating disturbances, motility and bizarre posturing. Even in early life the child shows signs of wanting to be alone; he is unusually apathetic or cold to responses made by parents and aspirations of isolation and withdrawal. One strong indication of autism is that of subducting from anything that disarranges his isolation. This may include people, toys, and sometimes food. One interesting characteristic of the autistic child is his ability to relate well to objects. Even though he sometimes completely disregards his parents, he relates well with objects.

Rimland explains in his text that a child with autism is grossly impaired in a function basic to all cognition — the ability to relate new stimuli to remembered experience. This individual has a great amount of difficulty with or cannot relate to nor think in terms of abstractions. Symbols, concepts, or analogies cannot be readily understood by the individual afflicted with this major personality disorder.

Compulsive mannerisms such as sock-pulling, nose-picking, and grunting are also common symptoms. Grimacing is almost a routine symptom. Mannerisms and attitudes, often of the most bizarre nature, are very common. The head may be rotated a little and sit at an odd angle on the shoulders, which makes them unevenly disposed. The hands in repose are held in odd positions, perhaps with the fingers at different angles, and the wrists unduly flexed. The child may sit for long periods with the trunk bent forward or sideways in an uncomfortable position. Pulling the lips up into a snout, narrowing the eyes, or looking upward and sideways are among facial mannerisms seen, and the most important is *looking through* a person — gazing at him with apparently unseeing eyes with no evidence of any kind of emotion.

At birth and for the first few months thereafter the autistic infant develops normally except for an unusual amount of crying and the presence of a feeding problem. Around four or five months after birth the child may start banging his head in the crib and taking unusual positions in the crib and while being held; there is also noticeable rigidity of the child's body when touched. Coffey and Wiener (1967) point out that "after about 18 months and older, the parents will become quite concerned about the child's compulsion to have his environment left alone and unchanged, desire for aloneness, and ritualistic play." The autistic child, as stated earlier, has a great desire for routine and exactness of his atmosphere. This individual is so obsessed with routine and exactness that he sometimes reacts violently to changes.

Rimland (1964) reported that failure to pattern or to schedule toilet training and feeding are two major problems which cause parents to seek professional help. Toilet problems are not uncommon of the autistic individual. Autistic children have been known to have early toilet training, then completely lose it within a few years. Rimland also states that feeding problems are almost the rule. It has been observed that some of these children eat very little while others have tremendous appetites. One example of a feeding problem was a child who would not drink a liquid unless it was a precise temperature. Another example of a feeding problem was a child who loved chocolate candy, but would only eat it if it were cut into squares; round chocolates were not touched (Creak, 1953).

Another ability the autistic individual possesses that could help rule out mental retardation is good motor coordination and manual dexterity. Rothenberg (1960) remarked that one boy, at the age of fourteen months, could catch a ball with either hand. He could also throw the ball within an inch or two of an adult's hand from all the way across a room. Another boy at twelve years was taught the numbers on a typewriter. He could, without error, type a series to 1,000 at sixty words per minute.

The motor development of the child afflicted with autism is strange. Parents have reported that many are late walkers, but unlike normal children walk firmly and steadily right away. This very possibly could show the child's characteristic or nonrelation with people or parents whereas the unafflicted child shows dependence upon his parents for guidance.

Many autistic children function as mentally defective children. However, it is very important to distinguish them from the usual mental retardates since they occasionally demonstrate increments in intellectual ability and function adequately.

Mental retardation is a very unlikely diagnosis of autism. Due to the fact that autistic children have amazing memories, good spatial relationship, undelayed motor ability, and sudden walking as if they could have done it sooner, defective mentality is a very unlikely associated disorder (Rimland, 1964). The amazing memory of the autistic child contributes to the fact that he can tell when his surroundings have been tampered with or his environment has been upset.

The symbiotic infantile psychosis first described by Mahler (1952) is a functional psychosis of childhood which usually appears during the second, third, or fourth years of life. Its onset is more dramatic than that of early infantile autism because there has been more ego development. The symptoms are also somewhat different.

The roots of this psychosis lie in the so-called symbiotic phase of development, which is that period of ego growth following the autistic phase. It begins at about three months of age and is slowly replaced during the next two years by the separation-individuation phase. As the child begins to crawl, to walk and to talk he also begins to diminish this symbiotic relationship and becomes more of a separate individual. The normal child is able to accomplish this emotional and physical separation successfully; the child with a symbiotic psychosis is not.

Motor skills and language appeared at the proper times. The onset, as well as the symptomatology of a symbiotic psychosis varies, but initial regression is a prominent characteristic. The youngster begins to show increasing dependency upon his mother with exaggerated anxiety or even panic during her absences. His speech becomes less expressive and more difficult to understand. Neologisms may appear. His thinking begins to show evidences of primary process in that it is illogical and incoherent. Posturing and grimacing may occur. The child has difficulty maintaining contact with reality and wanders into flights of fantasy from which he cannot be recalled.

The history shows that up until the traumatic event, the child seemed to be progressing adequately. At some time, usually during his second to fourth year of life, a situation develops which threatens the symbiotic mother-child relationship. This crisis is often the birth of a sibling, but it may be illness of a parent or any other sudden upheaval in family life. The child's inadequate ego is unable to tolerate the trauma, and psychosis results.

Sleeping and eating habits become disturbed, and toilet training, although previously established, begins to break down and enuresis or encopresis may appear. This entire process may consume several months or it may be much more rapid. By the time the psychosis is well developed, the youngster is no longer able to mix successfully with his contemporaries. He has lost interest in most of the things that a child of his age would enjoy. It has become difficult if not impossible for him to carry on a logical conversation because he cannot maintain contact with reality nor relate normally to anyone. New situations are apt to produce overwhelming anxiety, and he clings tearfully to his mother. He lives an extremely inhibited life, remaining in the house and sticking close to his mother.

In evaluating the prognosis, the history of ego development is important. The psychotic four-year-old who is apparently without speech but who has a history of having achieved useful speech and some ability to relate in the past has a more favorable prognosis than a child with a history of completely autistic development.

Language Characteristics

Another characteristic of the autistic personality is the inability to use and to facilitate language. Speech and language form the means by which the child acquires socialization. The adjustment of the child to people and to objects in his immediate environment is accomplished through the mediation of language, both oral and written. A lack of socialization and communication forms one of the hallmarks of the emotionally disturbed child (Karlin, Karlin, and Gurren, 1973).

Probably the one feature of autistic children which is detected first and which is probably the best and most reliable indicator is the autistic child's reaction to sound, particularly speech. People often think that an autistic child is deaf because he tends to ignore very loud sounds (Wing, 1972).

Once parents begin to realize that their child's behavior and personality are not adequate, they almost always, without exception, consider the possibility of a hearing defect. The consideration of a hearing defect is attributed to the child's reaction to the spoken word. "A young autistic child's response to speech is just as unusual as the way he reacts to other sounds. He seems unaware that speech has a meaning, although he may attend if he hears one of the few words he knows that are linked with things he likes, 'sweet,' 'dinner,' 'orange drink' " (Wing, 1972).

Sometimes parents will abandon this idea when the child repeats part of a song or repeats some phrases that have been spoken to him at an earlier date. After this thought is abandoned, the next likely diagnosis by parents will be mental retardation.

Autistic children often show characteristically poor relationships to the human elements in their environments. As the autistic children may ignore speech, they quite often ignore people who speak to them. "The autistic child pays no attention to persons or to the activity of people around him. Kanner states that parents of autistic children refer to them as always having been 'self-sufficient,' 'like in a shell,' 'happiest when left alone' " (Karlin et al., 1973).

The normal individual learns from every experience and from his contact with different areas of our society. Each of these experiences contributes or helps to construct the world in which one lives. The autistic child who cannot think abstractly, integrate experiences, and cope with nonisolated experiences has difficulty developing a strong and healthy ego.

Since the autistic individual does not respond to people, he finds no use in developing communication (verbalization) skills. The demonstration of his desire to remain apart from people indicates his failure to develop and use language sufficiently. Research has indicated that some individuals remain aphonic several years after language is normally acquired. It also denotes that this type of child does not enjoy speaking and therefore speaks very little. Some autistic children never speak, but remain mute all their lives. Others (more than half) do learn to say at least a few words, although they almost always begin much later than normal (Wing, 1972). The classical case entails the child who learned to say a few words or was talking almost normally at the age of two and a half, and whose speech then stopped improving, the child talking less and less until in the end only a few words or none at all were left. Many of these affected children understand everything that is said to them, and one knows that they could talk perfectly well if they wanted to. The child does not learn to speak in monosyllables like *mama* and *dada* and *car*, but will remain mute until his emotional state has reached a point at which he is ready to resume speech.

The speaking characteristics of those autistic children who do speak are a mixture of features which seem to suggest a lack of abstracting ability, poor word understanding, and echolalia.

The children (who do speak) often muddle the order of letters inside words and may say acitt for attic, diccifult for difficult, pasghetti for spaghetti. The order of words in sentences may be reversed, for example "Put bed on blanket." "Have strawberry shake milk" (Wing, 1972).

Austic children, even those few who make good progress in speaking, cannot use words flexibly or to express subtle ideas. They tend to learn one meaning only for a word or a whole phrase and stick to that (Wing, 1972).

A very interesting and often-noted characteristic of autistic children's verbal language is their tendency toward echolalia, both immediate and delayed. An autistic child may repeat phrases he hears from other people with the correct pronunciation, accent, and tone of voice that was used by the original speaker. However, when the autistic child tries to say things which he has thought out for himself, his pronunciation may be very poor indeed (Wing, 1972).

A very interesting and seemingly contradictory element of some autistic children is their peculiar use of language.

> One of the most striking characteristics of early infantile autism
> is the baffling use of language by those autistic children who use

speech. Because of his early speech, the child is frequently regarded as being highly precocious or 'a budding genius.' Words are learned with great rapidity in these cases, and sometimes the child is suddenly found to be using complete sentences at one year of age, even before the component words have been used singly (Rimland, 1964).

Spending childhood in an intellectual atmosphere and with intelligent parents, the parents sometimes try to promote precociousness in their child. The autistic child, by having excellent rote memory, has often led parents to stuff him with more and more scientific data, names of great composers, leaders in intellectual fields, and the like. Language of this sort has not been used for meaningful and purposeful communication, but as a meaningless, valueless distorted memory exercise. Some of the speaking autistic children have both quantity and quality vocabularies and excellent memories for music, names, and dates.

An autistic child often has difficulty in controlling the loudness of his voice. He finds it hard to produce a smooth flow of speech, his voice goes up and down in the wrong places, and his voice may have a mechanical quality (Wing, 1972). It is pointed out that "The speech is generally of a peculiar noncommunicative kind, however, and is ordinarily produced in an empty high-pitched parrotlike monotone. Whispering is very common, little or no expression is used, and, as it generally turns out, the speech is elicited only as specific responses to certain stimuli, and not as a means of communication" (Rimland, 1964).

In Bruno Bettelheim's excellent, if rambling, long book on autism, *The Empty Fortress,* language development of these children is examined at great length. One facet of the language of autistic children which Bettelheim notes and stresses as being peculiar to these children is their use and misuse of personal pronouns. Bettelheim (1967) says, "Nearly all reports mention that where autistic children talk at all they do not use the pronoun 'I.' Kanner called this phenomenon 'pronominal reversal' — where the child uses the pronoun 'you,' but correct grammar would require the 'I.' "

An example of this would be the use of *you* for *I* in speaking. When spoken by the autistic child, he would say, "You want to go to the bathroom, you want to eat, or you want a drink?" It is held by one author that autism could be a deficiency in ego development. This would account for his inability to use *I*. Bettelheim described a *typical* autistic child. He said, "While he (the child) never came out of his autism, he began after a while to use personal pronouns in reverse, as do most autistic children. He referred to himself as 'you' and to the adult he was speaking to as 'I.' A year later he called his therapist by name, though still not addressing her as 'you' but saying, 'Want Miss M. to swing you' " (Bettelheim, 1967).

In the same text, Bettelheim also notes a peculiar tendency of autistic children to avoid the word *yes* as much as they avoid the word *I*.

Kanner is quoted in *The Silent Fortress*:

> "Yes" is a concept that takes the children many years to acquire. They are incapable of using it as a general symbol of assent. One child learned to say "yes" when his father told him that he would put him on his shoulders if he would say "yes." This word then came to "mean" only the desire to be put on his father's shoulders. It took many months before he could detach the word "yes" from this specific situation, and it took much longer before he was able to use it as a general term of affirmation (Bettelheim, 1967).

There is now a considerable amount of evidence in support of the view that infantile autism arises on the basis of a developmental perceptual disorder, in particular a disorder of language involving defects in comprehension. Retardation of speech and language is an almost invariable manifestation in infantile autism, and a lack of response to sounds is frequently the first symptom to be noted (Kugelmass, 1970).

The autistic child functions as a mental retardate, aggravated by social withdrawal at a period when the mind develops rapidly through inquisitiveness, interest, and experience. He loses the benefits of the stimulus equivalence of infancy with loss of perceptual constancy, loss of differential sensitivity of faces, loss of sequential display of anticipatory responses, loss of repetitive exploratory behavior, and loss of sensorimotor intelligence during the period of language deprivation. Later, there is further failure to develop communication and referential language because of self-imposed mutism with loss of benefit from the preconceptual stage devoted to the development of symbolic images for depicting the world (Kugelmass, 1970).

Implications of Language Development

In a study by Kanner and Eisenberg (1955) following forty-two patients from four to nineteen years after first observation, they found that speech disturbances in early years have useful prognostic implications.

Of nineteen children who did not talk at around four years of age, eighteen were still withdrawn in their shells and exhibited to lay observers traits of feeblemindedness. Seven of these children were at home in a helpless state, two were in hospitals for the insane, and seven were in institutions for the mentally defective. Only one of the nineteen patients was able to function in school.

In the same study, twenty-three speaking children seemed to do somewhat better. Ten of the twenty-three did poorly; of these, five were state hospital patients, three were in hospital schools for retarded children, one was on a farm, and one was at home. The remaining thirteen patients of the speaking group were able to function to a high degree at home and in the community and were able to maintain a continuous contact with reality.

When discussing language development of emotionally disturbed children, especially children who are extremely disturbed, it is important to note two points about this topic. First, language development or the lack of it is one of the primary indicators of the condition of emotional disturbance. Second, there is considerable professional dispute over specific emotional nomenclature and the nature of the disturbances.

There is disagreement over the nature of autism and childhood schizophrenia. Some authorities claim that autism is a form of childhood schizophrenia. However, for the purposes of this paper, autism and childhood schizophrenia will be approached as being related, but separate syndromes.

This position is supported by professional opinion. Kanner stresses the separation of autism and schizophrenia. He states,

"This differentiation relies upon a difference between the ages of the problems onset (DeMeyer, et al., 1971).

Some further differences between autism and childhood schizophrenia are that the sex ratio of autism is preponderently greater in males over females; childhood schizophrenia tends to occur statistically equally in the sexes; and a difference in the social class of the parents of autistic and schizophrenic children exists. Parents of autistic children tend to show a higher intelligence level than the general population and to be in such professions as teaching, medicine and law. The parents of schizophrenic children tend to be from a level common to the general population (DeMeyer et al., 1971).

Childhood schizophrenia characteristically exhibits itself at a somewhat later date than autism, which is often present from a preverbal stage. Sources almost universally agree that childhood schizophrenia is seen after the beginning development of speech by the child.

In childhood schizophrenia, language disruptions of a different nature than those of autism occur. Often, these children do use language while the classic autistic child may remain mute for life.

> Very early, schizophrenic children show a tendency to dissociate sign from function in their use of language. They have an exaggerated often obsessive interest in word forms detached from the emotional and intellectual content which these forms normally carry. They are prone to play with words which are either too difficult or abstract for children of their age, or words which are not relevant to the interests of young normal children (Despert, 1968).

A common characteristic of the language development of schizophrenic children is their tendency to create new words which carry meaning to themselves only and which may have considerable emotional content.

> Schizophrenic children frequently coin words, the meaning of which is peculiar to themselves, although not necessarily unintelligible when the background of the neologism is known. Their need spontaneously to communicate with the outside world by means of accepted conventional signs is limited; and

under such conditions, language structures are likely to develop
without regard to semantic rules and usage (Despert, 1968).

This tendency to make new words and phrases is frequently a
characteristic of these children. "The language of the group designated as schizophrenic would seem to show a greater tendency
to marked individual variations and a tendency to push the variation to the extreme of incomprehensibility" (Vetter, 1968).

Instead of the disruption of language serving as a basis of similarity in these children, it functions primarily in the opposite
way.

> With schizophrenic patients, scrutiny of language leads less
> to an awareness of similarity within a group. It emphasizes
> more sharply the individual differences within a group.
>
> The language of a schizophrenic child often appears to satisfy
> the speaker in that he is expressing his thought in the kind of
> words personally endowed with meaning . . .
>
> Schizophrenic language appears to function as a mode of
> expression rather than communication, as a mode of presenta-
> tion rather than representation (Vetter, 1968).

It might be mentioned here that normal children often play
games which involve the use of nonsense words and the formulation of new words (particularly secret words). However, there is a
difference, and a very important one between the word games of
normal children and the word formulation of schizophrenic children.

The difference between normal children's nonsensical talk,
which is a game, and a schizophrenic child's neologisms is principally the absence of playfulness in the schizophrenic child, giving
the activity its dissociated character. So the schizophrenic child
does not *play* with words for the fun of the sounds, but rather
makes and pronounces strange words which have profound and
serious meaning for him, and this is no laughing matter.

It may be stated, and evidence exists to support the statement,
that schizophrenic children do not rely upon the actual sound of
what they say to regulate what they say and how they say it. In
fact, these children really are affected very little by the sound of
their words.

In an experiment designed to compare the auditory monitoring
of normal children as opposed to children diagnosed as being

schizophrenic, William Goldfarb, through the use of head-phones, delayed the hearing of the child's speech by himself for one-half second. He writes,

> In normal children, the interference with self-monitoring by delaying the feedback of the individual's own voice almost always causes mild to moderate deterioration in voice and speech. In the case of schizophrenic children, the absence of such deterioration of voice and speech under conditions of delayed feedback has been interpreted as evidence of diminished use of auditory feedback as a self-monitoring tool (Goldfarb, 1974).

One often-noted characteristic of schizophrenic children is their memory for certain items. Schizophrenics have excellent memories for seemingly meaningless material, e.g. they may reproduce long TV commercials or unexpectedly and spontaneously produce words and sentences of a highly complex structure.

Behaviorism and Language Therapy

A somewhat different view of the symptomatology of autism is presented by researchers whose perspective is behavioral analysis. The authorities from behavioral analysis contend that there is insufficient and inconclusive evidence supporting the development of autism being caused by genetic and other constitutional etiologies. They contend that the behaviors which do frequently characterize autism are in fact learned behaviors which are supported, controlled, and reinforced by the environment. By the use of behavioral principles they have determined that the autistic child has a very limited repertoire of appropriate verbal responses which he emits on an infrequent level. Therefore, the available responses that he has will be either repetitious or emitted at inappropriate times and irrelevant to the context in which they are exhibited.

Those who support this notion have adopted a theoretical learning approach to change the autistic behaviors and to instill new behaviors in the child. These authorities have used either positive reinforcement (Ferster, 1961, and Ferster and DeMeyer, 1961, 1962) or have explored the use of discomfort or aversive therapy (Lovaas, 1968 and Lovaas et al., 1965).

Lovaas (1968) has been extremely successful in the shaping of new behaviors in autistic children with specific conditioning procedures. The most relevant behaviors that Lovaas and his co-workers have been able to shape are those which involve speech and communication. The following statements summarize the results that Lovaas has found through the use of his procedures:

1. Self-destructive behavior can be extinguished by withdrawing interpersonal contact contingent on its emission.
2. Self-destructive and tantrum behavior can be extinguished by the use of painful electric shock contingent on its emission.
3. Echolalic speech is decreased and appropriate speech is increased when adult attention is presented only for appropriate speech.
4. Appropriate social and verbal behavior seems to exist in an inverse ratio of self-destructive behavior and psychotic speech because, when appropriate behavior begins to strengthen under reinforcement, inappropriate behavior decreases without any direct application of reinforcement techniques.

As discussed earlier, language inadequacy represents a central deficit of the severely disturbed autistic child. The apparent failure in the development of functional speech is an especially important diagnostic behavior pattern. Browning (1971), for example, adopted the behavioral criteria of (1) an absence of spontaneous communicative speech, (2) a failure to develop attentional sets to verbal commands, and (3) the failure to follow verbal commands as important indices of the diagnosis of autism. He further contended that language acquisition was critical to any behavioral treatment of autism.

The literature has strongly suggested that the beginning or initial objective of a behavior modification program with autistic children should be to implant or to teach functional speech (Gardner, 1974). The application of behavior modification techniques have been previously used in the reinstatement of speech among mute schizophrenics (Pawlicki et al., 1973, Wilson and Walters, 1966, and Baker, 1971), to develop imitative speech among schizophrenic children (Lovaas et al., 1966), to train autistic children in following verbal commands (Schell et al., 1967), in the treatment of elective mutism (Straughan, 1968), to shape autistic children in speaking in complete sentences (Brawley et al., 1973), and the treatment of stuttering among schizophrenic children (Browning, 1971).

The available literature has demonstrated that certain behavior management practices have been successful in the shaping of functional speech among seriously disturbed schizophrenic and autistic children. The research indicates that the training — that is behavior shaping — should occur in an orderly sequence of stages. The first stage of training of conversational or functional speech involves attention training. Attention is the prerequisite behavior necessary for future motor and vocal imitative behavior (Hartung, 1970). The shaping of attention or orienting responses may be facilitated either by the use of an intensive auditory stimulus (Look at me) or physically turning the child's head in the direction of the therapist. The attending or orienting responses are reinforced in order to maintain attending behavior for increasing intervals of time.

Only after sufficient attentional training and eye contact training has been established should the therapist advance the child into the second phase of imitation training. It has been recommended that imitation training begin initially with the child imitating motor behaviors of the behavior therapist (Gardner, 1974, Hartung, 1970, and Risley et al., 1968). It was felt that motor imitation represented a lower-ordered sequence of imitative behavior that could be shaped with the least amount of difficulty. Shaping of motor imitation hopefully affects an internal awareness that receiving reinforcement is contingent upon the duplication or imitation of motor movements used by the therapist. It is hoped that the internal awareness of reinforcement contingencies will be generalized or transferred to the vocal imitation phase of shaping. The progression of imitation proceeds in a step-wise fashion from the imitation of the therapist's gross motor movements to fine motor movements, then continues to the imitation of facial fine motor movements which are prerequisite movements necessary for vocal imitation. Eventually, verbal imitations can be shaped because of the acquisition of the earlier approximations of motor and vocal imitations (Gardner, 1974 and Nelson et al., 1968).

186 Language Development of Exceptional Children

The shaping of vocal responses frequently involves reinforcing approximations of the vocal sound. Early approximations may involve the manual positioning of the child's lips to aid in the vocalization of a *visible sound*. For example, the formation of the vocal sounds of b and m are much more animated and, therefore, more visible than the sounds such as d, ng, and n (Lovaas et al., 1966, 1968, Hewett, 1965, Nelson and Evans, 1968, and Sulzbacher, 1972). Eventually the therapist can fade the lip positioning technique required to initially prompt the response as the child becomes more dependent on his own positioning to produce the sound (Risley and Wolf, 1967 and Sherman, 1965).

It is recommended that the therapist avoid the shaping of those sounds which have only auditory stimulus values. Such sounds would include the l, k, s, and t.

After the child has acquired many of the vocal sounds and has acquired some new words, the shaping of functional speech continues into imitation of verbal responses of the therapist, labeling of objects, giving appropriate responses to verbal commands, speaking in complete sentences (Brawley et al., 1973) and continuing to conversational speech.

Hartung (1970) indicated that it was commonly observed that nonverbal autistic children may, during the imitation phase of therapy, develop echolalia. Echolalia might be observed in the child's tendency to duplicate or imitate words or phrases. Echolalia may be found to be immediate or delayed. Immediate echolalia implies the imitation of a word or short phrase immediately after the child hears it, whereas delayed echolalia may be manifested by the child's repeating of a word or a phrase after the passage of a considerable interval of time (Premack and Premack, 1974 and Kanner, 1944).

BIBLIOGRAPHY

Baker, R.: The use of operant conditioning to reinstate speech in mute schizophrenics. *Behav Res Ther*, 9:329-36, 1971.

Bakwin, Harry, and Bakwin, Ruth: *Clinical Management of Behavior Disorders in Children*, 2nd Ed. Philadelphia, Saunders, 1963.

Bettelheim, Bruno: *The Empty Fortress: Infantile Autism and the Birth of the Self*. New York, Free Pr, 1967.

Brawley, E. R. et al.: Behavior modification of an autistic child. In Stedman, J. M., Patton, W. F., and Walton, K. F. (Eds.): *Clinical Studies in Behavior Therapy with Children, Adolescents and Their Families*. Springfield, Thomas, 1973.

Browning, R. M.: Behavior therapy for stuttering in a schizophrenic child. In Graziano, A. M.: *Therapy with Children*. Chicago, Aldine, 1971.

Coffey, Herbert S., and Wiener, L. L.: *Group Treatment of Autistic Children*. Englewood Cliffs, P-H, 1967.

Creak, Mildred: Discussion: Psychoses in childhood. *Proc R Soc Med, 45*:797-800, 1953.

DeMeyer, Marian, K. et al.: In Churchill, Don W., Alpern, Gerald D., and DeMeyer, Marian K. (Eds.): *Infantile Autism*. Springfield, Thomas, 1971.

Despert, J. Louise: *Schizophrenia in Children*. New York, Robert Brunner, 1968.

Ferster, C.B.: Positive reinforcement and behavioral deficits of autistic children. *Child Devel, 32*:437-456, 1961.

Ferster, C. B., and DeMeyer, Marian K.: The development of performances in autistic children in an automatically controlled environment. *J Chronic Dis, 13*:319-45, 1961.

Ferster, C.B., and DeMeyer, Marian K.: A method for the experimental analysis of the behavior of autistic children. *Am J Orthopsychiatry, 32*:89-98, 1962.

Gardner, William I.: *Children with Learning and Behavior Problems*. Boston, Allyn, 1974.

Goldfarb, William: *Growth and Change of Schizophrenic Children*. Washington, V. H. Winston and Sons, 1974.

Hartung, Jurgen R.: A review of procedures to increase verbal imitation and skills and functional speech in autistic children. *J Speech Hear Disord, 35*(3):203-215, 1970.

Hewett, F. M.: Teaching speech to an autistic child through operant conditioning. *Am J Orthopsychiatry, 35*:927-936, 1965.

Kanner, L.: Early infantile autism. *J Pediatrics, 25*:211, 1944.

Kanner, L., and Eisenberg, L.: *Psychopathology of Childhood*. New York, Grune, 1955.

Karlin, Isaac W., Karlin, David B., and Gurren, Louise: *Development and Disorders of Speech in Childhood*. Springfield, Thomas, 1973.

Kugelmass, J. Newton: *The Autistic Child*. Springfield, Thomas, 1970.

Lovaas, I.: Acquisition of imitative speech by schizophrenic children. *Science, 151*:705-707, 1966.

Lovaas, I.: A program for the establishment of speech in psychotic children. In Sloane, H., and MacAulay, B. D. (Eds.): *Operant Procedures in Remedial Speech and Language Training*. Boston, HM, 1968, pp.125-152.

Lovaas, I., et al.: Building social behavior in autistic children by use of electric shock. *J Exp Res Pers, 1*:99-109, 1965.

Mahler, Margaret: On child psychosis and schizophrenia. *The Psychoanalytic Study of the Child*. New York, Intl Univs Pr, 1952, vol. VII.

Nelson, Rosemary O., and Evans, Ian M.: The combination of learning principles and speech therapy techniques in the treatment of non-communicating children. *J Child Psychol Psychiatry, 9*:111-124, 1968.

O'Gorman, Gerald: *The Nature of Autism.* New York, Appleton, 1967.

Pawlicki, R. E., et al.: Increasing verbalization of chronic mental patients with operant techniques: Partial replication. *Percept Mot Skills, 37*:205-206, 1973.

Premack, David, and Premack, Ann James: Teaching visual learning to apes and language-deficient persons. In Schiefelbusch, Richard L., and Lloyd, Lyle L. (Eds.): *Language Perspectives — Acquisition, Retardation and Intervention.* Baltimore, Univ Park, 1974.

Rimland, B.: *Infantile Autism.* New York, Appleton, 1964.

Rimland, Bernard: Infantile Autism: The syndrome and its implcations for a neural theory of behavior. *Am J Ment Defic, 69*(4):4, January, 1965.

Risley, T., and Wolf, M.: Establishing functional speech in echolalic children. *Behav Res Ther, 5*:73-88, 1967.

Rothenberg, Mira: The rebirth of Johnny. *Harper's Magazine,* Feb., 1960, 57-66.

Schell, R. E., et al.: Development of language behavior in an autistic child. *J Speech Hear Disord, 32*:51-64, 1967.

Senn, Milton, J. E., and Solnit, Albert J.: *Problems in Child Behavior and Development.* Philadelphia, Lea and Febiger, 1968.

Sherman, J. A.: Use of reinforcement and imitation to Reinstate Verbal Behavior in Mute Psychotics. *J Abnorm Psychol, 5*:155-164, 1965. ·

Straughan, J. H.: The application of operant conditioning to the treatment of elective mutism. In Sloane, H. N., and MacAulay, B. D. (Ed.): *Operant Procedures in Remedial Speech and Language Training.* Boston, HM, 1968.

Sulzbacher, Stephen: A behavior strategy for language of a child with autistic behaviors. *J Speech Hear Disord, 35*:256-276, 1972.

Vetter, Harold J.: *Language Behavior in Schizophrenia.* Springfield, Thomas, 1968.

Weiland, I. H., and Rudnik, H. L.: Consideration of the development and treatment of autistic childhood psychosis. *Psychoanalytic Study of the Child.* New York, Intl Univs Pr, 1961, vol. XVI.

Wilson, F. S., and Waters, R. H.: Modification of speech output of near mute schizophrenics through social learning procedures. *Behav Res Ther, 4*:59-61, 1966.

Wing, Lorna: *Autistic Children.* New York, Brunner-Mazel, 1972.

Chapter 9

SPEECH IRREGULARITIES

WHEN writing about speech irregularities one must determine whether the child's speech pattern does indeed constitute an irregularity. If we use some definitions of speech handicaps we would have to say that accents and dialects constitute a speech handicap. These two conditions would constitute a handicap only if they deviate so far from the speech of other children that they call attention to themselves. Emerick and Hatten (1974) suggest that the following three aspects of the communicative act are very important in defining defective speech: "the acoustic characteristics of the individual's speech signal; the influence of the message; and finally, the handicapping condition that results from the first two aspects."

The acoustic signal would deal with the physical characteristics of one speech, pitch, tone, etc. — in other words, quality. The two authors mentioned above then look at how the quality of the child's voice affects the intelligibility of the message and, finally, how the quality and intelligibility of the message cause a handicap.

Speech and oral communication are the primary tools by which an individual relates to others in the world around him. Speech involves more than the ability to make sounds or to pronounce words; it calls for the assimilation of sounds into words, followed by a combination of words into units which make a meaningful whole. Therefore, speech becomes the basic tool which assists in developing a formalized language. It is the result of visual, auditory, kinesthetic and perceptual experiences and has as its aim the conveyance of an assembly of ideas to a listener.

The child having a speech handicap has always functioned adequately in the regular classroom, assuming of course he does not have other handicaps. Specialists should be available to help the speech-handicapped child in the regular and special classrooms and also to help the teachers work with speech problems.

Since the early history of man, society has been concerned with human communication. All societies use vocalizations in communicating, even though some societies do not have written forms of language.

The concern for individuals having defective speech predates man's concern for normal speech. As early as 340 B.C. man was trying to find a *cure* for stuttering. This concern, which began hundreds of years ago, has reached down through the ages to our present time.

Speech and the need to express ourselves adequately are of paramount importance in this most vocal of worlds. An agile tongue is to be envied. Oral speech forms the very core of our communication with our peers. It is something upon which we rely practically every day of our lives. The ordinary business of life presents many opportunities for the use of oral communication, and not only is it a transmissive thing, psychologists have shown that the ability to *think aloud* has become an economic necessity. We win and lose jobs, not on how little or how much we know, but rather on how well we are able to *sell* ourselves and our talents.

Obviously, then, there is a large responsibility on us as parents, teachers, and specialists in the field of speech to see that every child has the opportunity to develop his speech skills to the fullest — a facility which our society so highly regards both in school and in later life. And since these skills are a product of the learning process, it is only natural that many will fall by the wayside as the result of some hinderance. These latter ones will be the focal point of our discussion.

Since this chapter concerns correcting speech defects, it is deemed necessary to preface all remarks with a few facts and statistics concerning disorders of speech.

Recognizing Speech Disorders

In order to correct speech defects one must be able to recognize speech disorders. Let us consider, "What is a speech defect?" According to Van Riper (1963), speech is defective "when it deviates so far from the speech of other people that it calls attention to itself, interferes with communication, or causes its possessor to be maladjusted." Or, condensing this somewhat, we might say that speech is defective when it is conspicuous, unintelligible, or unpleasant.

Berry and Eisenson (1956), include in their definition, an additional subjective aspect. They propose that speech may be considered defective when the speaker becomes excessively self-conscious or apprehensive about objectively small deviations, or assumed deviation, however small, becomes a significant defect if it interferes with the speaker's social adjustment. We could sum it up in one sentence — Speech is defective when it deviates. But who is to judge? The cultural norms of society really determine how deviant speech must be before it is conspicuous. For example, we would not consider a child of three who said wabbit for rabbit as having a speech defect, whereas it would be uncommon among adults. Defective speech is characterized in the following descriptions (Barry and Eisenson, 1956):

1. It is not easily audible.
2. It is not readily intelligible.
3. It is vocally unpleasant.
4. It deviates in respect to specific sound (consonant, vowel, or diphthong) production.
5. It is labored in production.
6. It is linguistically deficient.
7. It is inappropriate to the speaker in terms of age, sex, and physical development.
8. It is visibly unpleasant.

Types of Speech Disorders

As one can easily see, it is apparent that much can be wrong with the manner in which an individual speaks. In fact, the range of defects is so wide, Van Riper (1963) has conveniently divided them into four categories: articulation, time (or rhythm), voice, and symbolization (language). It would help the reader understand corrective techniques better if we review briefly speech disorders in general. For this we will select one classification and describe corrective measures. It is far beyond the scope of the chapter to discuss them all.

Articulation

Under disorders of articulation we include all those disorders characterized by the substitution, omission, addition, and distortion of the speech sounds. A child who omits the *s* might say, "In the 'ummer I like to 'wim, 'kate, and ride my bi'ycle." One who makes additions would say, "My umburella is bluack and grueen." There are several concomitant terms related to these disorders, namely *baby talk*, sometimes called infantile perservation and characterized by sound substitutions during the early stages of child development; *lalling*, which is due to sluggishness of the tongue tip and characterized by defective *a, l, t, d*, or *s* sounds; *lisping*, a disorder of the *s* and *z* sounds (a frequent one); *delayed speech*, unintelligible consonants; and *oral inaccuracy*, a general term for any mild articulatory defect. One must keep in mind that these defects do not always occur independently, but may appear jointly in an individual's speech. For example, a laller may also lisp or a lisper may talk baby talk.

Many people tend to overlook articulatory defects as being serious, and some even think that they are cute in children. Although most children outgrow their speech difficulties, there are many who do not. Of the 5 percent of children having serious speech defects, 3 percent of the total have problems of articulation (ASHA Committee on the Midcentury White House Conference, 1952). One estimate states that there are approximately 120,000 children of school age that have functional articulatory defects (Berry and Eisenson, 1956). This figure justifies therapy. In working with speech defects, the number of articulatory errors is sometimes so great that the speech is nothing more than an unintelligible jargon (idioglessia). Corrective procedures for articulatory errors will be discussed later.

Time and Rhythm

The second major category of disorders is that of time and

rhythm. We speak language in a sequential pattern in that sound follows sound, syllable follows syllable. When something disrupts the spontaneous flow of speech to the degree that it is conspicuous, unpleasant, or unintelligible, we have a disorder of time. A prime example is stuttering, a disorder which has affected men through the ages and ranks second after articulatory disorders. About 280,000 school-age children are gripped by this perplexing problem. An interesting thing about stuttering is that it seems to be more of a communicative disorder than one of speech. Must stutterers speak fluently when alone or singing. The impediment appears while under emotional stress or while confronted with others in a speaking situation. There have been many books written on the subject, and presently several theories are being considered as to the cause or causes. Johnson (1956), an authority in the field, claims that stuttering is a symptom of psychoneurosis or is due to some physical difference. Early recognition and referral of a stutterer to a trained therapist is an excellent recommendation, for it may save much anxiety, frustration, and embarrassment in later years.

Cluttering is also a disorder of time or rhythm. Distinguished from stuttering, it is characterized by excessive speed in speaking, disorganized sentence structure, and slurred or omitted syllables and sounds.

Voice

The third category of speech defects is that of voice disorders (dysphonia). As mentioned previously, the sounds of speech may be articulated incorrectly, and the noises, sounds, and tones themselves may be defective. If so, we have a voice problem. Estimates indicate that less than 0.5 percent to more than 1 percent may have difficulties in vocalization (ASHA Committee on the Midcentury White House Conference, 1952, and Johnson, Brown, Curtis, Edney, and Keaster, 1956). Some of the possibilities for voice disorders are too-high pitch, too-low pitch, monotone, pitch breaks, and stereotyped inflections (Van Riper, 1963). There may be disorders in voice intensity or loudness and voice quality.

Examples might be voices that are too weak or too loud, hypernasal, strident falsetto, breathy, or hoarse.

Symbolization

The fourth category of disorders concerns problems of symbolic formulation and expression (dysphasia). Speech and all the language functions may be affected singly or jointly because of brain damage. Although these individuals comprise a small percentage of speech defectives, they are no less important. Aphasia is a handicap that is often difficult to diagnose. The aphasic may suffer from one or two types — (1) inability to express ideas through spoken or written language symbols (expressive) and (2) disturbance in the ability to comprehend language through spoken or written symbols (receptive) (Wepman, 1951). Therapy for aphasics presents many frustrations and challenges for the speech therapist.

Related Speech Disorders

Mention must be made of other related speech disorders. There are those of cleft palate, foreign accent, deaf and hard-of-hearing speech, and cerebral palsy. These disorders do not always appear as distinctive entities. One might have a combination of several defects. Although these latter ones comprise relatively small numbers, they, along with stuttering, present great difficulties in treatment.

Correction

With this potpourri of information it is evident that speech pathology is no simple matter. Volumes could be written on corrective techniques and methods for the above disorders. Time does not allow a comprehensive analysis of corrective measures for each disorder, however this brief look at speech disorders in general provides us a better understanding of the many types of defects and the difficulties that have befallen the speech clinician. Remarks will be restricted primarily to methods used in correction of articulatory errors, the ones most commonly found and a favorite of clinicians.

Diagnosis and Evaluation

The two most commonly used terms referring to the presumed etiology or causation of articulatory errors are dyslalia and dysarthria. The first refers to disorders of functional origin where the cause may be due to mislearning, imitation, emotional conflicts, or the like. Dysarthria implies a disorder of articulation due to impairment of the part of the central nervous system which directly controls the muscles of articulation.

Defects of articulation comprise the bulk of speech disorders. Hundreds of surveys prove this. Much to the clinicians' delight, articulatory cases respond most easily and quickly to therapy, but there are many exceptions to this rule.

Most parents want to begin immediately to correct a child who says whittle for little. They feel the child has made a mistake and should correct it. The speech clinician takes a different approach. He must come to grips with the problem. Like the detective or lawyer, he must get to the *facts*. He attempts to answer the questions: "Why does the child have articulatory errors? What are the errors?" and, finally, "What must be done to eliminate them?"

One of the first duties of the clinician in any thorough analysis is to consider the developmental factors. This is on the assumption that the child has been referred. He should explore the maturation or articulation in the child. This would come from parent interviews. All of the child's past history should be investigated to determine the origin of the problem. Any illness, accident, or abnormality in growth could be significant. The child's hearing acuity and intelligence quotient need to be known. Also it is helpful to know the amount of speech stimulation in the home and the attitude of the parents toward the defect. Often the cause is lost somewhere in the midst of speech development. An earlier cause that was highly effective in contributing to the defect may subside while the defect persists. Then, too, there is the possibility of speech being mislearned. A child may habitually say thoup because of poor teaching, and we must not forget emotional factors, often important in cases of delayed speech. This preliminary investigation and history taking is basic. Misdiagnosis is a curse to any true speech clinician.

Some parents believe that their child has faulty articulation due to organic abnormalities. Misarranged teeth, swollen tonsils, and a shortened frenum (tongue-tie) are often suspected. However, speech clinicians are usually conservative in attributing the defective sounds to organic factors (Van Riper, 1963). There are on record too many instances of good, intelligible speech when organic factors are present: there are those who have no teeth who produce all the speech sounds correctly and individuals with no tongue or with half of their tongue who speak intelligibly, so it is possible to compensate. A perfectly good *l* sound may be produced with the tongue-tip down or even outside the mouth. The difference lies in the extra effort in learning to overcome these obstacles. This does not mean that the clinician should discount organic deviations entirely, but he should consider them along with the many other possible causes.

Modern surgery has done wonders in the reconstruction of dental, palatal, and jaw structures. Although most undertakings of this sort are tremendously expensive, it is the duty of the clinician to refer those with marked mouth deformities to these specialists. Especially in cases of severe organic defects in children, the speech clinician should convince the parents of the need for corrective measures. One way is to point out the social maladjustment which such defects may produce.

Another important factor in any satisfactory diagnosis is a complete phonetic analysis of the individual's speech. This is vitally important for therapy. Van Riper (1963) gives three major objectives in making a phonic analysis: "(1) find the sounds which are defective; (2) the type of error in terms of substitution, omission, insertion, or distortion; and (3) the location of the error within the word (initial, medial, or final)." This gives us an idea of which sound or sounds are defective and how much ear training is needed. It helps the therapist understand better the scope of the problem. You ask, "What method do you use to find these errors?" Most therapists use a standard picture articulation test. For adults, special phonetically structured sentences are often used. One of the best is the Developmental Picture Articulation Test by

Henja. The Bryngleson and Glaspey Picture Articulation Test is also widely used among speech therapists. The pictures are arranged in sequential order of the development of consonant sounds. They begin with the plosives (*p*, *b*) and run through the completion of the blends like *sl*ed and um*br*ella. After gaining rapport with the child, he is asked to say aloud the pictures. On a scoring blank the therapist records phonetically any misarticulated sound, whether it is at the beginning, middle, or end of a word. This is getting the child's errors down on paper so that the clinician can see the problem in better perspective.

It is advantageous for the therapist to carry the evaluation a step further and get a kinetic analysis. It is not just enough to say a child has a lisp. We need to determine whether it is a lateral, occluded, interdental, or nasal formation of the lisp. In short, the important thing is the manner of production. An attempt is made to find just what the child is doing when he makes an error. One method is for the clinician to imitate or duplicate what the child is doing. Each of the speech sounds may be incorrectly produced in several ways. For example, errors of stop-plosives such as *k* and *g* seem to be due to (1) the wrong location of the tongue contact, (2) the wrong speed in forming the contacts, and (3) the wrong structures used in contacts. A child who says tandy for candy is using a tongue-platal contact, but it is too far forward. Too slow a release from a *k* contact may give a breathy, aspirate quality to the utterance. "Kuheep the kueys" is an example of this (Van Riper, 1963).

A common error is the use of the wrong channel for the airstream. This is seen when using an unvoiced *l* for the *s*. A lateral lisp is produced. Also, the airstream may be in the wrong direction as in the case of a nasal lisp. The *s* is inhaled. Too weak an air pressure may cause an omission of sounds.

The reproduction of the error enables the therapist to understand its nature. Only after careful analysis of the articulatory error and the breaking of the old habit can the clinician begin any thorough sessions. Most progress can be made after the subject understands clearly what he is doing wrong. Insight into error is a must before significant progress can be made.

A final factor to be considered in an evaluation is the condition under which errors occur. We need to examine each error in terms of the following: (1) type of communicative situation, (2) speed of utterance, (3) kind of communicative material, and (4) discrimination ability (Van Riper, 1963). Some lispers only have difficulty when under emotional stress. Children may imitate correctly but distort their own speech sounds. Knowing when a child makes his errors helps in the therapy.

At the end of the examination all of the information is put together in a systematic and meaningful way. If the therapy plan is to be successful, the information gained must be organizd. The following is a form commonly used:

Case: Age: Grade: Address: Phone:

Family history:

Developmental history:

Birth history:

Present physical conditions:

Behavior:

Type of disorder:

Phonetic errors:

Intelligence:

Hearing acuity:

Muscular coordination:

General observation of speech:

The clinician is now ready for therapy. So far this chapter has described defects that would be corrected in individual therapy. For the most part, this will be the major concern of speech clinicians. However, speech therapy can be accomplished by other methods. There are several approaches being used to reach and help those with speech handicaps. One could be referred to as a general speech improvement program.

A General Speech Improvement Program

What is meant by general speech improvement? Ainsworth (1948) states, "It is group work done with whole classes or grades. The objectives are to raise the general speech performance of the group and minimize and correct minor defects of some of the individuals in the group."

Van Riper and Butler (1955) propose,

> Speech improvement — is more than tongue exercises, memorization, vocal phonics, articulation, drills, and activities. It is more than instruction in the improvement of voice quality, pitch and intensity. It is more than training in the ebb and flow of speech rhythms. It is more than the sum total of all these parts. Speech improvement should go far beyond the mechanics of speech drills, into the area of meaningful language. One of the most important aims might well be to help the children to verbalize their thought — to be able to "think on their feet" efficiently and adequately.

This type of program utilizes group instruction as the basis for speech therapy. Used primarily at the preschool and elementary level, it emphasizes increased vocabulary, growth in concepts, meaning of words, and improved articulation and sentence patterns. The purpose is to develop better communication and language, not just improved articulation or speech production. A program such as this will utilize the classroom teacher and a trained speech pathologist acting as consultant and diagnostician. Only in the regular classroom situation can language development be made to meet the immediate needs of the children.

What is done in the classroom? The therapist may visit the classroom twice a week or more with sessions lasting fifteen to thirty minutes. Each group will receive planned language development programming worked out with the cooperation of the classroom teacher to fit the needs, interests, and present academic work of the group. The classroom teacher will remain in the room during the session so that the activities can be repeated at other times and recommendations for future sessions made.

The child is taught common language patterns appropriate in various life situations. Some particular speech patterns might be as follows:

"Yes." "May I get_____?" "Thank you."
"No." "Have a _____" "Hello."
"Look at _____." "Come _____."

These patterns are introduced through specific types of activities which encourage the child to take part in conversation and to express ideas or opinions. He needs to learn that speech is a tool for communicative relationships with other people.

Another approach used to reach those with defective speech is the organized speech correction program within the public school system. Ainsworth (1948) divides the work of the speech therapist into two principal categories — correcting speech defects and organizing and administering the speech correction program. From the therapeutic point of view this is similar to individual therapy in that children with pronounced speech defects are the objective rather than general speech improvement. In this program the majority of the work is done in small groups of three or four. Of course this does not rule out individual work. Each case will vary and require certain adjustments. Individual cases are usually those of a more serious nature such as stuttering, aphasia, or cleft palate. Most speech and hearing clinics provide services for these individuals.

For most people, the field of speech pathology is new. One might ask, "What do speech clinicians do in correcting a defect?" or "How do they go about it?" To answer these questions and to provide an illustration, let us take a hypothetical case of a child with an articulatory disorder. We will presume that he has been evaluated and found to have defective *s* sounds. Further, we will assume that the child has no significant organic anomally of the articulatory apparatus. As a rule, children with one-error sound present no major difficulty, but those who have many errors do.

A Hypothetical Case

The first task at hand is to convince the child that he has a problem which he must solve. This is easier said than done. Often speech defectives grow into adulthood without being made aware of their speech disorders. The quickest way of getting rid of an error is to make the child aware of it. After this is accomplished, we hopefully move on. The therapy itself is focused upon the defective sounds. Parents and teachers often focus their therapy on the word level. "Don't say thirtherth," they command, "say scissors." This is difficult for the child who has no concept that he is saying it incorrectly. Then, too, suppose he does happen to say it correctly by accident. There is very little carryover into other words. The speech clinician begins at the sound level (phoneme), then moves to the syllable, word, and sentence level. With this method, once a sound is learned, it is readily incorporated into words containing the sound. The child need not learn each word individually. Although other approaches are used, the majority of speech therapists seem to prefer this method.

Ear Training

In teaching a child to make a sound correctly, clinicians use ear training. The child learns the standard sound through auditory stimulation rather than repetition of syllables or words. The lisper can learn when the sound is distorted and when it is not. To accomplish this the speech therapist uses four basic sets of techniques: (1) isolation, (2) stimulation, (3) identification, and (4) discrimination (Van Riper, 1963).

In isolation, the clinician attempts to break down word configurations so that the correct sound may be heard by itself. To the speech defective, spoken words are lumps of sounds. Sometimes the correct sound is lost somewhere within the word. They do not hear it with clarity. The speech therapist attempts to motivate the child via games and play activities. Two exercises might be as follows: (1) The teacher hides, in different places about the room, nine or ten pictures of various objects, one of which begins with the *s* sound. The moment the child finds this picture, he can run to the teacher's desk and ring a bell. (2) The teacher sounds out words and asks the child to locate the appropriate picture, putting all *s* word pictures in a special envelope.

Second, the child's ear must be bombarded with the sound so thoroughly that it may almost be said to ring in his ears. This is stimulation. The child's attention must be focused on the sound. Parents, friends, and classmates can help. The child makes no attempt on his own to produce the sound. The all-important thing is learning to listen. Young children must be motivated to listen by interesting activities. It is a good practice to always let the child perform in some manner to indicate his efficiency in the reception of the stimulation. One activity among many would be the use of a hollow tube of sorts. It is held to the child's ear as he winds a string on a spool. The clinician makes the sound into the tube. The moment the clinician stops making the sound, the child must stop winding.

In identification, the therapist gives the sound a name. The *s* sound could be called the snake or the leaky tire sound. In this way, the sound takes on the identity of sounds with which they work. This helps the child in recognition. Identification is necessary before the final step — discrimination.

The first three steps in ear training must be successful before the therapist begins discrimination. Here, we attempt to compare and contrast the correct and incorrect sounds. It is important that the child be able to differentiate the correct sound from error. Activities are planned so that the child will have to perform to either the correct or incorrect sound by the clinician.

Upon completion of the ear training period, the child should have acquired a clear concept of the target sound. Until now he has not been required to produce the sound. Next comes the transitional step of self-hearing, a process where the child learns to recognize and identify his errors.

Reproducing the Correct Sound

At last comes the big day. The child begins learning to produce the new sound. Keep in mind that the new sound must have been mastered on all the previous levels. There are several ways to approach this task. The speech clinician selects one, often to discard it for another. One has to adapt to each particular case. Learning the new sound is a process of modifying the old sound. Rarely does a child suddenly shift from saying wabbit to rabbit. Change is gradual, for movement of the articulators and acoustical patterns has to be varied.

One method in teaching the new sound is progressive approximation. This method resembles the way that infants acquire normal articulation. The clinician makes the same error as the child. He then makes modifications in the sound and attempts several series of transitional sounds that come closer to the desired or correct sound. This is a gradual process but has been used with great success.

Auditory stimulation is another method. The child attempts to directly imitate the clinician. It works well with those who are ear-minded. Some say the sound perfectly on the first attempt. Others may repeat several times. If the child whispers the sound first, it helps to get the feel of it.

The traditional approach is that of phonetic placement. Many elaborate devices and diagrams have been made to show the individual exactly how the sound is to be produced. The disadvantage is that the mechanics of phonetic placement cannot be performed quickly enough for the smooth flow of connected speech. Also, many speech clinicians produce sounds in nonstandard ways. If used effectively this method can be an indispensable tool in the kit of the speech clinician. It can give a clear idea of the desired position of the articulators before any speech attempt.

Another useful approach in teaching a new sound is the key word method. Speech defectives need some standard with which to compare their speech attempts at correct production of the usually defective sound (Van Riper, 1963). Surprisingly, most speech defectives have a few words in which they do not make the error. If the clinician has a keen ear and can capture these words, they will prove to be a tremendous asset. By capitalizing on these key words, he can drill on them, demonstrating that the individual can make the sound correctly in some instances. It is hoped that the defective speaker will be able to produce the new sound in isolation and at will.

Using the Sound in Speech

After the child has learned to make the correct *s* sound, then comes the stabilization. The formation of a new sound is a weak creature and must be reinforced by constant practice. Even the therapy is not complete. It must now proceed through the syllable, word, and sentence levels. Until now we have been concerned only with the sound itself. As the child progresses from one stage to another, the idea is to make the sound habitual and consistent at all times. It must be unconsciously retained.

One successful method is the use of negative practice. Although it seems odd at first, this is the deliberate and voluntary use of the incorrect sound. Used more with adolescents and adults than children, it is an effective technique for getting the correct sound into an individual's speech. It helps make the sound habitual. The clinician never asks the subject to use the sound incorrectly unless he can produce it correctly whenever called upon. How does it work? (1) It helps make the speech defective conscious of his habit. This is a prerequisite for any elimination of the defect to take place. (2) Voluntary practice makes the error vivid, making the individual vigilant in guarding against it.

It must be remembered that an ideal situation has been discussed, one seldom encountered in therapy. Each individual case is different, requiring constant evaluation. What works in one instance may not be satisfactory in another. Also, the proper approach depends upon the type of disorder. There are many variables to be considered.

The possibilities for correction of a speech defect are considerably better than those several centuries ago. We know now that a stutterer is not really a creature possessed by spirits and that society will not be improved by ridiculing and alienating the speech-handicapped. Our enlightenment as to the nature and causes of speech defects and the recognition of them as obstacles to the emotional and social well-being of individuals give promise to those who constantly hide behind a wall of embarrassment.

Speech Therapy as a Profession

It must be stressed that speech therapy as a profession is still very young, with the American Speech and Hearing Association, its professional organization, being established less than fifty years ago. Nevertheless, this profession has branched out internationally. Speech and hearing specialists can be found in most countries throughout the world.

Because of the high standards demanded of the personnel in this field, parents of speech-defective children can feel confident of receiving competent treatment from certified speech or hearing specialists. Also, because of the newness of the field and the high standards enforced, the demand for workers is great. Many college students do not become familiar with the field as a profession until it is too late to start training in this area. However, students who do investigate this field find dedicated professionals working in a still young but rewarding field of service.

Remedial Speech Services

If all children who are of school age in the United States and who have serious speech handicaps were brought together in one place, they would make a city about the size of Philadelphia, which is the nation's fourth largest city. A conservative estimate of the number of these children would be 2,500,000, which exceeds the population of the entire state of Mississippi or Arkansas. As a matter of fact, this figure exceeds the population of twenty-three of our fifty states. This is a conservative estimate and includes only those children ages five through nineteen who have a speech or hearing defect which is so marked that they go through life with a serious handicap — vocationally, socially, and personally. Speech-handicapped children constitute the largest group of exceptional individuals within our total population and also the largest group who need special education services in the country's elementary and secondary schools. Most of these children are found in the regular classes in the schools of America. It is true that many of them are found in the special classes, too, because the lower the intelligence and the greater the multiple handicaps, the greater the relationship between these abnormalities and speech defects. Nevertheless, most of these children enter the first grade classes every year and stay in the regular classrooms with the regular classroom teachers. The majority of these handicapped children do not have the services of a speech pathologist. There is no doubt that if these children have average or above intelligence, or even below-average intelligence for many of them, they should be functioning in a regular classroom. There is also no doubt that a speech clinician should be available not only to help the teacher work with speech handicap problems in the regular classroom, but also to work with the severely speech-handicapped on a one-to-one basis.

There is an increasing awareness on the part of educators

concerning the shortage of speech specialists who are adequately trained to help speech-handicapped children and to help the teacher take care of children with mild defects in the regular classroom or in the special classroom. Today the requirement to meet certification as a speech clinician by the American Speech and Hearing Association is a master's degree. Other individuals who do not hold a master's degree can be certified with a Certificate of Clinical Competence for the members who desire it and can show adequate competence resulting from specialized training and experience. The American Speech and Hearing Association has more than 10,000 members who are actively employed; of these, 7,500 are in clinical work. This is not enough to meet the nation's needs. Therefore, the regular classroom teacher should take courses in speech pathology and language development to help him alleviate the mild problems which he will find in his classroom.

An adequate school program requires one trained speech clinician for each one hundred speech-handicapped children enrolled in that community. The adults should have two trained speech clinicians for every 50,000 of the total population of a city or community, therefore one can see that we have a tremendous shortage of speech clinicians in America today. The regular class teacher must in some way help to alleviate the mild speech problems which are found in the classroom. A speech clinician must be available in an adequate program to help the children having severe problems. Regardless of whether the speech clinician is available or whether the regular class teacher is trained to help alleviate these minor problems, we do have children in the regular classes, in special classes, and in other facilities who have mild and severe speech problems. Many of these children receive no service to help alleviate these problems. This is a tragedy and must be alleviated in the very near future if we are going to say that we have adequate programs in all phases of education in the American school system.

We must be reminded that the regular classroom teacher cannot be expected to undertake time-consuming tasks on behalf of pupils who have severe speech impediments. Naturally, a one-to-one relationship would distract the teacher from her main job —

that of taking care of the individual differences of all the children in the classroom. The kind of classroom or school system that has a teacher who is good for a child who stutters or has an articulatory disorder is good for all the children, too.

BIBLIOGRAPHY

Ainsworth, Stanley: *Speech Correction Methods.* New York, Ronald, 1948.

ASHA Committee on the Midcentury White House Conference: Speech disorders and speech correction. *J Speech Hear Disord, 17*(2):68, 1952.

Berry, Mildred R., and Eisenson, Jon: *Speech Disorders.* New York, Appleton, 1956.

Emerick, Lon L., and Hatten, John T.: *Diagnosis and Evaluation in Speech Pathology.* Englewood Cliffs, P-H, 1974.

Johnson, Wendell: *Stuttering in Children and Adults.* Minneapolis, U of Minnesota Pr, 1956.

Johnson, Wendell, Brown, S., Curtis, J., Edney, C., and Keaster, S.: *Speech Handicapped School Children.* New York, Harper and Brothers, 1956.

Van Riper, Charles: *Speech Correction Principles and Methods.* Englewood Cliffs, P-H, 1963.

Van Riper, Charles, and Butler, K.: *Speech in the Elementary Classroom.* New York, Harper and Brothers, 1955.

Wepman, J. M.: *Recovery From Aphasia.* New York, Ronald, 1951.

Chapter 10

PARENT'S ROLE IN FOSTERING
LANGUAGE GROWTH AND DEVELOPMENT
IN EXCEPTIONAL CHILDREN

THE chapters throughout this book have been written to inform prospective and experienced teachers of the idiosyncracies and disturbances in language development observed among exceptional children. The book has also indicated the possible role of the teacher in the facilitation and the management of verbal and other language behaviors and processes. Frequently, however, the teacher must serve in a consulting role to advise parents in the home management of atypical children. With the exception of the family physician it is perhaps an available teacher who is first consulted for help by parents of children who are apparently, in the parents' opinion, deviating markedly from normal growth and development. Parents who are becoming concerned that their children are not reaching or attaining the expected developmental milestones may seek a teacher's advice to either confirm their suspicions or help them reject the fears that their child is significantly lagging behind in certain areas of development.

With parents becoming increasingly aware that language is one of the most important tasks that children are expected to develop, delays in speech development in their children often produce antagonizing worry and concern. The worry and concern often center around the two possibilities of impaired hearing and mental deficiency. More importantly, the longer the child goes without developing speech, the greater the likelihood of confirming the parent's dread fear of mental retardation. The fear of mental retardation becomes even greater when their child reacts to noise and other startling stimuli suggesting that impaired hearing is not the basis for their child's delay in speech.

Since it is the position of the authors that the teacher can be a valuable source of information and advice for parents of exceptional children, it is the goal of this chapter to provide a systematic guide for teachers to use in their interactions with parents. The guide for teachers proposes the following three interrelated areas of parental counseling: (1) knowledge, (2) skills, and (3) information/referral.

It is at this point the authors present a basic philosophical premise which suggests that the more knowledge parents have concerning the exceptionalities, the more positive their attitude toward their exceptional children (Love, 1963). Therefore, at the knowledge level, it is believed that the parents should have a thorough understanding of what is considered to be normal or expected language development of children. With a model of expected language development, the teacher or parent could more closely determine the degree to which their child is deviating from some expected norm. It is important for parents to understand that their child's development occurs in stages and that certain developmental tasks should be occurring within specific stages. The following discussion will consist of categorizing the expected developmental language tasks under the stages in which they most frequently erupt. Since this discussion will be for teachers to relate to parents, the developmental tasks will be discussed in a very general manner.

Chronological Acquisition of Language

Birth to Six Months

The first form of prespeech behaviors that is observed among infants is crying. The crying behavior of the infant is initially reflexive and undifferentiated. This is especially true of the first month of life. Most children between one month and six weeks of age will begin to vary their crying behavior in terms of intensity, tonal quality and rhythm. The variation of crying behavior becomes a signal for the child's family to predetermine the reasons for the crying. It is at this point the child's crying becomes so differentiated that the parents can predict certain states of distress (hunger, cold, pain, etc.). Crying for the infant provides that necessary bridge to reduce the gap between nonlanguage and language. When developmental language gains are made by the child, crying to communicate his distress, needs, and desires will begin to decrease. Until the child can replace crying with verbal communication, his crying behavior is a trusted method to request the objects in his environment that will satisfy his needs and demands (Hurlock, 1964).

The four to six-week-old child should begin to show some observable response to human voices. During the period from six weeks to approximately six months, the parents should begin to notice vocal play in the form of cooing, babbling, and chuckling to demonstrate pleasure. Differential vocalizations should also be observed to demonstrate displeasure or distress. The vocalizations during this developmental period will consist primarily of initial or front vowels of *g, k,* and *l* although some of the infants will babble syllables such as *ba-ba.*

Six Months to Twelve Months

It is frequently observed that children at or around six months of age should be vocalizing or lalling with some intonation. Most of the vocalizing at this developmental age will consist of the initial vowels and consonants *m, n, b,* and *p,* with the possibility of some syllables. Much of the vocalizing will be used for socialization with the parents and immediate members of the family. These prespeech forms will also be used to acquire attention from the parents.

The speech of his parents is becoming an important cue for the child. It is during this period of speech development that the child becomes responsive to the speech patterns of his environment. The child begins to respond to his name and to human voices by turning his eyes or his head in the direction of the speaker. Frequently, the child responds to the human voice with a tantalizing smile if that voice is especially friendly or soft. Most children of this developmental level are also able to detect differences in speech patterns and will respond differentially to those speech patterns. His ability to detect differences in friendly and angry voices indicates a step-up in his comprehension ability.

Recognizable speech sounds of *ma ma* and *da da* are frequently observed during the latter quarter of the first year of life. These speech sounds are usually echolalic and the child may be somewhat inconsistent in the production of those sounds. Later, however, the child will use *ma ma* and *da da* more consistently and appropriately.

His comprehension of the speech sounds of adults is increasing to the degree that he comprehends some words and some inflections or intonations.

Twelve Months to Eighteen Months

It is during the period of twelve to eighteen months that one observes the child's readiness to consistently imitate an adult model that would be considered echolalic and echopraxic behavior. Echolalic and echopraxic behavior represent infantile modes of duplicating the verbal and the physical gestures of an adult model. There is, however, an intentional use of speech in which certain words, as for example *ma ma*, may have different meanings. The use of *ma ma* may be generalized to include such meanings as Where is ma ma? and I want ma ma. The child will often imitate physical communication gestures of the parents which initially begin with shaking the head to indicate no.

The child of this developmental age can comprehend simple sequences of instruction, especially if the parent provides adequate and understandable physical cues. It is perhaps the range of twelve to eighteen months that is considered to be the beginning of true speech. The child usually speaks in one-word sentences consisting primarily of nouns. However, during the later stages of this developmental period, a child's speech will include some verbs, adjectives, and adverbs. Most children in this age range will have vocabularies ranging from one to twenty words, with most children having approximately ten-word vocabularies.

Eighteen to Twenty-four Months

This step-up in development results in a significant increment in the child's receptive language. It is also during this period that the foundation of grammatical rules, which will eventually regulate his speech, is being formed. These rules are induced into the child's speech system through comprehension of the parent's speech. Due to his particular stage of development the child understands more of the language than he actually verbalizes. The child's vocabulary, though consisting primarily of nouns, may reach a maximum of three hundred words. His verbal communication will consist of two-word sentences in order to satisfy his needs and to explore his immediate environment. The child will, however, exhibit jargon (unintelligible speech sounds) frequently accompanied by emotional inflection.

Two Years to Three Years

Receptively, the child is beginning to comprehend the concepts of many, few, on, and under. The child also demonstrates his understanding of pronouns such as I, you, and me. However, there may be a tendency for the child to confuse the pronouns during this developmental stage. The child should also be able to point to and verbally label several parts of his body.

Expressively, the child's speech should be more socially usable and more intelligible. It is generally observed that children at this developmental level have mastered two thirds of the speech sounds of adults. That is, approximately two thirds of what the child articulates is completely intelligible. The child frequently uses three-word sentences for the satisfaction of his needs and in identifying objects in his immediate environment. The child's speech patterns, however, may be lacking in rhythm and fluency due to his particular developmental stage of growth.

Three to Four Years

The child in this age range demonstrates a step-up in the refinement of his number concept to include awareness of two, three, etc. He is also more fully capable of understanding the speech patterns of adults along with the understanding of prepositions and can demonstrate that he knows the meanings. The child at this age level has increased in his understanding of pronouns to include who, what, etc. His understanding of size relationships has expanded to include concepts of big, little, larger, smaller.

Expressively, the child most frequently uses sentences containing four to eight words and is more able to explain the activities occurring in his immediate environment as well as being able to abstract meaning from pictures. This abstraction of meaning from pictures is most frequently exemplified by his ability to tell a sensible story concerning the picture. The three-year-old child's speech patterns are beginning to exhibit the use of plurals and past tenses as well as increased proficiency in the use of verbs. The child's expressive language is becoming more refined, especially in his ability to describe imaginary events, and for explaining and narrating. During his third year of life the child has mastered approximately 90 percent of the adult speech sounds and demonstrates clearer pronounciation of the *j, s, v, l,* and *t* sounds.

Four to Five Years

The child's vocabulary at the four to five-year developmental level ranges between 1,500 and 2,500 words. At this age the child is gaining more complete and structured sentences. The child may frequently use sentences containing seven or more words. During the fourth and fifth year, the child uses his speech for information-seeking which is most clearly demonstrated in his asking questions about his environment. Due to his gain in the functional use of language, which allows him to ask many questions about his environment, the child increases in his ability to name familiar animals, define many common words, and understand more prepositions.

He has gained in the functional use of the questional organizers of how, why, and what, and he understands many nouns with derivational suffixes. The understanding of derivational suffixes notes an increase in the child's ability to abstract and generalize. The child understands that by adding the suffix *er* to such words as run, swim, paint, sing, dance, fly, he can convert verbs to nouns. The child can also repeat four digits and words containing four syllables.

Five to Six Years

The five-year-old child is increasing in his use of adjectives and adverbs, which adds continuing refinement of his expressive ability. His active vocabulary contains an excess of 2,500 words. However, he may understand approximately 6,000 words. The child's understanding of number concepts has increased to include four or more and has some money concepts. The child may be able to identify some coins with some relative understanding. The child can also demonstrate his understanding of such concepts as big, small, heavy, and light and has incorporated more time concepts in his vocabulary. Most five-year-old children should have understanding of time concepts such as morning, night, yesterday, tomorrow, today, and after a while. The child's expressive abilities are observed in his ability to use sentences containing nine or more words, however the children most frequently use sentences containing four to five words. The child at this developmental level should have mastered the *k, j, t, d, n, ng,* and *y* sounds. The child should be able to follow three sequential commands such as, "Pick up the red car, put it in my hand, and put the green car in your hand."

Suggestions to Parents

The following information is presented to provide teachers with guidelines for aiding parents in facilitating the language development of their children.

Initially, the parents should be encouraged to seek the available resources which might determine or eliminate the factors which are adversely affecting their child's language and speech development. The prominent factors which might be affecting the normal development of speech would include impaired hearing, central nervous system damage, auditory perceptual disturbances, faulty speech mechanisms, and subnormal intellectual development. In order to determine or eliminate the organic factors that might be interfering with the normal acquisition of speech and language, the parent should be encouraged to solicit the services of professionals who may be prepared to identify the source of the problem.

Parents may often think of a speech and language disorder as primarily an output or an expressive disorder. In other words, their understanding of delayed development of speech is that the child is simply not talking. Therefore, it could be the responsibility of the teacher to aid the parents in understanding that their child's problem may lie within the area of a receptive language disorder — that is, their child may be lacking in his ability to internalize and, therefore, respond to verbal cues within his environment.

If a determination has been made that the child's receptive language disorder is not likely the result of organic or constitutional factors, the possibility of what Van Riper (1963) refers to as "functional causes" may be the contributing reason for the speech abnormality. Functional causes might include such conditions as emotional disturbances, unfavorable environmental conditions, negativism, elective mutism, poor speech standards, and improper teaching methods. It is perhaps in the functional cause listed as improper teaching methods that the teacher's expertise in parental advisement may be more clearly defined. It is imperative that parents understand that a receptive language disorder may be a consequence of an impaired or a developed inability to comprehend what is expected of him. This problem is frequently exemplified by the child's inability to follow directions given by the parents as in "Place the ball in my hand" or "Drop the ball in my hand." As Lenneberg and Long (1974) stressed, "... a patient who can recite television commercials has not given us evidence of his understanding of language; to demonstrate such understanding, he must respond correctly to commands such as 'Put the box under the table,' or questions such as 'Is the chair something one can eat?' "

If one analyzes the above instructions in terms of stimulus complexity, it becomes apparent that the level of the child's receptive integrity may not permit the understanding of place or drop. As a consequence, he cannot produce the desired response triggered by the instruction. The child's inability to complete the response is not the result of inattention, negativeness, or unresponsiveness, but the result of his lacking or comprehension of verbal cues given by the parents, at which point the parents must be aided in understanding that much of their child's behavior is regulated by his level of receptive language. He can only respond correctly to verbal instructions which contain words that he clearly understands.

Luria's (1961) research on regulation of behavior by speech and language development provides an interesting insight into the dilemma described above. Luria, along with Vygotsky (1962), presents the idea that meaningful or understandable language is the basis for the child's ability to plan, organize, remember, think and reason.

The following list is presented to serve as a guide for organizing the teacher's plan for advising parents who have preschool children exhibiting deficiencies in receptive language development:

1. Parents should be advised to employ what is sometimes referred to as *parallel talking.* That is, the parents should, while performing an activity, describe in clear and simple language precisely what they are doing. For example, the parents should provide a clear and vivid description of objects that are being manipulated such as "I am closing the door," "I am giving you the yellow ball." This procedure not only exposes the child to a language model, but offers a means for the child to begin pairing verbal cues with exact activities.

It is extemely important for the parent to be consistent in describing the activities they are engaging in to avoid confusion of verbal cues. If, for example, the parent on one occasion says "I am closing the door" while on the second occasion says "I am shutting the door," the differences in the verbal cues may create confusion and, as a consequence, disturb the child's conceptual learning of the language cues which describe that action. It is extremely important that parallel talking in the initial stages of working with the child have the greatest of consistency.

2. The parents should be encouraged to speak to their child slowly and clearly without an overpowering and overstimulating use of verbal instructions, directions, and commands.

3. The parents should be encouraged to use such child care

activities at bath time as a language-learning experience to teach the major parts of the body. For example, "I am touching your nose," "I am touching your ear," "I am touching your arm," etc.

4. The parents should be informed that the repetition of words and phrases should always be consistent to insure the child's understanding.

5. The parents should be encouraged to teach the child the correct names of people and objects.

6. The parents should be encouraged to avoid baby talk because of the danger of teaching incorrect language concepts. Erroneous use of labels as pippy for pillow, banky for blanket and nankie for drink contributes to the inappropriate learning of names of objects.

Toys and Aids

Toys and other learning aids are priceless tools in building a child's language success. Parents should be advised to choose materials appropriate to their child's interests and current needs.

When presenting a new toy the parents should be encouraged to always take time to introduce it to their child. This will hopefully create an atmosphere for friendly communication between the parents and the child. The following is a list of play materials that may be useful in the parent's language-teaching activities.

1. Riddle-a-Rhyme Lotto® (Childcraft Equipment Co.)
2. Pick a Card® (Berkley Card Co.)
3. The Farmer Says® (Mattel, Inc.)
4. Language Lotto® (Appleton Century Crafts)
5. Play and Say® (Stanwix House, Inc.)
6. Learning to Develop Language Skills® (Milton Bradley's Early Childhood Enrichment Unit)
7. Phonoviewer with Language Arts/Oral Development Programs® (General Learning Corp.)
8. Talk-a-Fun Phone® (Sears)
9. My Books That Talk® (Sears)
10. *Things to See,* a book published by Platt and Munk
11. *I Am a Bunny,* A Golden Sturdy Happy Book
12. *My Book About Me,* Dr. Seuss

13. *I am a Puppy*, A Golden Sturdy Happy Book
14. *Mother Goose Song Book*, Garden City Publishing Co., Inc.
15. *A Treasury of Songs for Little Children*, Hart Publishing Co.
16. *Songs for Today's Children*, Clayton F. Summy Co.
17. *Songs Children Like*, Association for Childhood Education International
18. Records, for listening and responding
    Jean Barnett Records
      George Stanly
      1225 Biscayne Point Rd.
      Miami Beach, Florida
    Young People's Records
    Basic Listening Program
    Decca Records
19. Provide toys which symbolize everyday life.
Example: cars, airplanes, community helpers, family members
20. Provide toys which encourage use of the imagination.
Example: puppets, flannel boards, people figures, toy animals
21. Provide toys which spark creativity.
Example: crayons, paints, finger paints, clay, yarn, paste, art paper, old magazines, blocks and other building toys
22. Provide toys which develop insight.
Example: puzzles, jacks, juvenile card games
23. Provide musical toys for accompaniments to music.
24. To find out where Montessori-type learning aids and materials can be purchsed, write to:
    Children's House Creative Center
    437 Pompton Avenue
    Cedar Grove, New Jersey 07009

The following books and other publications are recommended as potential sources of helpful information and suggestions for those working and/or living with a child with delayed speech:

Academic Therapy Publications, Books Department, 1543 Fifth Ave., San Rafael, California 94901 provides parents with extensive lists of recommended books and pamphlets for the remediation of specific learning disabilities.

Battin, R. Ray: *Speech and Language Delay: A Home Training Program.* Charles C Thomas, Springfield, 1964.

This workbook, designed primarily for parents, explains normal speech and language development and causes of delay. It offers simple instructions and outlines for a day-to-day therapy program.

Beasley, Jane: *Slow to Talk.* Bureau of Publications, Teachers College, Columbia University, New York, 1956.

Many practical procedures are discussed that can be used with the child with delayed speech.

Berry, Mildred F., and Eisenson, John: *Speech Disorders.* Appleton-Century-Crofts, New York, 1956.

Written primarily as a textbook on major speech disorders, the three chapters on retarded development of speech contain a great deal of information which parents find useful and informative. Finger plays, toys, books, phonograph records, and group games to motivate speech are given.

Blumerfield, J., Thompson, P. D., and Vogel, B. S.: *Help Them Grow.* Abingdon Press, Nashville, 1971.

This small paperback is directed especially to parents and seeks to provide suggestions for teaching handicapped children in the home. The section on communication skills is very good.

Chamberlain, Naomi H., and Moss, Dorothy H.: *The Three R's for the Retarded.* National Association for Retarded Children, New York, 1960.

This booklet is a compilation of suggestions for help in training the mentally retarded child at home. The procedures are applicable to any child who is delayed. Each suggestion included has been successfully tried with some child, and it may help yours. Step-by-step procedures are given for teaching speech sounds.

Egg (Egg-Benes), Maria: *When a Child is Different.* The John Day Co., New York, 1964.

This is a reassuring book about what a retarded child is and how the family can learn to cope with him (her). It stresses the importance of maintaining good medical care and has specific suggestions for parents for various aspects of life.

Fauna, Albert, Furth, Bol H., and Smith Joseph M.: *Growth Through Play.* Prentice-Hall, Inc., Englewood Cliffs, 1975.

Games and songs for various age groups are given in this book.

Goodwin, F. B.: "A Consideration of Etiologies in 454 Cases of Speech Retardation." *Journal of Speech and Hearing Disorders,* Vol. 20, p. 300-303, 1955.

Available at University of Central Arkansas.

Greene, Margaret, C. L.: *Learning to Talk: A Parent's Guide for the First Five Years.* Harper and Brothers, New York, 1960.

This book tells parents how they can help a child learn to talk from birth on. What can be expected each year from one to five and good advice about how parents can help the child are offered. It includes pointers for the parent on the deaf child.

Hainstock, Elizabeth G.: *Teaching Montessori in the Home.* Random House, New York, 1968.

This book was written especially for parents to familiarize them with the methods of Dr. Maria Montessori, the Italian physician educator, and to help them work with the child(ren) at home. It is useful to any parent looking for more interesting and challenging activities for any child.

Harris, Grace M.: *Language for the Preschool Deaf Child.* Grune and Stratton, New York, 1963. HV 2443 .H3 1963, UCA.

This book gives background information and suggestions for the person who is trying to help the preschool deaf child. Johnson, Wendell (Ed.): *Speech Problems of Children.* Grune and Stratton, New York, 1950.

Charles Van Riper's chapter, "Children Who Are Slow in Learning Speech," discusses attitudes, causes, and techniques of correction.

Karnes, Merle B.: *Helping Young Children Develop Language Skills.* Council for Exceptional Children, Washington, D.C., 1968.

This manual was developed for teachers of three, four, and

five-year-old disadvantaged youngsters. Many of the activities can be utilized by parents at home. It is also a rich source of games, materials, and books.

Kirk, Samuel A., Karnes, Merle B., and Kirk, Winifred: *You and Your Retarded Child.* The Macmillan Co., New York, 1958.

Although somewhat dated, this book still contains a great deal of valuable material. Chapter 8, "Helping Your Child Learn to Talk," has excellent suggestions to parents.

Larsen, Lawrence A., and Bricker, William A.: *A Manual for Parents and Teachers of Severely and Moderately Retarded Children.* IMRID. George Peabody College, Nashville, 1968.

Although written for those working with the lower-functioning child, the behavior modification techniques and speech production activities can be applied to any child with delayed speech. This book is easy reading and contains step-by-step directions and pages of suggested rewards.

Malloy, Julia S.: *Teaching the Retarded Child to Talk.* The John Day Co., Inc., New York, 1961. 371.927M L.R.P.L.

The purpose of this book is "to help parents and teachers of very young retarded children who have not started to talk or who talk poorly." The book deals with why children do not learn to talk and how an interested person can help. The book is aimed at the trainable mentally retarded child, but would be useful for working with any child with delayed speech.

Myklebust, Helmer R.: *Auditory Disorders in Children.* Grune and Stratton, New York, 1954.

Myklebust, Helmer R.: "Training Aphasic Children, Suggestions for Parents and Teachers." *Volta Review,* 57:149-157. April, 1955.

Patterson, Gerald R., and Gullion, M. Elizabeth: *Living With Children.* Research Press, Champaign, 1968.

This book was written to give parents a practical technique to deal with children's behavior. It is in down-to-earth language in programmed instruction form to make it especially easy to read and use. Using this technique will greatly increase the chances of success in getting a child with delayed speech to talk.

Richardson, Sylvia O.: "Early Teaching for Children with Minor Central Nervous System Dysfunction." United Cerebral Palsy Association, New York, 1964. UCA

This is an excellent discussion of the use of materials designed for use in the Montessori method of teaching.

Shreiber, Flora Rheta: *Your Child's Speech: A Practical Guide for Parents for the First Five Years.* C. P. Putnam's Sons, New York, 1956. 136.72883S L.R.P.L.

This book is a reassuring description of how the child develops language. It vividly describes the accomplishments of each year from birth to age five and explains some of the special characteristics of the slow-developing child, the child with a speech defect, and the gifted child.

Sklar, Maurice: *How Children Learn to Speak.* Western Psychological Services, Los Angeles, 1969.

This is a short, concise, easy-to-read pamphlet offering advice to parents of children with delayed speech, telling what to do and where to seek help. UCA

Slaughter, Stella Stillson: *The Mentally Retarded Child and His Parents.* Harper and Row, New York, 1960. 136.766S L.R.P.L.

This book is a very complete description of the mentally retarded child. It tells how the parent can help the child and outlines how the child can learn language, reading, writing, arithmetic, and social studies. It also deals with the child's leisure activities, his personality and attitudes, and the outlook for his future.

Valett, Robert E.: *Prescriptions for Learning: A Parents' Guide to Remedial Home Training.* Fearon Publishers, Palo Alto, 1970.

The main intent of this book is to provide a series of sequential programs that will help parents identify, understand, and do something about specific learning problems.

Wood, Nancy E.: *Delayed Speech and Language Development.* Prentice-Hall, Inc., Englewood Cliffs, 1964. UCA

The pattern of language development and causes of delayed speech are described in this book.

Van Riper, Charles: *Helping Children Talk Better.* Science Research Associates, Inc., Chicago, 1951.

A relatively simple discussion of how children learn to speak and how to prevent defective speech is presented in this Better Living Booklet.

Van Riper, Charles: *Teaching Your Child to Talk.* Harper and Brothers, New York, 1950. 136.72883 V357 UCA

A good discussion of how a child learns to talk and how the parent can help is found in this book by a well-known authority in speech development.

Van Riper, Charles: *Your Child's Speech Problems: A Guide for Parents.* Harper and Row, New York, 1961. 618.92855V L.R.P.L.

This book gives good information about the nature and causes of various kinds of speech problems. It tells how the family can create a favorable climate for good speech at home and how the parent can help his child at home.

Agencies

The following local and national agencies are recommended as sources of help and information. Seek help as soon as you suspect there is a problem, and do not hesitate to consult your family physician.

The American Speech and Hearing Association
9030 Old Georgetown Road
Washington, D.C. 20014
> Lists all members in the United States with certificates of clinical competence in speech and hearing.

Arkansas Association for Retarded Children
University Shopping Center
Asher and University Streets
Little Rock, Arkansas

Arkansas School for the Deaf

2400 W. Markham Street
Little Rock, Arkansas

Center for Early Development and Education
814 S. Sherman
Little Rock, Arkansas

Central Institute for the Deaf
818 So. Euclid Avenue
St. Louis, Missouri 63110
   This institute is the foremost research center for the study of
   hearing disorders in children and adults.

Department of Health, Education, and Welfare
The Children's Bureau
Washington, D.C. 20025
   Publishes many low-cost pamphlets for parents of children
   with special handicaps and sponsors research projects.

John Tracy Clinic
806 W. Adams Blvd.
Los Angeles, California 90007
   Specializes in providing correspondence training for parents
   of hard-of-hearing children; carries on research with deaf
   children.

Little Rock Council for Children with Learning Disabilities
2915 Youngwood Road
Little Rock, Arkansas 72207

National Association for Retarded Children
386 Park Avenue South
New York, New York
   Can supply a list of speech and hearing clinics.

National Society for Crippled Children and Adults
2023 Ogden Avenue
Chicago, Illinois 60612
   Distributes a variety of pamphlets and books on rehabilitation of speech and hearing disorders.

Office of Vocational Rehabilitation
Department of Health, Education, and Welfare

330 Independence Avenue, S.W.

Washington, D.C. 20036

Can provide information about rehabilitation resources nearest your home.

Pulaski County Association for Retarded Children

P. O. Box 3844

Little Rock, Arkansas

University of Arkansas Medical Center

4301 W. Markham

Little Rock, Arkansas

Pediatric clinic can do referrals.

Child Study Center may be a source of help.

BIBLIOGRAPHY

Hurlock, Elizabeth B.: *Child Development*, 2nd Ed. New York, McGraw, 1964.

Lenneberg, Eric H., and Long, Barbara Susan: Language development. U.S. Department of Health, Education and Welfare/Office of Education. *Psychology and the Handicapped Child*. Washington, 1974.

Love, Harold D.: "A Study of Certain Characteristics of Parents Who Have Mentally Retarded Children as Compared with Parents Who Do Not Have Mentally Retarded Children." Unpublished doctoral dissertation, University of Northern Colorado, 1963.

Luria, A. R.: *Speech and the Regulation of Behavior.* New York, Liveright, 1961.

Van Riper, C.: *Speech Correction: Principles and Methods*, 4th Ed. Englewood Cliffs, P-H, 1963.

Vygotsky, L. S.: *Thought and Language.* New York, John Wiley, 1962.

INDEX

A

Abnormal EEG, 63
Academic functioning, 149
Academic tasks, 20
Academic Therapy Publications, 218
Achievement testing, 165
Advantaged children, 118
Adventitiously deaf, 131
Advisory Committee on the Deaf, 138
Ambidexterity, 63
American Foundation for the Blind, 76, 77, 84
American Indian, 98
American Psychiatric Association, 170
American Speech and Hearing Association, 206
Amphibians, 16
Analytical method, 157
Anxiety, 28
Aphasia, 138
Articulation, 195
Articulatory disorder, 207
Asian-American, 97
Association for Children with Learning Disabilities, 148
Ataxic, 87
Athetoid, 86
Auditory
  acuity, normal, 11
  area, 49
  decoding, 65
  integration, 51
  learner, 44
  measures, 52
  memory, 51
  perceptual efficiency, 51
  perceptual level, 52
  processes, 51
  receptive language, 8
  retention span, 119
  tracking, 51
Auditory-visual integration, 51
Auditory-vocal association, 66
Auditory-vocal automatic ability, 67
Auditory-vocal sequencing, 67
Autism, 169
  infantile, 170
Autistic behaviors, 183
Autistic child, 35, 171, 173, 174, 176, 179, 185
Automatic-sequential level, 66
Automatic tests, 66

B

Barsch, Ray, 18, 155
Bees, 3
Behavior
  autistic, 183
  bizarre, 12
  echolalic, 211
  echopraxic, 211
  expressive, 147
  humanistic, 38
  language, 60
  maladaptive, 164
  measurable, 28
  modifications, 162
  reading, 27
  verbal, 36
Behavioral changes, 114
Behavioral discipline, 104
Bell, Alexander Graham, Association for the Deaf, 143
Bender Gestalt, 59, 63, 69
  designs, 58
Bender Visual Motor Gestalt, 57, 61, 62, 70
Bible, 4
Binet, 103
  Intelligence Scale, 108

Ego development, 174
Elective mutism, 215
Emotional liability, 62
Emotionally disturbed child, 175, 180
Emotional problems, 63
Encoding Tests, 66
Engineered classroom, 164, 165
Environment, nonstimulating, 12
Exceptional children, 38, 48, 50, 69, 208
Expressive abilities, 214
Expressive disorder, 215
Extinction, 36

F

Favorable situation, 32
Feedback system, 18
Fernald, Grace, 53, 157
Fitzgerald, Edith, 159
Freidus, Elizabeth, 155
Frostig, Marianne, 67, 160
  Center of Educational Therapy, 68
Frustration, 28

G

Gallaudet College, 135, 144
Gallaudet, Thomas Hopkins, 126, 134
Gate's reading test, 61
Gesturing, 13, 36
Getman, Gerald, 13, 155
Glen Haven Achievement Center, 20, 154
Goodenough Draw-A-Man, 57
Gutherie's, Edwin R., theory, 26

H

Habit formation, 25
Hand movement, 79
Haptic learner, 44
Hard-of-hearing, 131
Hearing-impaired child, 130
Hemispheric dominance, 15, 16
Hirsch, Katrina de, 158
Homogeneous grouping, 44
Homolateral movement, 16
Hyperactive children, 63
Hyperactivity, 63

Hyperkinesis, 62

I

Illinois Test of Psycholinguistic Abilities,
  60, 64, 65, 70, 116, 160
Imagery, 10
Imaginative pursuits, 119
Impulsivity, 62
Initial approximations, 34
Inner language, 7
Inner speech, 7
Institute for Developmental Studies, 91
Institute for the Achievement of Human
  Potential, 15
Instrumental conditioning, 28
Intellectual
  assessment, 64
  development, 61
  factors, 44
  processes, 90
Intelligence, 46, 61
  assessment, 49
  measures, 115
Interindividual concept, 43
Interindividual variation, 42, 43

J

Jastak Wide-Range Reading Test, 57
Johnson, Doris, 9
Joints, 21
Journal of Learning Disabilities, 151
Judeo-Christian theology, 4

K

Keller, Helen, 6, 145
Kephart, Newell, 20, 154
Kinesio-perceptual abilities, 54
Kinesthetic
  ability, 54
  avenues, 53
  elements, 53
  learning, 53
  perception, 50, 54
  perceptual efficiency, 54
  reading approach, 54